THERE'S MORE TO LIFE
THAN POLITICS

WILLIAM MURCHISON

THERE'S MORE TO LIFE THAN POLITICS

Foreword by William F. Buckley Jr.

SPENCE PUBLISHING COMPANY · DALLAS
1998

Published in the United States by
Spence Publishing Company
501 Elm Street, Suite 450
Dallas, Texas 75202

Library of Congress Cataloging-in-Publication Data

Murchison, William P.
    There's more to life than politics / William Murchison : foreword by
William F. Buckley.
      p. cm.
    ISBN 0-9653208-3-9 (hardcover)
    1. United States—Social conditions—1980-   2. United States—
Politics and Government—1989- 3. United States—Economic
conditions—1981- 4. United States—Moral conditions. 5. Quality of
life—United States.
    HN59.2.M88 1998
    306'.0973—dc21   98-22732

Printed in the United States of America

For Nancy, Will, and John,
lights of my life;
and
for Dorothy Ann Bivin Murchison,
tough of mind, soft of heart, wise in all things.

Contents

Foreword

WILLIAM MURCHISON was born in 1942, in Corsicana, Texas. He graduated from the University of Texas twenty-one years later. From there he went to Stanford for an advanced degree (in history) arriving just in time for the Woodstock Decade. He has spent a productive life (half-life—we assume he will live out the biblical allotment) recording, in lively journalism for the *Dallas Morning News*, his thorough disapproval of many of the recent tendencies of the society he grew up in. Will you, on reading this book, opine that he is preoccupied with what is going wrong? No, much that he approves of us is warmly commented upon. But as a commentator his attention is naturally drawn to that in the society that is especially in motion. And this is, of course, the mad-cow disease of the 1960s and, always, the thump-thump-thump of increasing government.

He contrasts, in his introduction, the relatively modest appurtenances of a start-up legislator in Texas, back when he was a young man, with the grandiosity of the circumstances today. It seems more merely than a generation ago that a legislator could make do with simple office conveniences, but the easiest test to measure the portentous growth of government is also the most reliable. How much do they spend, and what percentage of the national income do they consume?

My own perspective on his alma mater is at second hand, but not irrelevant, inasmuch as I take every opportunity I can to remark that my father was also a graduate of the University of Texas. I was invited to Austin as a visiting fellow the same year that Bill Murchison graduated. I do not know whether the tradition endures, but I was then invited as what was called a "Last Chance Fellow." The idea dates back I don't know how long, but the gist of it was that the visiting fellow would participate fully in the life of the university from Sunday until Friday at which point he would deliver his "last chance" lecture. The idea was for the lecturer to give voice on that Friday night to the very last speech he'd ever give. To generate that terminal sense of theater, my hosts contributed mightily. When a fortnight before my arrival I examined the proposed schedule I wired (Western Union existed in those days) to say it was just too heavy: I would make myself available only beginning at noon every day not, as the planning committee had arranged, beginning at eight o'clock every morning.

What happened—I counted—was ninety-five public appearances. They ranged from seminars to fraternity initiations. They included public debates and press reviews and participation in history and literature and political science classes. When I staggered on to the stage on the Friday evening I knew exactly what a dying man felt like: such was my fatigue, I had every reason to doubt I would live another day.

I recounted the experience to my two aunts who lived on Lavaca Street and had gone to UT with my late father. They were amused by the sheer "size" of their alma mater and advised me that when they were there, a few years after the turn of the century, the university had 750 students. That figure suggested anew to me something about the largeness of Texas—a largeness that manages also the wholesomeness one comes upon in this collection of Murchison's newspaper columns. But it is characteristic of Texas that its largeness is quite naturally expressed; it is taken for granted.

I recall an experience, during my Last Chance week, with the university's librarian. She headed toward the collection of personal papers left to the library by my father. En route to that cache she passed by an issue of *Life* magazine, a few months old, lying there on the library ledge. She stopped and turned the cover page exposing a dull-white sheet of parchment paper ornately addressed and written in rococo Castilian. It was a letter written by Christopher Columbus to Their Majesties, King Ferdinand and Queen Isabela. I asked how many holograph from Columbus to his sponsors survived, and she gave me the answer quickly and matter-of-factly: four. The librarian had not yet decided exactly where to house the letter, so she stuck it in an old magazine. What was it worth, I asked? She related that one had recently been auctioned and fetched four hundred thousand dollars. That episode, I thought, was in the grand Texas style. A letter from Columbus? Where else likelier to find a copy than at the library of the University of Texas, in Austin, stashed in an old magazine?

Bill Murchison tacitly celebrates everything that is grand and expansive about his home state and his native country, and his religion and his heroes. But what is distinctive is the naturalness with which he deals with them, which goes hand in hand with the fervor with which he elects to protect them. He came back to Texas from California and decided to take the world head on. He doesn't, in this volume, dwell at any length on his days at school, but the reader is not left in doubt about what, in modern college life, the author approves of and what he deplores. The University of Texas, during the crazy campus years, was relatively civilized. Decorum means a great deal to this author, because he recognizes it as related to intrinsic satisfactions. He is eloquent on developments in his beloved Episcopal Church. It has tended, in the years here examined, to go in doctrinal directions he judges to be awry. But always it is there to give him the satisfactions he here communicates.

The medieval churchmen talked about right reason, which is the thought, and the action, taken after deliberate time spent on the moral dimensions of alternatives. Bill Murchison has a natural sense of the direction of right reason. "While billions of us the world over were clawing, scratching, scraping away at the business of life," he writes, "Malcolm Muggeridge attained his fondest wish. He gave up life entirely, finding the fulfillment for which he has thirsted throughout a busier lifetime than most of us can conceive." Muggeridge died, yes, but he left his very large flock with serial satisfactions, in his books, articles, and documentaries. Murchison celebrates that achievement as he does that of other men he admires, most strikingly the late M. E. Bradford, whom he knew and revered. Muggeridge, as is the case with so many who leave us with the excitement of epiphanies experienced, had to live out the delusions he would subsequently reject, and disdain. Murchison skipped all that. There cannot have been a moment—I think the reader would agree with me—when, staring at something black, he pronounced it as white.

You will, I predict, experience that sense of balance, of moral well-being, of utilitarian certitude on reading these pieces, so happily collected and providentially published. *There's More to Life than Politics,* he calls this book—and proceeds to prove it. Like many of us, Bill is a political junkie in the sense of taking in what politics thrusts out at us. But only to examine, and usually to reject, one more heresy. What is it lying around that is more to life than politics? Well, there is the satisfaction and pride one can take over this book. It is a tribute to the author, to the daily newspaper that sponsors him, and to the state that engendered him. It is nice to reflect that this will not be a last chance to read and deliberate over the work of William Murchison, but grab the opportunity when you have it.

WILLIAM F. BUCKLEY JR.

Introduction

THE CLASH OF PRINCIPLE, the flash of rhetoric; maneuvers and countermaneuvers; deals, coalitions, lonely stands; victory and heartbreak; the whole of it related intimately to the public weal. I am talking of politics, every tasty morsel of which we journalists love to consume.

Well. . . . don't we? . . .

Growing uneasiness heads off easy assumptions. Certainly the general expectation is that journalists—to a man, to a woman—adore the political trade for the folderol and foolishness it offers us, and through us, our customers. H. L. Mencken set the tone long ago with his elegant excoriations of the political craft.

Without politics, how do we fill up newspapers and magazines, and stretch out the Sunday morning talk show formats—with chit-chat about gardens, cooking, and movies? (It remains to be calculated how many empty church pews a cessation of Sunday morning political shows would fill. Arguably, a fair number.)

Contemporary society has invested politics with vast importance, and because contemporary society is what journalists observe and report, political news and prognostication assumes vast importance. There is also the sheer fun of the thing: the nonlethal combat, grown men and women bashing each other in the rhetorical snout: cries of "oooof!" "ow!" "hit him again!" In our higher toned moments we curl our lips at such bawdy stuff; the truth remains that, as entertainment, all this stuff beats watching the cars drive by on Saturday night.

Politics enjoys an additional cachet: The whole, occasionally sordid, disgusting business matters. This would seem a truism. How could an enterprise not matter whose flour and yeast is the people's liberties and economic resources? The citizens of the ex-Soviet Union are willing to testify that politics can cancel out citizenship itself, not to mention life. Clearly politics has meaning. But politics as meaning itself? The insight is pure twentieth century (though chronologically antecedent to the twentieth century). In the view of one political commentator—I can speak for no other—the insight is disagreeable and dangerous.

Politics, in its classic sense, concerns the means by which we order life: the rules, the regulations, the laws, the statutes; not so many of them as actually to impede life, just enough to afford common protections. On which point everyone agrees. Disagreement sets in at just the point one set of politicians or another begins arguing about how life could be improved.

A lifelong attachment to politics, and a passionate commitment to its outcomes, has not rendered me indifferent to politics. I stand before you, gentle reader, a recovering political junkie. As a high school speech student many years ago, when called on to edify my classmates, I delivered political orations. *Time* magazine I read cover to cover, on the day it arrived, red-bordered, at our home; my car I decorated with political bumper stickers; my viewpoints I interjected, finally making their defense my profession.

Do I still care about politics? I care greatly. Do I still regard politics as central to human concerns? Not in the least. There is too much else out there. And that is what this collection of columns is about—all the other things that are out there in the culture, shaping, informing, affecting life in decisive ways.

Our chief political problem is that we think our problems are political. They are not. Nor could they ever be. Politics, at the root, is about power: its distribution and exercise. Politics concerns itself with who decides in the community's name what the community ought to do, and for how long, and at what cost. This is, of course, is what elections are for.

Another "of course": We can't escape from politics. All we can do is withdraw, which merely means others besides ourselves will make the basic decisions. There is after all a common life to be pursued. Rules are necessary; those rules proceed from politics. But politics as secular salvation? Behold the great heresy of modern times: the earnest belief that the collective power of society is perpetually available for banishing human vexations. There is a naive charm to the assertion. All of us, liberal or conservative, have fallen for it at one time or another. That this no wonder, because, like all heresies, this one carries the germ of truth. Human power, the power of the state, can indeed be harnessed for good, and has been on more than one occasion. Even libertarians (I hope) wouldn't quarrel with the necessity of traffic lights and stop signs!

The politicians won't save us. Bless 'em, they can't even save themselves. How many fewer problems has the United States—has the human race—got in the era of big government than back when, for entertainment and inspiration, we looked to preachers and poets rather than to the wielders of state power? There are various ways of measuring human afflictions, but the sheer quantity, at the end of the twetieth century, is hardly less than at the century's start, when Theodore Roosevelt began putting government forward as multi-purpose arbitrator and adjuster. The federal budget approaches two trillion dollars, versus one hundred billion on the eve of the Great Society. Even taking into account wage and price inflation, are our lives, say, ten or twelve times better than in 1965? Are we ten or twelve times happier than when the Beatles descended on us and bread was a quarter a loaf? As subjective as standards of value may be, it is hard to answer yes to such questions.

Semi-politicized we are all the same: the consequence of inviting government to do all manner of wonderful things for us, and not asking rude questions about where the money was coming from. How fascinating that this politicization has taken place in the United States of America. Life as politics, politics as life, has been in our time the hallmark of the totalitarian regimes—Nazi Germany, Soviet Russia, Communist China. Into every corner of domesticity the totalitarian state reached in its heyday—the 1930s through the 1960s—plucking up people by the scruff of the neck, subjecting them to whatever treatment the authorities found appropriate. How the people were taught was a political issue; how, or whether, they worshiped was a political issue; likewise what jobs they held, how much they earned, whom they married, what they named their children.

The world is done with most of that for now, despite the persistence of communism in China. Yet, while totalitarianism languishes abroad, state power in our own country rocks and rattles forward like a freight train—at the state and local, as well as the federal, level.

I would offer a couple of homely examples. Early in the 1960s—a time, in spirit, more like the 1950s than the ugly period into which we were ambling unsuspectingly even then—I attended the University of Texas, in the state capital of Austin. My hometown legislator hired me part time for some light chores connected with constituent service. The neighborhood through which I strolled to work—eight or so square blocks between the university and the Capitol—consisted of early twentieth-century homes and boarding houses. What does the passer-by see there today? State office buildings, and parking lots to serve the workers and constituents who populate the office buildings. Government was not big time in the early 1960s. It is big time in the 1990s, that's for certain.

A reinforcing example: My legislator, on the day I first reported for work, invited me to seat myself at his desk on the House floor, because, well, being a first-termer, he didn't—that was just how it was, you know—have a regular office. To paraphrase the Gospel, foxes had holes, but the tribune for Navarro County, Texas, had not where to lay his briefcase. Do times ever change! A couple of years ago, the state proudly opened for use an underground addition to the Capitol, consisting of more than six hundred thousand square feet; every legislator, you may be assured, has ample room to do the people's will—though of course a corner second-floor office still isn't guaranteed!

Thus has government swollen up in the midst of a people—Texans—prickly as a cactus plant concerning their rights and liberties, critical of "government" almost as a matter of principle. Imagine what things must be like elsewhere. Or, rather, don't imagine; just look around. It takes little time to catch on to the proposition that, no, these are not the 1950s.

Formerly the reference points to which we looked were church, family, and community (the latter variously defined as Rotary Club, PTA, Junior League, Shakespeare Club, and so forth). The reference point that has come to dwarf them all, as measured by our attentions, as well as by what it spends, is government. The raw material of government, naturally, is politics—the same politics that fascinates, titillates, entertains, amuses, sometimes even inspires.

Ah, well, that's just how it goes! You hear this disclaimer constantly. The world is different: more complex, more interrelated, and in regular need of professional tune-up and balancing. And there are so many more of us now—billions more than when dust clouds and the jingle of bridles marked the daily arrival of delegates to the Philadelphia constitutional convention.

All of this is so self-evident, we have largely accepted the politicians' word that we are unable to get along without them. The old wheeze, "There oughta be a law," has become fact. There is a law—regulating, touching, impinging on practically everything to one degree or another. A large number of our laws are, of course, good and useful, but many are bad and, if not totally useless, then counterproductive to the end allegedly sought.

Charles Murray's strictures against the welfare state are case in point. Murray, the libertarian scholar, blames false incentives: To reward joblessness and sloth with a government check is to turn joblessness and sloth into viable choices. It is true that comparatively few people starve to death under the welfare state. It is true that comparatively few starved to death in the Bad Old Days before FDR; it wasn't the federal government, but someone fed them. The point is, there has been serious moral deterioration under the present regime of dependence and open-handed spending. Families fall apart, and children grow up only partially instructed in what it means to be human. Perhaps, on balance, things weren't better in the Bad Old Days; still, the Bad Old Days were not the product of blueprints depicting how wonderful and joyous human life could be, once particular changes were implemented.

It would be unfair to say the politicians have pretty well mucked up everything (the Democrats by making the original mess, the Republicans by talking unceasingly about the mess without ever doing much to clean it up). Every age has its problems, and every place. What characterizes modern America is the deep persistence of problems—moral, cultural, racial, even economic—amid the general impression that problems are being addressed, compassionately and efficiently, through politics.

Help may be on the way. Over the past few years there has sprung up all around the country, not quite a movement—more like a broadly based concern for the revival of virtue and civic spirit. Thinkers and doers, not all of them "conservative" by any means, are raising, and trying to answer, questions such as, how do we reinvigorate our community-based institutions, how do we persuade people to do good, or at least refrain from doing bad? Such questions proceed from the conviction that virtue cannot be compelled by regulatory enactment or judicial diktat. Why, it cannot be compelled at all, goes this old-fashioned assumption. It arises rather from the moral understanding, which understanding is nourished by our lives together as family members, as workers, as worshipping members of religious bodies. To which understanding we pay inadequate attention these days.

I happily second the motion. In this book, do I seek to foreclose conversation about politics? Not for a minute. No one can talk about the late twentieth century without talking about politics. My hope is to redirect the conversation just a bit. I seek to consider politics in a larger context. What's really the problem here? Is it too little trust in those secular princes the Psalmist (No. 146) warns us against? Or is the problem altogether too much trust and faith in the power of laws and regulations to serve the community's basic interests?

Over the past three decades, I have written hundreds of columns about the raw stuff of politics and government: elections, inauguration, bills conferring power, bills taking power away. You write this sort of thing when you hire on as a public affairs commentator. Additionally, as I have noted, politics can be enormous fun. However, politics, like bread left out overnight, can grow stale. The great villains, the great heroes one singles out; the great causes and movements over time, these often seem less, shall we say, momentous than when talk of them filled the TV screens and the front pages and supplied the late-night comedians with instantly recognizable topics.

Such-and-such a political figure, we are wont to say at such-and-such a moment, would do such-and-such things, providing such-and-such benefits for the public weal. Or thus-and-so should happen in terms of legislation, and if it doesn't happen, woe and alas! And if it does happen, pass the champagne! Then, in just a bit, it's something else again—a new crisis, a new challenge, a new messiah. The TV screens and front pages fill with different matter. The joke factories lay on extra shifts.

Amid the hurly burly of electoral politics, the changes in allegiance and attention, what endures? The generally less visible marks of human life endure: marriages, births, deaths, family, friendships, classes, clubs, religious worship, acts of mercy, acts of anything-but-mercy. At just this level life, real life, is lived; real people go around making something of their opportunities or making absolutely nothing of them, but performing in either case "off camera," outside the reach of reporters and analysts, who, if they were told that such matters were of enduring interest, would likely yawn.

The enduringness of life suggests a defect of the political approach to life: the futility, in other words, of supposing that governmental measures make much impact on daily existence. Some impact they make, certainly. Taxes bite—hard. Regulations affect the way business is done, hence the way income is earned or spent. An elaborate system of welfare, as we have noticed, can provide false incentives. Nonetheless, Dr. Samuel Johnson's couplet is profoundly to the point: "How small of all that human hearts endure/ That part which kings or laws can cause or cure."

Granted, Dr. Johnson lived under a "small-government" regime that had not attempted, far less failed at, the task of reshaping society. His observation remains incorrigibly true, however: human life is lived, for the most part, outside the ambit of politics. Only the politicians live within that ambit—a major problem for all of them, what with the need for incessant fundraising, the wear-and-tear on family relationships, the divorces, the frequent sense of loss when the political life ends. The movement to limit terms of office strikes me as a boon for the very politicians who fear and oppose it the most. All that the term-limit folk propose is that representatives be allowed to lead normal lives!

What, then, is this book—the author's prescription for the dis-

mantling of politics, for the explosion of the political vision? Ah—
not quite. For one thing, there is no extended argument here. The
columns and essays included are occasional pieces, written to fill
specific holes in newspapers. They reflect little more than my perception (and my editors') of what topics are of particular interest
and consequence in a discrete moment of time: e.g., the day on
which deadline falls. It seems hardly necessary to explain this to
consumers of daily journalism; I remark it and pass on to a larger
matter, which is that, never mind what journalists say, never mind
what politicians say in their more lucid moments, the political vision is here to stay. If men were angels, James Madison famously
observed, they would need no government. It turns out there is
lots and lots of government, and always has been. What does this
tell us about Mr. Madison's understanding of human nature?

The question is not, shall we have government? The question
is how much government shall we have, and what shall we do with
it? Specifically, do we make government large and costly in order
to coerce a particular worldview into existence? That approach
has been tried, and not just by the totalitarian powers. The New
Deal of Franklin Roosevelt, with government as social and economic overseer, was an attempt to enforce a new, supposedly more
efficient order of things, with daily life left far less to chance than
had previously been the rule.

A different kind of view—one bound up nonetheless with the
exercise of power—is that of using government in order to minimize government and strengthen the private sectors of life. Such
is the vision of Ronald Reagan: pass laws that minimize the reach
of law, fill government offices with men and women committed to
moving government nearer the periphery of existence. You can't
get away from government, in other words, without using government to get wherever it is you want to go. This suggests the ongoing necessity of politics, however much or little one may enjoy
political processes.

That necessity conceded, it remains for Americans of varying political outlooks to reflect on how much "of all that human hearts endure" (or even rejoice in) is invisible to my own profession, with its love of eavesdropping on power. What this particular journalist loves—the one whose book you hold—is flagging down the politically obsessed in order to point out a few things. Such as what? Oh, the limitations of politics, for one thing; the general frustration to which those limitations give rise; and the comparative irrelevance of politics, measured against matters like, especially, family and religion.

We slight the "big stories" not just of our time but of all time when we pay only perfunctory attention to family and religion. Not that such "stories" lend themselves readily to conventional treatment. Journalism, responsive to readers and viewers, thrives on conflict. This is why sports and politics dominate news coverage; here is where the action is. There are winners in each of these endeavors; and naturally there are losers. Loyalties are engaged, and primal human emotions. The identities of the victor and the vanquished matter to the spectators, at home or on the scene. The resolution of the conflict moves the action to another, if not necessarily higher, level: in sports the next game, in politics the next vote. There is one problem here: the intensity of the conflict makes the conflict, much of the time, seem more far urgent than it really is. Sports and politics come to represent and embody life. It becomes hard to shrug: win a few, lose a few.

Things clearly should not be so, but consider the competition: chiefly, family and religion. In both bailiwicks sweetness and light theoretically reign—and bore to tears any outsider silly enough to eavesdrop. The point is only in part that theory has little to do with practice: that, for instance, husbands and wives sometimes fight more, and hurt each other worse, than Democrats and Republicans try to hurt each other.

The real point, the underlying point, is that the main business of mankind gets conducted in these settings—religion and family. Here you get born, here you grow up, here you honor (or, alternatively, reject) historic teachings as to what life is for, how a man or woman should live, what principles guide our footsteps, where our primary allegiances lie. These, you might think, were urgent matters, bearing on the basics of life. On the other hand, flip through a newspaper, and what impression do you normally take away from it? Why, that next week's vote in the House of Representatives, or the upcoming fall elections, or the balance of power on the city council, matter more than all these generally invisible considerations.

"Out of sight, out of mind," turns out to be sound social, as well as romantic, counsel. In the age of instant communication, what rarely gets talked about disappears from view. On the other hand, what gets talked about unceasingly moves forcefully to the center of the universe.

And yet. . . . and yet. . . . the matters that provoke most conversation lack power to influence life; those that draw less (far less) notice are the pivotal matters.

Where did we come from? Where are we going? For what purpose are we made? How must we live? And who says so, anyway? Fundamental questions, you would certainly say: the kinds of questions no politician can pose or address without embarrassment. Where do we come from? To a politician, that means what's our congressional district? For what purpose are we made? The politician, without scratching his head, can name at least one fundamental purpose of life: keeping those taxes pouring in, because, without taxes, how do we keep the government going, solving all those problems, binding up all those wounds, employing all those people? The basic purposes of life, in other words, are not exactly the stuff of political discourse (even though the highest political wisdom of the past—e.g., Edmund Burke's *Reflections on the Revolution in France*—enjoins respect for those purposes). The higher purposes of life are sought, we discover, under the aspect of eternity—beneath the gaze of God. Or such was the case up to our own feverish time and maybe ought to be again, the politicians having failed so conspicuously to make us happy.

Did God make us happy? Back when Western civilization found him more or less at the center of everything? Did we kick up our heels with greater abandon, knowing He would somehow work things out for our benefit? Not quite. Happiness figured less prominently in human calculations than since, well, perhaps since Thomas Jefferson, in the Declaration of Independence, grafted the word onto our collective consciousness. Happiness was thereafter something we had a right to "pursue"—which right we exercised with growing enthusiasm over the succeeding decades and centuries.

The larger question, actually, respecting the relationship of humanity to Creator, was what does He want of us? Here we are—what now? The question sprang up logically enough: God had created us. He had thereby laid upon us a set of obligations. Upon these obligations—the Ten Commandments provided a good, if not quite exhaustive, summary—we were to center our lives. This would not be easy. Getting down to brass tacks, it could get a man, or a woman, killed. Happy? Where was the "happiness" in facing hungry lions in the arena?

That is to say, where was the worldly happiness? The word "worldly" turned the conversation in a different direction. "The pursuit of happiness" suggested vistas of drowsy, late-summer contentment: end-of-the-month profits counted, creditors happy, half an hour more to sit before returning to work, and a new shipment of ale coming in later. From what the theologians knew and taught about God, a different set of priorities emerged: satisfactions occurred in service, and sometimes in sacrifice; to gain was to lose, to lose was to gain—all for the sake of drawing closer into unity and comity with the Creator. "Happiness"? Oh, dear. Could someone have heard wrong?

It all depended on how you looked at things, and on what deductions you drew from what you looked at. The religion-centered world of early America was a land of small and limited government only in part because the Divine Right of Kings had no purchase on the settlers' minds. It was a world in which the satisfaction of earthly objectives played some part but not the whole part. Government was not yet a means of enfleshing social and cultural visions. The commonwealth built by the stern, occasionally fierce, Puritans was designed to honor divine purposes, in the way they were understood by the designers. Its instruments of retributive justice—public stocks, ducking stools, and so on—were meant to make the ways of the world look less appealing than ever.

The burgeoning of state power puts that power at the service of the state's objectives, never mind the real worth of those objectives. And look where we are: economically triumphant, morally attenuated. The state can do it all, we hear. The state can do about half what it claims it can do, we discover.

Under the sway of the state, divorce and family breakup reach astounding heights; public—i.e., state-funded—education falters; and we rejoice to find (as was the case recently) crime dropping to levels we would have deemed intolerable not many years ago. The state wrestles helplessly and unhappily with cultural questions of the deepest importance—abortion, homosexuality, euthanasia. Some say, do as you like; others say, do what's right. The suspicion grows: These are not matters suitable for referenda; you cannot, with much purpose, take votes on right and wrong. Yet voting is the stuff of political judgment, and politics is what life centers on in the late twentieth century, and if the politicians can't help. . . .

I have remarked that the main business of life gets conducted, out of sight, out of mind, in the domains of religion and family. These domains are on my mind in this book: their extent, their claim on us, their redemptive power—a power denied the state because the state's legitimate claims on our attention and resources lie elsewhere. I have not sought, as I hope I have made clear, to set out a worldview in the course of plugging holes in newspaper opinion pages. I have sought to speak to discrete concerns. I find these concerns dovetail, nevertheless. Columns on family underline over a period of time the essentiality of the family, not just biologically, but culturally. Here is where you learn what you learn—or fail entirely to learn it. I have included in the present collection a series of columns written nominally to my own children, from birth to the present day. Of all the columns I have written since 1968, when I first ventured into the opinion trade, these are the ones that draw the most attention and enthusiasm. I hope that it is because they are true, not just because (another thing that is true) my children are quite wonderful. It seems to me a hopeful sign that people remember these columns better and longer than they remember any attempts on my part to whip up enthusiasm for this political candidate or that one.

I have written much also about schools and about education. I come from an educating family, knee-deep in public school teachers. For the teaching profession I retain deep respect. As for why the schools don't work as we seem entitled to expect they would work (given how they cost us!), I blame the general collapse of standards during the 1960s and afterwards. Egalitarianism undercuts the whole basis on which education—with its commitment to merit and achievement—rests. The schools have accordingly deteriorated: not physically, because the state keeps pouring in the money, but rather in terms of their mission to stretch minds. The retrieval of education—good education—is among our chief tasks. Education is in large measure a state, hence a political, endeavor. The challenge is to extract the politics from it without severing a state connection there seems no reason to argue against, given the depth of popular commitment to state schools. Unless the state, in this connection, behaves even worse than it has up to now!

A word about religion, and perhaps more than a word. Very

few journalists indeed are theologians. I am no exception to that rule. On the other hand, it is hard not to notice that major questions turn out eventually to be religious questions: questions of ultimate loyalty, questions of origin and destination. Who are we, where do we come from, where are we going? These are religious queries, begging religious answers. The state is unable to answer such queries and when it tries to, the answers it gives are usually false or misleading. The state's answers are consensus answers, proceeding from the inevitable show of hands. These answers speak not to right or wrong and good or evil but to preponderant opinion at a given moment in time. It is an insubstantial basis on which to offer social guidance.

How can a "secular" society, such as we style ourselves, use religion for its benefit? In much the same way we have used it throughout most of our history—as a mark of validity and verification. Salvation is for God to impart, according to His will and pleasure, and for the beneficiaries to accept. The means of achieving it are not for writers in the secular prints to worry their heads about. But there are various things, respecting religion, that our society in general and my profession in particular can do. Possibly the most important is, respect it. This comes hard, unfortunately. There is no point using up valuable space detailing the reasons the secular-minded mistrust religion. The shaky authority of an invisible God is among those reasons. Against such authority, that of politicians, who, if you want to talk to them are always glad to speak and glad-hand, has a nice resonance. A poll of leading Washington journalists, back in the 1980s, indicated that 86 percent never darken the door of a house of worship. It seems all too natural that, in assessing the needs of the nation, they prefer politics to pie in the sky. If our paid communicators see no special point in communicating a sense of religion's centrality, we need not wonder when competing voices—the voices of politicians and entertainers—carry farthest in the media.

Over the years I have written extensively on religious topics, generally with the idea that topics such as these touch us the most deeply and the most lastingly. Some columns of this sort are included here. Several focus on the Episcopal Church, of which my family and I are longtime communicants. Whatever the Episcopal Church's failings—and they are manifest—most of the time it keeps its eyes trained high above the Capitol dome, toward heaven, thus performing an important affirmation; to wit, that God, somehow or other, is in charge of the whole loopy human enterprise.

A very good thing, too. With politicians and journalists in charge of everything, working their way with us, laying on the flattering unction day after day, what hope would there be for the world?

I leave that provocative question to dangle loosely, enticingly.

I OWE A DEBT OF THANKS to the *Dallas Morning News* for its kind permission to reprint these columns, not to mention for having provided me with my jouralistic home these many years. In the compilation of the collection, my editor, Mitchell Muncy, read through, evaluated, and classified an astounding number of newspaper columns: more in fact than I could remember having written. This vital job he performed with tact and taste. John A. Murchison, to whom a number of the birthday letters herein are addressed, expertly typed much of the manuscript, never pausing to raise a philosophical quibble with his father. The staff of Spence Publishing has been uniformly helpful and encouraging throughout this venture. I thank one and all.

I

Cause and Cure

IN MY POLITICAL WRITINGS over the last fifteen years or so, I have found myself saying, wait! What do we expect from all this anyway? Why are we asking mere politicians—people with our own foibles and crochets, not to say malignancies and incapacities, to do important things for us? How do these things pertain to them? They don't, one crochety, malignancy-burdened observer begs to report.

Rejecting Secular Salvation

One thing the critics of Promise Keepers don't get: the group's stated, reiterated disdain for politics.

Aw, come on, guys, don't give us that! Feminists, liberals, secularists, gay-rights activists, earnest editorialists, etc., just know these guys have a political agenda. Yeah, come on: They marched in Washington! "When members of Congress look out onto the Mall," says Pat Ireland of the National Organization for Women, "they see the same thing I see: hundreds of thousands of constituents and voters."

Well, yeah. Voters, taxpayers. Also husbands, fathers, boyfriends, workers, managers, sports fans, guitar players, weekend gardeners, roller bladers, Jaycees, Scout leaders, bird-watchers, poets, amateur chefs, who knows that else? The variety of life, outside its political expressions, is rich and infinite. The problem is getting the politically obsessed to understand as much. Among modernity's high crimes is that of pigeonholing people by their imputed relationship to the political order. This exasperating habit wrongly puts politics at the center of human affairs.

Let me tell you, speaking as a political reporter and commentator of thirty-three years' experience: Promise Keepers have it right. As one of them, a United Parcel Service driver, told the *New York Times*, "We can't change people through politics. Our job is to have a lifestyle of integrity. I do it with my customers on my route, with my bosses. I don't call in sick if I'm not sick. My bosses know that."

A slender boast? Hardly comparable to: "I stuffed five thousand envelopes for my congressional candidate"? Or "I attended a White House coffee and wrote a big check"? Such a judgment would have to rest on the assumption that human laws shape destiny, when the whole of human history refutes that proposition. Dr. Samuel Johnson's couplet comes powerfully to mind: "How small of all that human hearts endure/That part which laws or kings can cause or cure."

Modernity sees politics as secular salvation. The Promise Keepers see right through that great heresy and moral imposition. They don't believe for a minute that the collective power of society is perpetually available for banishing human vexations.

How many fewer problems has the United States—has the human race—got in the era of big government than back when, for inspiration and entertainment, we looked to preachers and poets rather than to the wielders of state power? The sheer quantity of modern afflictions—centering on alienation and moral rot—is hardly less than ninety-odd years ago, when Theodore Roosevelt began battling economic inequalities through the instrumentality of government power.

The federal budget approaches two trillion dollars, versus one hundred billion on the eve of the Great Society. Even taking into account wage and price inflation, hardly anyone would say our lives are ten or twelve times better than in 1965. Yet we remain semi-politicized—the consequence of inviting government to do all manner of wonderful things for us, while ducking rude questions about who pays the tab.

So, then, politics is meaningless? Political endeavor is vain? Fat chance of that, given government's historic and indispensable purpose of maintaining order and justice. The modern brand of politics—politics as secular salvation—is what the Promise Keepers seem at this stage rightly to reject. The rest of society should participate heartily in that rejection.

Yes, vote; yes, donate money and sign petitions; yes, communicate with duly elected leaders and give unshirted hell to know-it-all pundits. Just don't expect such activity, pleasurable as it may be, to alter the basic conditions of life. These remain immutable: birth and death, love and hate, joy and sorrow, victory and defeat.

Find a legislative proposal intended to render fixed realities otherwise, blotting out tears and ushering in the reign of joy. Then take said proposal in your fingers, crease it, commence tearing from top to bottom . . .

October 8, 1997

Massaging the Moral Climate

So, we wobble toward a balanced federal budget, and meanwhile, Social Security gallops toward bankruptcy.

In May's *Atlantic Monthly*, Peter G. Peterson, the former Commerce secretary, projects that Social Security will run 766 billion dollars in the red by 2030, when an unprecedented number of us geezers will be awaiting our checks.

Peterson, not unreasonably, suggests reform. There may be an antecedent requirement, which is to ask how we got here, the federal government taking such tender care of us. That would include the millions who never bade the government take care of anything but its own business, yet who today, nevertheless, find their futures jeopardized.

Certainly, the government didn't take care of nineteenth-century geezers. Why, if some slick-haired youth from Washington, D.C., had shown up at the average American home of a century ago, conveying the government's desire to hold our hands and provide for us evermore, the average American homeowner would have slung said youth over the fence rail. Who was this interloper to suggest that an American citizen needed his hand held, his brow wiped?

That was—alas—then. This is unmistakably now. In 1996, unlike 1896, we define ourselves in terms of government. The government is a permanent backdrop to our struggles and exertions. We can't bend over to tie our shoes without seeing it.

While Social Security flops around like a beached whale awaiting retrieval, President Bill Clinton goes to Miami, and there he instructs us What We're Going to Do About Drugs. It seems we're going to spend more federal money on treatment, enforcement, and interdiction.

The federal government not only solaces our old age, it massages the moral climate.

You can rightly object, on constitutional grounds, to this governmentalizing of everything. But other grounds are no less feasible and attractive, such as: Does all this governmentalizing help?

In the case of today's elderly, maybe so. Their Social Security payments are no more in doubt than rheumatism. It is their grandchildren's payments that are in doubt. Social Security, whatever kindnesses its founders may have intended, has neatly governmentalized retirement. We define ourselves, many of us, in terms of how we'll live, using the government check.

Drugs, you might suppose, is a more logical field of endeavor for government. Drugs cause crime. Crime is a governmental function. OK? Not quite OK.

Clinton himself, in Miami, hinted at the basic problem. "Ultimately," said he, "it is (the children's) job to say no to destructive forces in their lives and yes to the future."

Why do children take drugs? Because there aren't enough federal agents on the job? Because, rather, there isn't enough joy and idealism and moral uplift in the non-governmental arrangements we make: not nearly enough to sidetrack the search for artificial joy and escape.

The war on drugs is less a legal than a moral and cultural undertaking. If people didn't like drugs, they wouldn't take them. Show them something better—family, religion, a nurturing community of some other sort—and they likely would stop. But we define ourselves these days not by church and family but rather by government. The signal from Washington constitutes our marching orders. It's easier to arrest than to nurture.

Identification with government and its purposes has badly warped American culture, but we seem not to notice. It's what we expect: The Social Security check waiting for us, drug czars and presidents plotting strategy against emptiness and despair.

The congressional Republicans wonder why they've been bashed over the heads for trying to cut government. Here's why: Because over the past six decades, government has become as snug and comfy as underwear. We can't imagine ourselves bereft of it. How do we rectify that debased condition—just go nuts and strip down to our lost innocence? How drafty! And how essential!

April 29, 1996

Service with No Smile

In the warm, woozy Clinton vision, thousands of young Americans are pounding police beats, teaching mathematics to the poor and feeding the hungry. Our new president hopes by 1997 to have one hundred thousand fresh-faced kids engaged in "national service." He might. There is broad sentiment in Congress and at the backyard-hibachi level to go ahead with this idea that has kicked around Washington for two decades.

I rise like the Grinch at Christmas to say, what a lot of malarkey! This lame idea exists only because it sounds so good—like dietetic pizza. The country neither needs nor can afford national service but may get it anyway. This is one time we can be thankful for the deficit, without which national service might become a bureaucratic monster of Great Society dimensions. Maybe it will anyway, given the human emotions it seems to arouse.

What's wrong with serving one's country? Nothing whatever, in time of war. We pull together as one people to frustrate the opposed designs of another people. Yet to equate wartime service, a national function, with peacetime service, a local or private function, makes no sense. For one thing, there already is peacetime service. It happens every time Joe or Jane Doe reports for work. Making a living is national service—that and paying the taxes that make it possible for presidents and congressmen to devise national-service programs.

There are still other kinds of service, normally uncompensated. Volunteers of all ages and races go into hospital rooms, homeless shelters, museum gift shops—wherever there is need for service.

America's volunteer corps is the largest in the world. I emphasize the private and local nature of these forms of service. Congress has not said, do these things (though the tax code provides a small deduction for charitable giving). The beauty of it is, no government bureaucracy—yet—coordinates the hundreds of millions of private service activities that take place daily.

Now comes Clinton, trying to muscle in on this mostly uncontrolled sphere of human endeavor. The Clinton tax hikes—not to mention the efflorescence of regulation we may expect in the next few years—narrow further the scope for making a living; and national service would be just the first step toward federalizing the concept of volunteerism. If one hundred thousand volunteers are good, aren't one millon better? What about ten million?

We need to remember something about this country. It *is* a country, but one made up of discrete parts as large as Texas and as tiny as 79 Wistful Vista.

The national government's missions include, theoretically, the things we can't usefully do as smaller communities. That's why "national service" doesn't apply—because not only *can* we do it, we *are* doing it. Maybe not precisely the way Bill and Hillary Clinton, looking down from Mount Olympus, would prefer we do it, but since when did the small things of life become the bailiwick of government?

We know the answer of course—during the New Deal. That's what is disquieting about the Clinton administration. The president and his wife have a quasi-Rooseveltian vision they mean to impose on us—government as the One Great Nanny. National service would give the federal government the key to yet another mostly unregulated, unsupervised realm of human existence, on top of all the others it now oversees.

An infinite number of practical problems shrouds this matter, such as how do we pay for national service? (Each volunteer will cost the government around twenty thousand dollars.) Would anyone want the trainees? What quality work would they perform?

But the philosophical problem is just as knotty. What makes "service" a national concern? Why does more authority need to be concentrated in federal hands? A curmudgeonly but accurate answer is, it doesn't. We're doing pretty well right now on the service level. The last thing America needs is a new tax-supported bureaucracy to figure out what America needs and how to supply whatever It Is.

March 8, 1993

Survior Syndrome: The Nixon Story

Some Fort Worth legal lion recently offered in behalf of an accused murderer from a high-crime neighborhood the ultra-modern excuse that the lad suffered from "urban survival syndrome." About two seconds is how long the jury entertained this novel argument.

Yet this odd vignette brings to mind no less a figure than Richard Nixon, whose picturesque public career the pundits have been dissecting like a biology lab frog. The formidable task is to reconcile the late fallen president's historic achievements with his historic moral obtuseness, the Watergate cover-up.

We need our friend the Fort Worth legal lion to start us off properly. Ladies and gentlemen of the jury, consider that President Nixon suffered from "'6os survivor syndrome."

In the year of disgrace 1968, America, like the temple veil, was rent in twain, from the top to the bottom. War, social revolution, campus takeovers, marijuana, long hair, the works: Richard Nixon was the man we sent to fix it. How he was to do it, we didn't really ask. All we knew was, things had to change.

In 1972, the rout of George McGovern—whose possible election had otherwise sober Americans jabbering about massive evacuations to Australia—gave Nixon his chance to reassert authority in government and start working on some overdue priorities, like budget-balancing. He blew it.

The Nixonites—like so many others in that apocalyptic time—underestimated the essential strength of American society. They resorted, clumsily, erratically, to Old-World methods of deceit and trickery. The Nixonites no more menaced democracy and civil liberties—which after all they were trying to save—than the man in the moon. Still, they broke various laws, got found out, and paid the price. Ditto their countrymen, who had to live with the consequences: stagflation, military decline, and Jimmy Carter.

It might well have happened to any president elected in 1968 as successor to Lyndon Johnson and then reelected in 1972. The times were that feverish, that muddled.

Richard Nixon's essential tragedy was to lose the 1960 election to John F. Kennedy (very likely through Mayor Dick Daley's tactical intervention in the Chicago polling places) and miss the chance to stabilize the 1960s before they went awry. Would Richard Nixon have sent American troops to Vietnam? Almost certainly not. Would the 1960s have proceeded as they did without the aggravation of a foreign war? Unquestionably not.

And what does all this teach us?—because if it teaches nothing, the pain and misery remain abstract. It teaches us to guard against the corruptions of power, which poison the good and decent and patriotic—such as Nixon was—equally as they infect the weak, perverse or already ill-disposed.

Dr. Samuel Johnson, in the only novel he ever wrote, *Rasselas*, penned a profundity that resounds across two centuries: "if power be in the hands of men, it will be sometime abused." Not bad men alone but also good men will abuse it—for purposes they deem good and right and useful.

Ends don't justify means, we used to say in more sanitary times, when ordinary people sat still for moral instruction. It doesn't much happen now—serious conversation about power and its dangers. Certainly it doesn't happen in Washington, D.C., where the measure of a man and, these days, a woman as well, is the amount of power at that person's disposal.

April 25, 1994

Save Your Congressman!

Amid the tumult and shouting over budget balancing, let us pause in sympathy for our congressmen. No kidding. This is serious.

Service in our national legislature is not all joy and gaiety. Consider two Texas congressmen, Jack Fields, a Republican from the Houston area, and Pete Geren, a Fort Worth Democrat. Both men are retiring when their present terms expire. They want more time to spend with their families. Congressional service doesn't permit such indulgences. The nation's business needs attending to nearly every minute of every day.

"I was touched several years ago," Fields said, "when another member retired and said that his one regret was that his wife raised their children and that he felt the most important part of his life had been missed and could never be retrieved."

A long story on Geren by the *Dallas Morning News* shows how life in Congress becomes life, period. On August 2, it is recorded, Geren began his day with a 6:45 AM jog. Then followed meetings of every description—a gathering of fellow Democratic moderates, a Small Business Committee hearing, a meeting about the V-22 tilt-rotor aircraft, the weekly luncheon of Texas House Democrats, a conference call concerning a proposed NAFTA superhighway, and chats with constituents and reporters off and on throughout the day.

At 7:15 PM, the congressman was in his office, answering mail. There were five roll-call votes at 9:40 PM. A debate on the telecommunications bill spilled over into the post-midnight hours. At 1:47 AM, Geren headed for his rented bedroom. His wife lives with his children in Fort Worth. He spoke with her by phone at 7:30 PM. His appointments for August 3 were to begin at 8:00 AM.

This is not life. This is a robotic existence—a blur of activity that passes for thoughtful, deliberative labor. But all for the greater good of the United States of America, yes?

One wonders. Just what *is* being accomplished at this level of, ah, service? Is anything? The government, notwithstanding the gridlock and shutdowns, goes on. But the deeper question is, must it? Is so much government, so much whirl and blur and fevered doing, necessary to the republic's well-being?

It didn't used to be, and we managed to get by. Of course, there didn't used to be so many Americans—a third more now than in the 1950s—requiring protection or service. But more than the population has grown since then. As we head toward the two-trillion-dollar budget, it is instructive to recall that only thirty years ago, the federal budget was one hundred billion dollars. Factor in nearly 400 percent inflation since then and still the federal government's growth astounds. You wonder how we peons got along for 175 years with a government we noticed only intermittently! Somehow, we did.

Congress chews up and spits out members like Fields and Geren because Congress undertakes too many projects, legislates too much, and spends too much. How can a normal human understand and deal intelligently with the range of problems to which Congress routinely addresses itself? A normal human can't. What, accordingly, do we get in Congress too much of the time? Abnormal humans.

You have to wonder long and hard about people who want to serve—or at least serve long—in such an institution. Are they sick? Some certainly are. Heaven help us, these folk are making our laws!

Term limits—an excellent idea despite the large number of voluntary retirements—would bring us part of the way toward a solution to the problem. But there is a more fundamental solution. It is the reordering of our desires as voters. The less we ask government to do for us, the more scope we give government to act intelligently.

The Congress that Fields and Geren are leaving resembles the Keystone Kops more than it does a body of great minds legislating in behalf of the world's dominant nation.

How's this slogan as a remedy: "Save your congressman's life—cut his job in half"?

December 28, 1995

Too Many Years in Washington

Republican Representative Henry J. Hyde of Illinois views term-limit proposals—which he helped the other day to crush—as part of a "corrosive attack on the consent of the governed." Some proponents of term limits, Hyde told his colleagues in a blistering speech, "really in their hearts hate politics and despise politicians."

The gentleman from Illinois, who has served twenty years in Congress, manifestly doesn't hate them. "I love politics and politicians. They invest the one commodity that can never be replaced—their time, their family life, their privacy and their reputation—and for what? To make this a better country. . . ."

Well, er, um . . . To hear an honest man like Hyde spout nonsense is always unpleasant. This particular morsel of nonsense, however, has an interesting aftertaste. It reminds us why we need term limits—because even honest men, after too many years in Washington, lose sight of their purpose. They come down with Potomac fever. They lay to their souls the flattering unction of indispensability and self-importance. "The country needs *me!*" is their cry. Often coupled with: "I love the power!"

This baseless egoism makes it easy and logical to sacrifice, as Hyde says, time, family life, privacy, reputation. But to what end? Making this "a better country"?

If that were so, America should be the Promised Land. We have never in our history had so much government or so many politicians. Yet we live with an insupportable national debt, a brush thicket of regulation and social and moral tensions unparalleled for more than a century.

Hyde, a conservative, is against the policies that created these phenomena. Yet he apologizes for those who created the policies.

He identifies authentic concerns about the effects of term limits—the presumptive loss of experience and institutional memory, the voters' absolute right "to chose who will represent you in Congress." He forgets that, despite these considerations, 80 percent of Americans tell the pollsters they want term limits. There must be *some* reason.

Hyde puts his finger on it: "The case for term limits is a rejection of professionalism in politics—'career politician' is an epithet." You bet it is, congressman. Career politicians have made it so.

It isn't that one wants stupid, bumbling, incompetent politicians—one wants modest politicians, who think they have neither the answers to everything nor a divinely ordained right to a permanent entry in the District of Columbia phone book.

Hyde interposes that the voters hold the ultimate check on career politicians: the right to throw them out any time they come up for election. This is technically correct, but the right needs reinforcement. We need not just to defeat time-servers like Dan Rostenkowski and Tom Foley but also to stigmatize the whole class of politician that regards Washington as the center of the universe. Sorry, but we can't trust frail human nature to resist the kind of power whose home base is Washington. We limit our presidents' terms—it makes no sense to treat congressmen differently.

Hyde, intending to excite sympathy for professional congressmen, notes the range of responsibilites they face: "environmental issues, health care, banking and finance and tax policy, the farm problems, weapons systems, Bosnia-Herzegovina, North Korea, foreign policy, the administration of justice, crime and punishment, education, welfare, budgeting in the trillions of dollars, immigration. The list is endless. . . ."

Too true! The challenge isn't simply to limit terms. It's to limit the power of the term-servers and thus to empower, as of old, the working, tax-paying citizens of this country.

Hyde says the term-limits people hate politics? Bully for them. In our time we've had far too much politics and far too little individual responsibility. The congressman reminds us of a physical phenomenon: too many years in Washington, like too much sun at the beach, can dry out the brains. In his own case, let's hope, just temporarily.

March 30, 1995

In Praise of August

The tribulations of August are manifold and notorious: searing, sizzling days made more obnoxious by humidity; school, and homework resume (a dire event that, in more civilized times, didn't happen until September), and a feeling of lethargy and ennui sets in.

World War I began in August. The wonder is that anyone on either side could find the energy to fight.

There is one thing, at least, to be said for August: it is the month freest of politics.

Consider this. Congress is out of session. Even our workaholic president makes specious claims to be resting in Martha's Vineyard. (We must not lean too hard on this claim, inasmuch as Clinton finds work inherently relaxing.) Health insurance bubbles on the stove, but the coming Great Debate has yet to commence.

The *Wall Street Journal*, with the best informed, most biting editorial page in America, decided on Monday of this week to lead with a caustic putdown of China's anti-democratic old-guard regime.

China! This focus on the sins of distant despots shows how relatively little goes forward in America, politically speaking. We should strive to keep it this way.

Henry David Thoreau's rule of thumb—that the least government is the best government—has never had more relevance than today, when we are weighed down by the biggest and costliest government in our national history. For this we can thank the politicians.

Politicians have a disagreeable habit of positing a political solution for every problem that comes down the pike; there is no other kind of solution, so far as they know. We are told we must pass this law or that one and set up one program or another—in this manner, all will be made well.

It never happens. What happens normally these days is that the new laws and programs make things worse, and certainly more expensive, than before. The politicians always overestimate their own wisdom and competence.

The underlying fault, nonetheless, is not politicians so much as it is politics: the eternal fascination with manipulating other people's lives (always, naturally, for people's own good). Politics, by nature, is meddlesome. Any civilized society has to have a little of it. But too much of it turns a country into Communist China, where, according to the *Journal*, "a lone figure who says China shouldn't host the [Olympic] Games is arrested" and "birth controllers have the right to monitor every woman's body cycle." Among other things. Communism is and was politics to the Nth degree: Everything is the state's business, and nothing is left to chance or choice.

One odd thing about America is that while nations from Chile to Czechoslovakia—yes, and some of the time China—have learned the hard way that central control doesn't work, the present U.S. government is lurching back toward statism, with Uncle Sam as Big Brother. Bill and Hillary Clinton set out to repeal the expansive, tax-cutting, enterprise-oriented 1980s. Oh, the fun they are having!

It would be worse, but for August. The more insistently Martha's Vineyard calls, the stronger the republic grows. When at last the federal helicopters rise into the sky and head back toward the capital, wise taxpayers will know what to do. The first thing is to grip their wallets tighter.

August 23, 1993

The Urgency of Delay

Let's hear it for gridlock! May it overrun and terrify Washington, D.C., like the monster in a Japanese movie! May its fetid breath pollute the political atmosphere from coast to coast.

"Gridlock"—the black beast Bill Clinton slashed at in next-to-every campaign speech two years ago, the horror we were supposed to avoid by electing him—has saved us, to this point at least, from nationalized health care.

Unable to agree on what kind of health care bill to pass—if any at all—the Senate has quit and gone home for a couple of weeks. Prospects are dim for the establishment of a consensus between now and the start of the campaign season. The coming election is expected to swell the ranks of congressional Republicans, making passage of any major health care bill next to impossible. No grand scheme that tinkers with one-seventh of the U.S. economy, in addition to our lives, is going to pass this Congress. Hooray, hooray for gridlock—one of democracy's deepest blessings!

The thought of a Congress wallowing in in-house rivalries, partisan conflicts, ego tangles, and the like has its repellent side, all right. There are times, legislatively speaking, to get it on and get things done.

Likewise, there are times *not* to get things done: times when there's no consensus, not to mention money to spend if there *were* a consensus. There are times when the leadership is rushing off faster than the people are willing to go. This is one of those times.

The Clinton health care bill, hatched in secret, peddled like detergent, was a national necessity if you cared to believe the president. The present system had let us down, Clinton claimed. It left too many people out. We had to start over.

It sounded fine at first. Start over? OK. We mentally fingered our checkbooks. Could we do it? Maybe, just maybe? Then we began to think about it. The fabled "Harry and Louise" ads ran; non-administration experts on health care began to weigh in; the National Federation of Independent Business, voice of the little guy and gal in capitalism, expressed its strong dislike of employer mandates. Second thoughts, then third ones, set in.

Whereupon gridlock, as Clinton would call it, commenced. Here was this fine plan the president had offered, and it wasn't moving. That could only be because of the intractability of The System and the bad people who composed it.

The president and his wife and their multifarious advisers could use a little historical perspective. When particular measures that particular people want go down to dusty death, that's not gridlock, it's the democratic process. Government doesn't exist to enact laws and regulations, period. It exists, first of all, to sift proposals for laws and regulations; to balance them in the hand, determine their weight, their tolerability. The constituted authorities, everywhere but a dictatorship, may *ask* that a thing be done, but no one is obligated to do it—least of all if the whole idea smells.

How bad may an idea smell? Sometimes, you have to keep it around a while, in order to find out. We call this process debate and education. It can drag on to incredible lengths, exhausting the onlookers and participants. Better this than too rapid passage of half-digested legislation.

Delay is all the more urgent when you've got a government as top-heavy as this one—weighing down all aspects of life. Often enough, the best thing such a government can do is—nothing, or next to it. Which is just what Congress appears ready to do in the case of health care, Clinton style.

As Patrick Henry might have put it, "If this be gridlock, make the most of it!"

August 29, 1994

II

Statesmen and Rogues

THE POLITICAL ENTERPRISE, like all human endeavors, throws onto the beach of life a variety of specimens: some appealing, some quite the opposite. Of these I sing—reserving the sweetest tones for those who understand and acknowledge the limits of political salvation.

George Washington

The bicentennial of George Washington's presidential inauguration, April 30, falls amid the Jim Wright brouhaha. We turn from the contemplation of book deals and borrowed Cadillacs to the commemoration of one who was first in war, first in peace, first in the hearts of his countrymen. How times do change over a bare couple of centuries!

Not that this hadn't been long suspected. Henry Adams, a century ago, observed that the descent of the presidential species, from George Washington to U. S. Grant, alone stood Darwin's theory of evolution on its head.

Washington personified the ideal of public service: meaning that he saw himself bound to serve the public, not his own interests and aspirations. Americans, if ever they wonder whether God loves them, may take satisfaction in that their very first president was precisely the right man at precisely the right time. How could this be mere coincidence? There had to be something providential in it.

There was never a national leader more personally disinterested than George Washington, less committed to ego (a Latin word not commonly used then) and personal gain. These are the commonplaces of the Washington myth, and yet, like so many other commonplaces, they are true.

Today, politicians lust to be president. Years ahead of time, they plan and plot their campaigns, positioning themselves for maximum advantage, raising money, drawing followers into their orbit. It is extraordinary, in 1989, to remember that Washington never wanted to be president, any more than he had wanted to be commander in chief of the revolutionary armies. He accepted these exalted positions not from ambition or hope of gain but rather from a sense of patriotic duty. His duties accomplished, he stepped aside in a timely fashion.

Washington it was who initiated the tradition of standing down from the presidency after eight years. The chief executive who breached the tradition—foxy, power-loving Franklin Roosevelt—was not precisely cut from the Washington mold.

For all his courage and abilities as soldier-statesman, Washington loved no pastime so well as agriculture. He was happiest at Mount Vernon, cultivating his acres, expanding and remodeling (with considerable skill) his now-famous house.

He was in this a noble Roman of the republican era. A statue, housed in the Smithsonian, depicts him in Roman toga and sandals. The sight is a little startling at first glance, but the viewer, if he looks for a moment, understands that the sculptor meant to depict not the reality but the ideal. Or did he mean perhaps that in George Washington's unique person, ideal and reality met for once?

Washington proved not only a patriot and an honest man but an energetic and gifted chief executive. He filled the Cabinet and the courts with individuals almost as able as himself—Alexander Hamilton, Thomas Jefferson, John Jay, Edmund Randolph, among others. He gave Hamilton scope to order and invigorate the republic's financial arrangements. He kept the country neutral during the French revolutionary wars. He vigorously suppressed the armed threat posed by backwoods Pennsylvania farmers resisting imposition of a tax on whiskey.

When he was done, and his task laid aside, the United States was not only prosperous, it was comparatively united—though unity would soon give way in the kind of partisan feuding Washington abhorred, and which still afflicts us.

The vision of national unity to which George Washington held was in fact an unrealistic one. It would have perished sooner or later. Thomas Sowell has lately shown that two different visions—one "constrained," the other "unconstrained"—divide Americans. One vision emphasizes natural limits on human endeavor; the other plays down, or obliterates, those limits. So it was to some extent even in Washington's time.

But what if a man less high-minded, less committed to unity had presided over the republic's creation? The governmental arrangements that would have flowed from this circumstance might have guaranteed civil war years before the two American nation, North and South, finally flew at each other.

"His integrity," wrote a grateful Jefferson, long after Washington's death, "was most pure, his justice the most inflexible I have ever known, no motives of interest or consanguinity, of friendship or hatred, being able to bias his decision. On the whole his character was, in its mass, perfect, in nothing bad, in few points indifferent."

No myth is George Washington; he was flesh and blood. The cherry tree, the silver dollar—these are rather silly, if understandable, embellishments on a legend. They do not mask for a moment the truth that at our country's most crucial hour, our greatest man rose, not to profit or aggrandize, but to serve.

April 29, 1989

Thomas Jefferson

As was to be expected, the best line of the late presidential campaign came from Ronald Reagan, who kidded William Jefferson Clinton about the latter's imputed resemblance to Thomas Jefferson. "Well, let me tell you something," quoth Dutch, "I knew Thomas Jefferson. Thomas Jefferson was a friend of mine. And, Bill Clinton"—across the country, grin muscles tightened in expectation of the inevitable punch line—"you're no Thomas Jefferson."

Well, who is, if you get down to it? Jefferson, whose 250th birthday the nation observes this month, was Jefferson. We try vainly, all these years later, to take his full measure.

Jefferson the friend of agrarian democracy and France's revolution, Jefferson the states' righter, the architect, the literary draftsman, the president, the religious skeptic—each is out there, awaiting appreciation. Everyone, to one degree or another, can identify with Jefferson. His twentieth-century patrons have included left-wing radicals and right-wing conservatives. The former profess admiration of his spaciously democratic principles; the latter echo his distrust of centralized government.

For instance: "When all government, domestic and foreign, in little as in great things, shall be drawn to Washington as the center of all power, it will render powerless the checks provided of one government on another, and will become as venal and oppressive as the government from which we separated."

I found this in a Jefferson anthology I bought in 1959, as a college student. In the intervening years, I have quoted it many times. No less bracing, back in the Earl Warren years, were Jefferson's strictures against the federal judiciary, "the subtle corps of sappers and miners constantly working under the ground to undermine the foundations of our confederated fabric."

Jefferson's views on the yeomanry as national backbone were popular in his day but lost out as the industrial revolution advanced. Ironically, now that hardly anyone lives on the land, we are better prepared than in a long time to agree with Jefferson that, "Those who labor in the earth are the chosen people of God;" likewise, that their independent spirit keeps at bay "subservience and venality." This is romantic stuff in the computer age, but it scratches an itch.

The best way to understand Thomas Jefferson is as a member of the most brilliant generation ever to live in, and influence, the United States. Both fortunately and unfortunately, it was the first generation; in a sense, we have been going down ever since the deaths of Washington, Adams, Hamilton, Jefferson, Madison, George Mason, Patrick Henry. If even one star of their magnitude twinkled in our modern political firmament, it would go far toward restoring faith in the political process.

To say the least, not all members of this extraordinary generation agreed with one another. Hamilton, man of the monied interests, and Jefferson, the farmers' friend, saw the world very differently. The seeds of their dispute blossom today in the divisions between those who believe in strong government and those appalled at just how strong the government has become. It is the difference likewise between political optimists and political pessimists. Jefferson trusted the people, Hamilton feared what the people might do if envy ever got the better of them.

What made the early republic glorious was the creative tension between these viewpoints. Neither viewpoint is wholly right, neither wholly wrong.

Jefferson, for instance, was profoundly wrong about the French Revolution, but Hamilton was too sanguine about the benefits likely to flow from promotion of commercial activity. Each viewpoint balanced the other—until the Hamiltonians won the War Between the States and paved the way, for the New Deal, a redistributionist enterprise they would have detested.

Our historical memory today isn't much, owing to the decline of education (in which Jefferson had such a touching faith). This is why these anniversary occasions do us some good. Junior and Sis— touring this big house with the dome—can gasp in amazement that there was so many-sided a man as Thomas Jefferson. The next step, a big one in the MTV era, is to take a book by or about him, open it, read, and think—as he himself thought, using that mind which Providence gave both to him and his country.

April 8, 1993

Edmund Burke

The talk, this summer of 1989, is of the summer exactly two centuries ago when the French Revolution erupted like Vesuvius. There is no sense adding to the conversational buzz. Let me talk instead about a book that is among the revolution's chief legacies; a book, nonetheless, that displays stunningly, luminously, that very spirit the revolution sought to strangle.

The book is Edmund Burke's *Reflections on the Revolution in France*. No work of philosophy, written to throw light upon a single event, has cast more light on the collective past.

When Parisian mobs stormed the Bastille on July 14, 1789, and their earnest middle-class friends undertook subsequently to dismantle the old regime, there was rejoicing throughout Europe and America. Nothing of this sort had ever happened before. A new day was dawning; a new thing was being made.

Across the English Channel, a member of Parliament honored for his many eloquent defenses of liberty looked on with growing horror. Edmund Burke loved liberty, but he defined it differently than did the French.

Liberty, as Burke saw it, came not from the clouds but from deep roots in the social soil; it was to be exercised prudently. The French were acting on the basis of abstract principles concocted by metaphysicians. It would all come to no good. "But what is liberty without wisdom, and without virtue?" Burke asked. "It is the greatest of all possible evils; for it is folly, vice and madness, without tuition and restraint."

Reflections on the Revolution in France, published in November 1790, is a work of profound prophecy as well as deep, if occasionally afactual, analysis. Heads were still on royal French shoulders when Burke set pen to paper. He saw nonetheless what was coming—namely, upheaval, bloodshed, and terror. "The red fool fury of the

Seine" would engulf Europe. Liberty, fraternity, and equality would give way to tyranny.

Burke, a Whig who had befriended the American colonists during their disputes with King George III, was no reactionary. He was for change—gradual, sensible change; change respectful of inherited wisdom and institutions. "Rage and phrenzy," he wrote, "will pull down more in half an hour than prudence, deliberation, and foresight can build up in a hundred years."

Burke's ideal was "never wholly new," "never wholly obsolete." No decent provision for the future could be made without resort to the wisdom of the past. Unless generation linked with generation, "men would become little better than the flies of a summer."

For the abstract principles of the revolutionaries, summed up in the claim that everybody was exactly equal, Burke felt only contempt and dismay. Where did these so-called "rights of man" come from? They were inventions. Yes, man had rights—the right to property, the right to protection, and so forth. These were rights of a very different order, rooted in institutions and community.

Society, to Burke, was a great oak. It grew slowly but grandly. The French, so as to plant a new oak, laid their axes to the old one, but in time would be sorry. They would miss the old tree's sheltering branches, its odd, interesting contours.

Reflections on the Revolution in France made a sensation, though not necessarily the kind Burke desired. Former admirers like Thomas Paine flew at him in fury. The great friend of liberty, it was said, had turned against liberty: the difficulty here being that "liberty" of the French sort quickly turned on people like Paine. Burke's forecast proved accurate: The revolution duly devoured its children. The guillotine became its symbol, until in due course a new Caesar, named Bonaparte, stepped in to restore order.

Two centuries after his death and burial in an unmarked grave (he feared the revolutionaries would conquer England and take vengeance on his corpse), Burke is revered as the father of modern English and American conservatism. His principles, put to the test, proved true—as they would again in 1917, when revolution engulfed Russia.

We may be or may not be exiting the age of revolution, but Burke's relevance remains total. The social rootlessness he deplored is the chief feature of modern life. Flies of a summer buzz around aimlessly, disconnected from each other because disconnected from a common tradition.

What do we do? Here is Burke again, his Irish voice booming across the centuries: "To be attached to the subdivision, to love the little platoon we belong to in society, is the first principle (the germ as it were) of public affections."

We rebuild from the ground up—the family, the church, the community. Liberty, and all things meaningful, grow from the bottom up; oppression descends from the top, like Dr. Guillotin's blade, lopping off what is venerable, ancient, and lovely.

The twentieth century needs Burke as much as the eighteenth century needed him. That is how it is with truths—they never wither, never grow old.

July 14, 1989

Margaret Thatcher

"I am not a consensus politician," said Margaret Thatcher. "I am a conviction politician."

And so she was, and is, God bless her; and though in the end firmness of conviction brought her down, so for a season it made her great; and her country greater than it had been in decades; and her countrymen freer and more prosperous than in long, long years.

The poet Yeats—not quite a countryman, being Irish, but not so distant in spirit from Mrs. Thatcher—had observed bleakly many years earlier, in *The Second Coming*, how "the best lack all conviction, while the worst are full of passionate intensity."

The West, by the 1970s, wore a "Kick me" sign on its back. The West hated itself—its history, its traditions, its religion. Its enemies, full of passionate intensity, denigrated Western values—like freedom—virtually without fear of rebuke.

So that when Margaret Hilda Roberts Thatcher, in 1979, became the queen's first minister, the world didn't know what to make of a conviction politician. She couldn't be serious, this lady? All that talk about freedom and responsibility? About hard work and old-fashioned values?

It turned out she was deadly serious. With all her heart she believed. No sly builder of consensus here: rather, a political leader with the delicacy and instincts of a Sumo wrestler.

Not since Winston Churchill had a British politician believed with like intensity and fervor, or attempted with such verve to show a stumbling nation to its feet; to prod it back to the path of growth, freedom, and mission.

Her polar opposite was A. J. Balfour, the languid, aristocratic prime minister of eighty years earlier. Churchill, back then, had said of Balfour: "Office at any price was his motto, and the sacrifice of any friend or colleague, at the sacrifice of any principle." Maggie Thatcher was famous for sacrificing colleagues—in behalf, not in spite, of principle. Office, as she saw it, had no meaning apart from the principles that officeholders should uphold and work for.

Britain, in 1979, was ridden with strikes, inefficiency, and burdensome government. The socialists, with Tory acquiescence and sometimes connivance—tut, tut, old boy: all for The Common Good—had reduced British splendors to drabness.

British hands, which had fashioned the Industrial Revolution, no longer had time to build; they were stuck out perpetually, in quest of public charity. A whipped, defeated people lived sullenly in the chambers of those Britons who, when the century opened, claimed lordship over a quarter of the earth's people.

Then came Maggie Thatcher, scourging the temples of ease. She hectored a people sorely in need of hectoring. She sold off inefficient, government-owned enterprises. She reinvigorated free-market processes and private ownership. She sat on bloated, arrogant labor unions until they hollered uncle. She took back the Falkland Islands and stood up to the Soviets, who called her the "Iron Lady." About time, Britons reasoned, that a Western leader possessed a spine made of something more durable than aluminum foil.

"I came to office," said she, "with one deliberate intent: to change Britain from a dependent to a self-reliant society; from a give-it-to-me to a do-it-yourself society; a get-up-and-go instead of a sit-back-and-wait Britain." Ronald Reagan spoke the same way, if in more avuncular tones. Maggie proclaimed herself Mr. Reagan's biggest fan. She knew another conviction politician when she saw one.

The 1980s—the Reagan-Thatcher era, when two tough conservatives dominated the West through conviction and force of character—are gone. Reagan is gone. And, yes, to the world's astonishment, Margaret Thatcher is gone. Her party proved more willing than she to see Britain sucked untimely into a new, speciously united Europe.

Likely Mrs. Thatcher wore out the very people she labored to save. Saviors, after a time, begin to irritate ordinary folk who just want to be left alone to drink their tea. Saviors keep the pot perpetually stirred up. We start saying waspish things about them to the opinion surveys. One day, all of a sudden, poof!—no more savior.

This is of course to miss the present point: Modern Britain's savior saved. Not for always, but long enough, and conspicuously enough, to lift conscience and spirits, the world around.

For a decade, a British prime minister and an American president evoked the human possibilities inherent in free choice and the shouldering of personal responsibilities. Maggie Thatcher and Ronald Reagan, just by being themselves, probably did more than Mikhail Gorbachev to undermine communism and liberate Eastern Europe.

"Hail and farewell" is paltry under the circumstances. For the

Iron Lady, three dozen cheers. No public figure of our time worked harder to deserve the Western world's sadly ephemeral gratitude.

November 28, 1990

Ronald Reagan

As his party rumbled along toward a star-spangled Election Day triumph, the man who made it all possible announced to the world that he has Alzheimer's disease.

Life without Ronald Reagan seems unthinkable, but his announcement makes us wrestle with the thoroughly disagreeable prospect. We know the time is coming—as it must, in theological as well as physical terms, for all men. It is moral to pray that the time should be short, so that the eighty-three-year-old former president might be spared needless suffering.

It is odd, it is agonizing, this withness and apartness: Ronald Reagan here but less "here" with perhaps every passing day. He says he hopes to "promote greater awareness" of his condition. We may be certain he will do exactly that.

His announcement, for all the pain it brings, has political symmetry. For days, the Democrats have in strident tones urged rejection of—in Bill Clinton's words—"policies that failed America in the past."

Policies such as what? Like cutting taxes, for instance; like sloughing off federal powers to state and local government and even—gasp!—to private enterprise; like maintaining a generally high moral tone as example to the country; like maintaining American military strength at whatever cost seems necessary.

Such are the "failed" policies of the Reagan years and, to a lesser degree, of the Bush years that followed. Clinton thinks the voters are amenable to rhetorical yelps depicting the Reagan-Bush years as grim and ghastly. The gentleman has another think coming.

The Reagan years were in fact wildly successful. Prosperity and military strength, both neglected under Jimmy Carter, were restored. Patriotism and love of country, under a president neither so high nor so mighty he couldn't mist up on a good flag-waving occasion, came back in fashion. A few months after Reagan left office, the Soviet empire began to crack and crumble. A few months more, and it lay in ruins: America's Carthage overcome by its own flawed reading of human nature, and of American determination to remain free.

Was it, then, the kingdom of heaven in which we lived during the 1980s? Certainly not! The kingdom of heaven cannot and will not be found on this fallen earth, and in any case, the Reagan administration had its problems: weakness or hesitation at critical moments; a reluctance to press home its agenda; too many weak, watery officials in charge of policy. The Reagan administration achieved less than it might have achieved, given its opportunities. Where, for instance, was the overwhelming assault on government spending? Still, we ended up stronger in 1989, and more united, than in many a year.

What did old Dutch have as president that his successors failed to emulate? A vision, first of all; and the personal attributes to sell it. At the worst of times, Reagan knew what he was *trying* to do, even if he couldn't do it. The people understood, and largely forgave. Second, he had faith and courage, which united to form that most American attribute, optimism—the expectation that, yes, sir, things were getting better, and just try telling an American otherwise.

And brains—what about those? More than ample; enough certainly to distinguish good policy from bad, and, most of the time, friend from foe. Dutch, as president, knew viscerally what was good and right; he didn't have to puzzle it out—in sharp contrast with the man who would occupy his office a scant four years later.

In short, behold a true leader, Ronald Wilson Reagan: the only man who could have done what he did when he did it. What a joy to say these things outside an obituary. No black crepe hangs hereabouts. If the former president, as his letter says, enters the sunset of life, his achievements leave the sky brightly glowing for his nation. Ronald Reagan's life recalls what politics, the despised profession, can achieve—provided you have the right politicians.

November 7, 1994

John Paul II

Fortunately, just as the O. J. Simpson mess was getting out of hand, the pope landed. There couldn't have been a better time for the world's preeminent moral leader to stick his nose into our affairs.

Hard-shell fundamentalists used to wring their hands over the "Pope of Rome." This was during a time of religious consensus. It could be taken for granted that however people might divide on theological questions, they accepted religious-based truth as the great guide in human affairs.

No more, that's for sure. The O. J. mess—what else do we call such a mixture of media-driven acrimony and sleaze?—makes plain how morally confused we have become. In these secularized times, the moral law doesn't "resonate" (to borrow a fashionable word).

It doesn't bind either. If it bound and restrained and guided, as it once did, fallout from the O. J. mess would be hugely different.

To begin with, O. J.'s celebrity would never have dazzled us. Not his fame but his conduct would have been the touchstone. Celebrity purchased for him perhaps not immunity from criticism but certainly the benefit of the doubt on various questions, starting with wife-beating and proceeding to capital murder. The authorities were obliged to tread gingerly in the matter of a jerk who happens to be world-famous.

And also black. The race question distorted everything. Blacks and whites, it became evident, couldn't trust each other. Or refused to, which came to the same thing. Guilt, innocence, credibility—in practice if not in theory, race continues to influence all such matters.

It wasn't the moral law's finest hour, the O. J. mess. ("Hour"? If only it could have been so brief!)

The pope's visit is like air freshener in the fetid environment of the O. J. mess. One doesn't have to be Roman Catholic—as I'm not—to smell the effect. John Paul II reminds us of something that formerly was much plainer than it has become in modern times. He reminds us of the true standards for judging.

How do we measure the worth of a man or woman? According to fame? According to income? The great virtues the pope preaches are faith, hope, and love.

What has any of them to do with TV contracts and book deals? The pontiff would rebuke us for flopping on our stomachs before the altar of worldly achievement.

How do husbands and wives treat each other? The moral law speaks powerfully to that question. They treat each other with enduring love and respect. There is no room for abuse of any kind in a relationship sanctified by God: not physical assault and, above all, not murder.

And how do the races treat each other? There is an old Sunday school song: "Red and yellow, black and white, they are precious in His sight." Religion alone erases differences of color and culture with the knowledge and the conviction that God has made every single soul in the world. There is no surer tonic for racial division. Nonetheless, it gathers dust on the supermarket shelves. Witness all the pre-verdict tensions between blacks and whites, not to mention the post-verdict ones (which, among other things, may sink Colin Powell's presidential candidacy).

There is serendipity in Great Events. All the attention directed at the pope's coming will not obliterate all the righteous anger over the O. J. mess. What it may do is put into some minds an idea in two parts.

The first part is that a society dedicated to celebrity and preening and raw acquisition and the venting of personal—or group—grievances is a society in mortal danger.

The second part is that there's a better, safer way that is based on acknowledgment of common humanity and the obligations and responsibilities that flow from such an acknowledgment. We call that way the moral law. At least, we did in the days—not all that distant—when faith, hope, and love were more central concerns than choices, preferences and rights. They are the O. J. style and the John Paul style—for a few days, we can watch them operate side by side. I wouldn't bet on its being much of a match.

October 6, 1995

William F. Buckley Jr.

I've been neglecting the matter of Bill Buckley's new book, and I'm not sure why, unless it's that when you say "Bill Buckley" to some people, a superior look spreads over their faces, translatable as "Hmmmmph, these people who can't communicate except by thumbing through *Roget's Thesaurus* . . ."—and so you put off raising the matter, and in the end, all you can do is apologize because the truth is, *Buckley: The Right Word* (this being the book's title) is compelling and irresistible, and I can't keep from picking it up to thumb back through it, which could also be the reason I haven't written about it. Oh, well.

I wouldn't suggest there is any constitutional requirement actually to like Buckley's famous prose style: one of the most famous prose styles since Macaulay's. The main chore is to appreciate the Buckleyan style for what it is: language-loving, word-caressing, syntax-adoring. We need more such love in this age that specializes in just about every other kind of love (besides celebrating them in five-buck magazines with centerfolds).

If there were more genuine love of English, there might be more lovable English writing instead of the loose and humdrum stuff in which the best-seller lists abound. (No examples; you know who wrote *The Bridges of Madison County*.) The very title, *The Right Word*, suggests the current dominance of wrong words, profitably bound between hard covers.

The public service that Samuel S. Vaughan, Buckley's editor through twenty-two books, has undertaken is the gathering together, in five hundred pages, of his client's best writing about writing. I doubt there has been so useful and lively a book issued since the sainted James Jackson Kilpatrick's *The Writers Art*, and that was a decade ago. (Buckley rightly praises it here.)

The Right Word, despite issuing from a man of the right, isn't about conservatism or conservative politics. It is about the imaginative and effective use of English. Can, shall we say, non-conservatives learn from it? Only by turning the pages.

What is the Buckley trade secret? Use big words like "congeries" and "ratiocination" and then everybody will say how smart you are? That's a canard the author refutes convincingly (at least in my own understanding of "convincingly"). But not as convincingly as his writings refute it: page after page after page of prose you might actually call conversational. Pomposity? Less of that rears its head in Buckley than in the average Al Gore speech. What is less pompous, less rococo, than an editorial beginning, "I first laid eyes on her in 1948" (from his obituary for Clare Boothe Luce)?

There arise in our media-saturated culture myths and fables for which there is no clear origin, and certainly no basis. Among these is that William F. Buckley's writings are hard going. No, they aren't — they're fun. Yes, fun: the kind of fun that proceeds from watching a pool champion run the table and, equally, the kind that flows from plain old good cheer and humor. Buckley's writing abounds in these latter commodities. The man loves life. It shows.

This was always Buckley's genius when he was active at *National*

Review—infusing with joy a serious philosophical enterprise, like saving Western civilization. That which, in Buckley, is pure English cavalier—jollity and toasting and talking—is the thing his liberal-Roundhead adversaries seem most to hate. Why can't he be what they want him to be? Then they truly could grind him down.

Am I writing more about Buckley than about his writing? Can't help it. Misconceptions have to go. Hate his politics, if you will, but accord proper respect to the language in which he frames his convictions and to the wit and grace and precision with which he deploys that language.

Some of the best writing of our time is in this fat volume, as in the dozens of previous volumes Buckley has given us. Buy one (this one especially). See how it's done. Try it. It won't work—for any of us. Try anyway.

March 17, 1997

Vaclav Havel

Out of the East comes Vaclav Havel, Czechoslovakia's playwright president, urging Congress to help the Soviet Union wobble toward democracy. But then, in a passionate passage, he points beyond ballots and bullets both.

"Without a global revolution in the sphere of human consciousness," Mr. Havel tells Congress, "nothing will change for the better in the sphere of our being. We still don't know how to put morality ahead of politics, science, and economy. We are still incapable of understanding that the only genuine backbone of all our actions, if they are to be moral, is responsibility—responsibility to something higher than my family, my country, my success."

It is indeed a new day. A world statesman is standing on tip-toe, peering into the human soul. He can't be much encouraged by what he sees.

The twentieth century has largely succeeded in stamping out the whole notion of responsibility. The lack of a governing moral and social ethic is modern society's most conspicuous characteristic.

Conspicuous, I say, now that competing distractions are passing from view. For instance, we no longer call for building more stately mansions of federal power. The Reagan revolution took care of that.

Likewise the crumbling of communism—once the whole worm-eaten edifice is really and truly down—will free us from standing round-the-clock sentry duty. It is hard, with finger on trigger and eyeballs skinned for bad guys, to think about "responsibility to something higher."

The fact is, communism does not cause AIDS. The budget deficit is not at the root of divorce, desertion, drugs, child abuse, rape, abortion, suicide, and other horrors, none particularly modern but all growing fast in currency.

What Havel calls "the sphere of our being" suffers because of the decline of religion as the major factor in human existence. The last two centuries are an unedifying chronicle of human beings trying to free themselves from responsibility to anything higher than their own appetites.

For eighteen hundred years, Western man considered himself under obligation to his Creator. This did not mean we had for eighteen hundred years a society of saints, or even that Christians weren't ready to kill each other over a point of doctrine. It meant that there existed a higher point of reference than mere appetite or human insight.

There were the Ten Commandments, for instance, which were posted in classrooms until the Supreme Court stopped this horrid threat to constitutional liberties. There was also the Catechism, a sample of which I offer in its Anglican version:

"Question: What is thy duty towards thy Neighbour? Answer: My duty towards my Neighbour is to love him as myself, and to do all men as I would they should do unto me; to love, honour, and

succour my father and mother; to honour and obey the civil authority; to be true and just in all my dealing; to bear no malice nor
hatred in my heart; to keep my hands from picking and stealing, and
my tongue from evil speaking, lying, and slandering."

Wouldn't that go over big in today's church, assuming it wouldn't
be sandwiched in between the "U. S. out of El Salvador" rally next
Sunday and the new weeknight class on Christian T-bill investing?

Religion is not pie in the sky; its place is the here and now. Religion has here-and-now effects, as does its absence or, sometimes
worse, its complacence.

Pulling the Ten Commandments off the classroom wall did not
precipitate the present moral crisis; it merely symptomizes that in-
difference to religion which undercuts all hope of moral order.

Vaclav Havel was not in Washington to whomp up a foot-stomp-
ing Baptist revival, or even to argue out the basic question of religious transcendence. He raised nonetheless some fundamental
considerations, such as, what happens when we make ourselves—
our jobs and our pastimes, our tastes, our aspirations—the center of
the universe? What then of responsibility? Does irresponsibility
bring joy and success, or sterility and despair?

We have just begun to think on these matters. Havel, with his
artist's eye, would suggest they are the only matters that matter.
Amen, brother.

February 24, 1990

H. L. Mencken

Poor old Henry Mencken, thirty-four years dead, has been caught
with his rhetorical pants down.

His newly published diaries seep with racism, anti-semitism, and
not-so-latent admiration of the Third Reich. It is as though virtuous Uncle Ned, the pillar of the community, an inspiration to young

and old, had been indicted for unbecoming familiarity with Girl Scouts.

The diaries reflect, among other unsightly things, the author's unappreciative opinion of Jews, his loathing of Franklin Roosevelt, his respect (at one point anyway) for Adolf Hitler, and some condescending judgments on blacks.

Disillusioned Menkenites aren't sure they shouldn't turn the old boy's picture to the wall. The National Press Club, in ever-righteous Washington, D.C., is considering changing the name of its Mencken Library and Reference Center.

I am having the time of my life with all this, how about you?

We talk here about the Great Liberal Folk Hero of the early twentieth century. Walter Lippman called him "the most powerful personal influence on this whole generation of educated people"— meaning liberal people, the kind who read improving books and wash under their arms.

Yes, yes, of course it was an everlasting hoot when Mencken blasted religion, morals, piety, and traditional literature. And when he jeered at the farmer as "a tedious fraud and ignoramus, a cheap rogue and hypocrite, the eternal Jack of the human pack."

Mencken didn't admire Jews? He didn't admire Anglo-Saxons— "a mongrel and inferior people"—either. The Anglo-Saxons of Dayton, Tennessee, site of the Scopes trial, were "morons, yokels, peasants, and a genus homo boobiensis." Ho, ho, ho; a "whole generation of educated people" could hardly rise from the floor for laughing.

Ah, then comes 1989, and publication of the Mencken diaries (written in the 1930s and 1940s). The laughter fades in mid-chortle. "Racially insensitive" remarks? As the little girl said when she stepped on a caterpillar: Oooooo! Icky!

I trust that as a charter non-devotee of the H. L. Mencken cult I have the standing to say: Lighten up, everybody, lighten up.

First, because, as I hope the foregoing helps to demonstrate, hypocrisy is unappealing. Is Mencken funny and enlightened only when his fingers are wrapped around conservative windpipes? That's what his liberal devotees, the ones raising all the fuss, seem to be saying. If that's what they truly think, they're nuts.

In the second place, nothing in the diary should surprise anybody. Mencken was boastfully German-American. All his acolytes know very well the master's devotion to Nietzsche, Hitler's favorite philosopher, about whom he wrote a book. Similarly, Mencken adored Wagner, Hitler's favorite composer. It never occurred to me to wonder whether Mencken liked the führer. He had to.

Indeed, Mencken apparently saw himself as a sort of Nietzschean superman, ordained to give law to the Great Unwashed. An individual of great personal kindness and generosity, Mencken nonetheless despised the mass of humanity.

Finally, we should keep in mind that, for all his defects, Mencken was a brilliant writer and stylist. I am too much the gentleman to name names, but some of the journalistic gentry who have been beating up on the old man couldn't write a stylish thank-you note. They are bores and dullards.

Mencken never bored. His tools were brass knuckles and the hot poker; he gave, wrote Frederick Lewis Allen, "the sort of intense visceral delight which comes from heaving baseballs at crockery in an amusement park."

Ladies, gentlemen—the statute of limitations has run on our brother Mencken's offenses, real or putative. All together now: "Free Henry Mencken"—from enforced relevance to an age he would have enjoyed even less than his own. Judge him on what he meant to the 1920s and 1930s, not the 1980s.

As the old boy himself said, in a mild moment, "I set up my pitch in life on a busy and interesting street. I did a good business, and I have no regrets."

Why should we?

January 3, 1990

Robert McNamara

But *of course* he's right, Bob McNamara is. Most Americans were onto the sulphurous truth prior to its reaching the defense secretary's nostrils.

A war of escalation through air strikes—succeeded by de-escalation whenever the North Vietnamese seemed in a peaceful mood—was inherently unwinnable. "Park it or drive it" was Paul Harvey's crisp advice to a White House that seemed to be joyriding in circles.

In a real war, two courses are open: Give it everything or get out. McNamara and Lyndon Johnson shrank from both expedients. They said, in effect, we would win by *not* winning. So we lost, and the bitterness took root in our national soul. There is no reason other than this for a book about Vietnam to engage attention the way McNamara's not-quite mea culpa, *In Retrospect*, has engaged it.

As the McNamara-bashers bash away with zest and zeal, one point about the war needs underscoring. It does not expiate McNamara; it explains him.

The point is that Vietnam was the kind of war likely to be waged by the kind of politician we had in the 1960s. Our public men in those days, now mercifully behind us, practiced the politics of expertise.

David Halberstam, the reporter and author, was onto it when he gave his book about the Vietnam warmakers the fetching title, *The Best and the Brightest*. The common people—voters, taxpayers—might not know what was what about Southeast Asian strategy or even where Southeast Asia might be. No matter, that was what we had intellectuals for; well-groomed people with Ph.D.s in management or Asiatic studies. Ivy League-trained eyes would set computers to whirring. It remained only to read the printout, then act.

And why not? The age of liberal bureaucracy, which ripened after Dwight Eisenhower's retirement from the presidency, was the age of micro-management. In the 1960s, and for some time afterwards, it seemed there were no mysteries left—none, at least, that right-thinking, *New York Times*-reading intellectuals were incapable of penetrating.

Disciples of John Maynard Keynes drank in economic statistics with the delight that soothsayers formerly lavished on animal entrails. You could tell—supposedly—whether the economy needed speeding up or slowing down. The Federal Reserve Board, grave as Chinese mandarins, decided how much money the economy required in a given month, then took steps to make sure that that was the amount it would have.

Even social policy, formerly the province of philosophers, came under the influence of the micro-managers. X dollars in federal spending would produce Y quantity of wonderful effects. Poverty could be eliminated, the unemployed turned into productive citizens, the long legacy of racism extirpated.

The micro-managers, like McNamara, who was president of Ford Motor Company before joining the Kennedy administration, were long on statistical calculations, short on grasp of human nature—a commodity they thought to be pliable in any case. The North Vietnamese could be understood more or less as shorter Americans, subject to the same incentives (peace talks) and disincentives (bombings) as ourselves.

Johnson seemed never to grasp that you have peace only when peace is the thing all parties to a conflict desire. Our on again, off again war in Vietnam never had a serious chance. We wanted peace more than victory. We got—defeat. And with it social disruption on a scale that no one, during the placid Eisenhower years, could have foretold.

The good news is, it isn't that bad today. We are working our way through the horror of those times. We didn't like them, and we don't want to go back.

Technocrats and micro-managers are as out of style as capri pants.

Militarily, economically, culturally, the nation's respect for common sense seems finally to exceed its regard for smug micro-management and control-everything policy wonkery.

Does it seem that way to you, too, President Clinton?

April 17, 1995

Robert Packwood

Let me suggest, gentle reader, how society would have dealt with Bob Packwood back in the good old days. On learning of Packwood's exploits against one of their flesh and blood, the male family members would have foregathered in the parlor. After minimal conversation, they would have saddled up and paid an unannounced call on the senator.

"Senator," their spokesman would have said, solemn as a minister on Sunday, "our sister told us about you. Senator, you show your face around her again, you step out of line just the least bit, and . . ." There might have occurred at this juncture the eloquent brandishing of a horsewhip or knob-headed cane. Silently, the visitors would have taken their leave. Senatorial depredations against one woman, at all events, would likely have ceased.

I say all this not to commend extracurricular justice but to underline how the moral climate of the country has changed so as to accommodate—more often than to punish—the Bob Packwoods.

Packwood's fieriest accusers make him out to be just a typical man. The heck he is. The senator is a jerk—a cad, in good-old-days parlance. Of course, we don't speak in those quaint terms any more, the old norms concerning cad-dom having evaporated. In consequence of this, we get Bob Packwood, public servant and pawer of women. And Teddy Kennedy, one might add for the sake of bipartisanship.

No, the senators are not gentlemen. And does anybody care? Seemingly not. You wouldn't exactly call this an age devoted to the maintenance of codes such as gentlemen and ladies used to impose on themselves.

In counterculture America, gentlemen turned into mere men and ladies into mere women. Gentlemen and ladies have moral and spiritual rights as members of a civilized community; men and women have only political rights—a deeply inferior species.

Packwood's repeated offenses against women were political. He violated women's constitutional status as co-equals. Under the older, better dispensation, he would have been seen to insult their station as co-creators of life under the providence of God.

Co-*what*? The jerk from Oregon didn't spend long on such old-fashioned categories. Even before *Roe v. Wade*, as he boasted in his valedictory, he unsuccessfully introduced legislation asserting a federal right to abortion.

The jerk from Oregon was a prize specimen of Liberated Man. He cultivated the pose of sensitivity. Always, his ears were open to women's political claims—as long as those claims remained political and not moral.

Was Packwood, the cad, a prize hypocrite? It depends on what you mean by hypocrisy. Bless his heart, he did prize women—as soulless political cogs, as voting units. Did that preclude his violating their spiritual dignity, their moral rights? Under the old dispensation, it would have. Which is why the victims' brothers would have come calling on him.

Wouldn't they have trembled at his power and prestge? Hardly. The older dispensation was less impressed than ours is with politics —a largely debased profession useful mainly in keeping the streets repaired and crooks locked up.

Today's politicians consider themselves demi-gods; if yesterday's were more modest, it was because we asked less of the political class than is customary today.

The reason political dignity eclipses spiritual dignity is that we've placed politics, rather than religion, at the center of modern affairs. How are you going to breed Christian gentlemen, please, in an environment where the giver of all good gifts is government? Let's just say it's not easy.

Bob Packwood is a modernist of purest essence: Worse yet, as his recorded "diaries" make plain, he's a modernist politician. His type isn't going to respect anyone's spiritual worth, inasmuch as "spiritual worth to the Packwood type is rhetorical gas. That's where male relatives used to come in handy—but, of course, we're glad those barbaric days are over. I mean, aren't we?

September 11, 1995

III

In Memoriam

THE OBITUARY is often the best format, journalistically speaking, for the appraisal of the principles that particular individuals happened to exemplify. This is true whether the subjects were famous—as many of these were—or "known only to God"—no mean commendation, come to think of it.

Mother Teresa of Calcutta

"Let us do something beautiful for God," said Mother Teresa of Calcutta again and again. And so she did infinitely beautiful things, again and again: a joyful, perpetual offering of body and spirit and worldly means for God's glory and his people's relief.

She argued gently with the spirit of the age and even with the age's leaders: for life, against abortion, against pointless suffering. "Every child is God's child," she said.

To prove it, she roved the gruesome streets of Calcutta. Here, an abandoned child; there, a dying woman. Her Missionaries of Charity took them in and did what they could, which was as much as God required of them. The missionaries swelled in number, and their areas of endeavor reached nearly five hundred worldwide. Mother Teresa won the Nobel Peace Prize.

Are we to look, as she goes to rest, for the flower-mountains, the armies of correspondents, the long funeral procession that figured, and may figure for a long time, in the world's goodbye to Princess Diana? Not likely. The worldwide wake for the radiant princess and the long-anticipated death of the wrinkled nun are separate events, fused chiefly by the coincidence of time. Searching for comparisons between the two women would be pointless. They lived on different planes of existence and traveled on separate trajectories.

Another way of putting it would be this: The world understood Princess Diana better than it understood Mother Teresa. Why? Because the world only imperfectly understands saints—when it condescends to acknowledge their existence.

An English book still read and consulted after two centuries is Alban Butler's *Lives of the Principal Saints. Deaths of the Principal Saints* could serve equally well as title.

The saints always seem to be dying: suffering torments unimaginable to folk who feel discommoded when the air conditioning goes out. Lions, axes, saws, crucifixes, Luger pistols, the gas chamber—the means of dispatching the saints seem endless and probably are. Saints, for keeping the faith, are dispatched today—in the age of MTV and the world wide web!—in lands like Uganda and the Sudan.

The point with the saints is not so much their physical dying. What they have let go of already—long before the gleaming of the executioner's blade in the sunlight—is the life of appetite and ambition, power and perquisite. To do "something beautiful for God" is the whole and only wish of the saints.

Small wonder an age that barely understands God has trouble understanding the saints: messy, often bothersome people who are uninterested in conventional rewards, never dependent on riches, never beaten down by poverty or suffering.

A writer in Calcutta, dealing with the Mother Teresa phenomenon, fulminates over the little nun's "relentless ascent to sainthood." "Relentless"—hmmm. All those children taken in off the streets, wounds bandaged, lives transfigured. A little more relentlessness, please!

Meanwhile, the quest for meaning goes on and on—the quest to reconcile joy and suffering, pain and achievement, long life and sudden death, a two hundred thousand–dollar ring in the wreckage of a luxury automobile. The quest is to fit all these factors into some kind of rational framework. A princess, fairest of the fair, suffers, struggles, dies—millions mourn. No, no,—not Diana, not "England's Rose." The blow that can fell one of fortune's favorites can fall any-where—on you, on me. And if so . . . ?

The saints catch our eye at such a moment. The saints know how to transcend and transfigure the pain of this mortal existence. How? By doing "something beautiful for God."

The punishing secularity of the late twentieth century—no age was ever so indifferent to God or gods—makes the Mother Teresa solution difficult to receive.

"Something beautiful for God"? Why? What's in it for us? "Only everything," Mother Teresa might have responded—joy, fulfill-ment, even immortality amid death and sorrow and sacrifice.

September 9, 1997

Iza Murchison Wallin Conine

At last, a month and a half after my aunt's funeral, it dawned on me: There was nothing wrong with this lady.

I do not mean in the physical sense. The bodies of eighty-six-year-old women wear out in due course. I do not mean in the spiri-tual sense. Original Sin, if the theologians are right and I do not see human history refuting them—has us all in its grip.

With my aunt, nonetheless, there had been nothing basically wrong: nothing you wanted to knead or pummel into shape.

This came to me some weeks after the funeral, as we nieces and nephews closed down her Austin home—International Headquar-ters of the Murchison Family, I liked to call it.

What would any of us have changed about Iza Murchison Wallin Conine? Her gentle temper, her lack of guile and malice, her fondness for a good joke (and for a judiciously proportioned Weller-and-Water)? What about her devotion to friends and family? No, I think we would have changed nothing. She lived with love and did her duty as aunt, sister-in-law, friend, hospital volunteer, and patient daughter of the church. Hers was a life of—here I invoke an unfashionable word—virtue.

Why did this not occur to me earlier? A life of virtue, entailing commitment to family and friends and community and God before commitment to self, might have made my aunt big news. Extra, extra! "Woman Puts Others First!" News for the 1990s, wouldn't you think?

Maybe not. News today is Madonna, selling—um, personal expression. Kneeling women who whisper to a very different Madonna (my aunt was Roman Catholic, devotedly so) have no hope of attracting notice. What are they doing—giving instead of receiving, refraining rather than expressing? Yawn. Do what pops into your head if the thing you most want is to get noticed.

Which is my point: the smoothness and plainness and regularity and everydayness of virtue. Is that not, paradoxically, an exciting thing? It seems so to me. The virtuous among us, so steady and still, may be more numerous than our cultural pessimism makes us suppose.

I tried to remember recently: Had my aunt ever snapped or snarled about life's way with her? Why, no—though had she done so, the psychotherapists would have smiled benignly. She had been twice widowed. A miscarriage left her unable to bear children. Her response was to "adopt" nephews and nieces, and subsequently *their* children, to take life on its own terms rather than on any she might've dreamt up and to do her best, simply and quietly, with what she had been given. Her gifts of friendship were extraordinary ("Iza never meets a stranger," family members used to say), yet she seemed content that life in the political hotbed of Austin rarely threw her in with the world beaters and shakers.

Virtue is out there. Can't we see it? Perhaps we expect a dress-up show. Flourishes of trumpets! The beating of drums! A Disney-land parade down Main Street. Hail, Virtue! When finally virtue comes on foot, in a plain print dress and everyday makeup, our eyes pass anxiously over its head.

Virtue is unquestioning love, forgiveness extended even when unrequested, anger and acrimony snuffed out—the supportive hand, the search for Good Things that need doing. Virtue asks nothing for itself, least of all for the chance to get one's hands on someone, or something, and turn it inside out. Virtue is all modesty.

God bless my aunt Iza, there was nothing wrong with her. Everything about her, humanly speaking, was right. And so her remarkableness went unremarked. It was too quiet for comment—too patient and daily.

Perhaps this helps explain how life proceeds as successfully as it does. The big shots do their respective things; the quiet and loyal and loving and diligent say their prayers, look for occasions to serve, refuse complaint, do their duty, make the rest of us look often enough like boobs, ninnies, and ingrates. The power of our glory is varnish and scuff polish to those with the gifts of love and sacrifice— bless 'em all, bless 'em forever.

September 1, 1997

Whittaker Chambers

The death of Alger Hiss, at ninety-two, cracks the door for rehashes, and rehashes of rehashes, of the Case of the Century. It cracks the door at least as wide for mention, in this Thanksgiving season, of a book for which to be profoundly thankful.

The book is not by Alger Hiss; it is by Whittaker Chambers, the man who in 1948 threw away security and esteem to identify Hiss as a Soviet agent.

Witness is about honor and treason and good and evil and man and God and the conflicts raging eternally among them.

With the end of the Cold War, subject and title have lost some of their resonance. Yet *Witness* made its distinctive contribution to the ending of the Cold War by identifying the stakes in the contest and the ground on which the honorable and just were to stand.

Whittaker Chambers, the *Time* magazine editor and ex-communist agent, was more than a great heart; he was a great writer. "Foreword in the Form of a Letter to My Children" should be assigned reading in all public schools for its ache and beauty.

The letter recalls the furor surrounding Chambers's congressional testimony that the dapper New Dealer Alger Hiss had been (and might still be) a communist agent. The furor almost swallowed the witness himself.

He speaks softly, lovingly, to his children. He tells them what a witness is: "a man whose life and faith are so completely one that when the challenge comes to step out and testify for his faith, he does so, disregarding all risks, accepting all consequences."

Why so willingly in this particular case? Because the Hiss case involved nothing less than "the two irreconcilable faiths of our time— Communism and Freedom. . . ."

"The Communist vision," as Chambers understood, "is the vision of Man without God. It is the vision of man's mind displacing God as the creative intelligence of the world. . . ."

The case enveloped the nation; it enveloped the Chambers family as Hiss's friends and well-wishers (who saw the case in part as an attack on liberalism and the New Deal) counterattacked. Chambers's morale sank. One day, after the milking on his quiet farm, he contemplated suicide. The voice of his young son—"Papa! Papa!"— called him back to life: "'Papa,' he cried and threw his arms around me, 'don't ever go away.'" Then, a few steps farther on, this sublimity:

> My children, when you were little, we used to go for walks in
> our pine woods. . . . you used instinctively to give me your hands

as we entered those woods, where it was darker, lonelier, and in the stillness our voices sounded loud and frightening. In this book, I am again giving you my hands. I am leading you, not through cool pine woods, but up and up a narrow defile between bare and steep rocks from which in shadow things uncoil and slither away. It will be dark. But, in the end, if I have led you aright, you will make out three crosses, from two of which hang thieves. I will have brought you to Golgotha—the place of skulls. This is the meaning of the journey. Before you understand, I may not be there, my hands may have slipped from yours. It will not matter. For when you understand what you see, you will no longer be children. You will know that life is pain, that each of us hangs always upon the cross of himself. And when you know that this is true of every man, woman, and child on earth, you will be wise.

There is nothing more beautiful in American writing—perhaps nothing *as* beautiful. And eight hundred pages follow!

Poor Alger Hiss. What could he say, in lawyerly rebuttal to such all-seeing eloquence? Forget the Woodstock typewriters and prothonotary warblers that transfix students of the case. In *Witness*, a book of such depth and richness no liar could have written it, Whittaker Chambers won the Hiss case forever.

May the God whom communists deny give rest to Alger Hiss. Whatever his defects and disloyaties, one service he performed: inadvertently inspiring the greatest moral testament of the late twentieth century.

November 25, 1996

M. E. Bradford

Public occasions—this is one—rarely call for blubberiness on the part of their initiators; but on the other hand, Dr. Mel Bradford is dead at fifty-eight, and I make no promises.

A beloved friend, dinner-table companion and soulmate of two decades' standing is gone. This is not even the whole of the matter. My trousers rustle in the bitter winds from which his vast presence— six-foot plus and 350 pounds—shielded comrades struggling to save the soul of the West. He was our intellectual Hector, ready with a gesture, a quotation, a closely reasoned allusion from history to give the infidels a swift kick in the pants.

Melvin E. Bradford, professor of English at the University of Dallas, loved the simple culture of an earlier America. This had nothing to do with nostalgia; it had everything to do with philosophy.

In a dozen scholarly books (with titles like *Against the Barbarians*), in hundreds of articles, in speeches galore, in table talk as rich and nourishing as I hope to hear this side of heaven, Mel Bradford stuck up for the old virtues as against the new debaucheries. He believed in duty, piety, respect, moral courage, self-denial, and the now-unfashionable like. His ideal social order was one whose members lived as free men and women in relationships based on mutual obligation.

He saw glimmerings of this ideal in the culture of the old republic, and especially that of his native South, whose history and literature he knew inside out. Leviathan government he viewed as a disruptive and poisonous force. People needed to be respected for what they did and said; politicians were a hindrance—always inventing abstract "rights" for purposes of electoral bribery.

Though Mel lived in a Dallas suburb, his voice carried the length and breadth of the nation, and occasionally across the Atlantic, to Europe. The scope of his interests was astounding. He had read everything; better still, he remembered ninety-nine percent of it.

Mel was that queer and sometimes contradictory creature, the activist professor. Ah, but not on the side inhabited by today's leftist professoriate: the side of government interference and endless hand-wringing over the alleged offenses of our forebears, a.k.a. the Dead

White Males. Any side but that one for Mel! The Dead White Males, from the Greeks and Romans up through the founding fathers and beyond, were his folk. Not because of sex, race, or inability to interrupt his rhetorical flights, but rather on account of their wisdom and prudence.

Few such folk were to be glimpsed in modern political thickets. From duty and inclination alike, Mel took a hand: as stump speaker, organizer, motivator, theoretician. He promoted, sequentially, the causes of Barry Goldwater, George C. Wallace, Ronald Reagan, and Patrick Buchanan. And paid the price.

For a time, Mel's own University of Dallas didn't know what to make of him. He was too much the man of action for more self-effacing academic types. In 1981, his hero Reagan would have named him director of the National Endowment for the Humanities but for vicious attacks launched by Mel's enemies. The professor had made bold, in widely read articles, to fault Abe Lincoln for grafting onto the American political tradition a specious equality ("dedicated to the proposition that all men are created equal") which most of the founders would have repudiated.

Well, one just didn't say such things in the civil rights era—even if they were true. Mel's detractors tried to deck him out in king-size Klan robes. More open-minded observers saw that the Dallas prof had courageously raised a delicate point bearing on a central problem of the day: whether equality must be earned or whether it can and should be spoon-fed. In any case, Mel's *elan* never recovered entirely from the abuse heaped on him. Prophesying, he had met the fate of the prophets—persecution and hardship.

And was he sorry? Not a bit of it. Anyway, not so sorry that he would have spoken otherwise. In the great civilized tradition Mel Bradford esteemed, a man—if man he was—had glimpsed the truth, spoke it, accepted the consequences and, with head held high, walked toward whatever lay ahead.

March 5, 1993

Russell Kirk

"An irritable mental gesture" was what the literary critic Lionel Trilling called conservatism, and there was worse, much worse, from fellow liberals, some of it actually printable. The American liberal establishment, in the high noon of its glory—the 1940s and the 1950s—was confident in its grasp of the ultimate truths, which were, in no special order, that the past had no claim on us; that man was basically good, as was government; that equality was written in the stars; and God . . . well, God was certainly a Congenial Idea.

Then came Russell Amos Kirk, of Mecosta, Michigan, and the intellectual life began to creak on its hinges, slowly, slowly turning.

Too few Americans know of Russell Kirk, who died last week at age seventy-five. Yet hardly any American is wholly uninfluenced by what he helped to launch—the conservative intellectual movement, which in turn launched the conservative political movement.

What Kirk gave conservatives was their heritage. It had been missing, stored in dusty library basements. The soft-spoken scholar found it, blew off the dust, committed his labors to paper, and, behold, the conservative intellectual movement was born. At forty-one, it is going stronger perhaps than ever.

Sensible people today know that the past has a mighty claim on us, that man isn't necessarily good, that equality isn't written in the stars, that God is exactly who He said He was, now and forever, and don't you go forgetting it.

Russell Kirk wrote an immense number of books and scholarly articles, hardly any of them for "mainstream" publishers. The most original, and most influential, was *The Conservative Mind*, in 1953. "Mental gesture," indeed! Conservatism had a grand intellectual pedigree, through which Kirk confidently guided his readers.

Kirk's heroes were not the conventional ones—Paine and Jefferson and Lincoln—but instead Edmund Burke, John Adams, John Randolph of Roanoke, John Henry Newman, Fenimore Cooper, Alexis de Tocqueville, T. S. Eliot. He assimilated Englishmen and Scotsmen into the American tradition as deftly, and convincingly, as the job market assimilated Lithuanians and Croats. He used them all to teach us "belief in a transcendent order," "affection for the proliferating variety and mystery of human existence," the need for social classes, and dislike for ideologues.

The last point was, with Kirk, a big one. Conservatism wasn't an ideology. It was, as Cardinal Manning had said, "the negation of ideology." Yahoos and badmen—e.g., Hitler and Robespierre—reared their little castles of air and blood: mere figments of the imagination, disconnected from human institutions. True conservatives were the natural enemies of skunks like these.

He was no man of the mainstream, Russell Kirk. He lived amid books in his family's old place, which, with exquisite fitness, he called Piety Hill; his mind, or, rather its habits, he referred to as "Gothic." Yet, the husband of a beautiful wife, he raised four lovely daughters to civilized perfection. Though hardly a golden-mouthed orator— he spoke, often too rapidly, in a soft, high-pitched voice—he loved missionary work. Over the years, he spoke at five hunded different American campuses, including, in 1962, the University of Texas, where a Gothic-minded junior (as I was then) with joy and excitement heard the master hold forth. Kirk helped Bill Buckley launch *National Review*, to which he contributed a column on education—its defects were for him a pet peeve—for nearly a quarter of a century.

With it all he was a gentle, kind, and civilized man; a devout Roman Catholic who, on learning that fire had gutted his beloved ancestral home, fell to his knees, affirming with Job: "The Lord giveth, and the Lord hath taken away; blessed be the name of the Lord."

With Russell Kirk, you never doubted who was in charge. It wasn't ideologues, it wasn't despots; it was Someone infinitely higher, infinitely more enduring.

May 2, 1994

Malcolm Muggeridge

While billions of us the world over were clawing, scratching, scraping away at the business of life, Malcolm Muggeridge attained his fondest wish. He gave up life entirely, finding the fulfillment for which he had thirsted throughout a busier lifetime than most of us can conceive.

He had suffered a stroke three months earlier, the obituaries said. His passing, I can only assume, was serene. How many times he had spoken and written of a recurring vision; floating out of his "aged carcass," watching with detachment and no small sense of relief the worldly scene below; only to return at last to that carcass, reluctantly to enflesh it one more time.

On this last occasion, there was no return, no enfleshment. His admirers, the multitudes whose lives he touched, are bereft. So are they overjoyed for him. So long, Mugg. See you one of these days.

Malcolm Muggeridge—author, Christian apologist, essayist, wit, television commentator, "knockabout journalist," to borrow his own self-depreciatory phrase—had bathed deeply in worldly praise and honors. But it was not the world he wanted, it was heaven. He knew the difference.

Born in England, in 1903, he grew up in an age and place where men exalted the earthly, not the heavenly, kingdom. He yearned to see Jerusalem built (his adored William Blake's words) in England's green and pleasant land. In the New Jerusalem, the state would abolish poverty, discrimination, and war.

He joined the Manchester *Guardian*, which dispatched him to the communist Jerusalem—the Soviet Union—as correspondent. He saw, not brotherhood, but tyranny, barbarism, and starvation; the deliberate starvation, by Stalin, of millions of Ukrainian peasants.

The socialism began to drop from Malcolm like snake's skin. Slowly, against his will even, he put on Christianity, socialism's polar

opposite creed. The old Jerusalem, city of the covenant, where earth
for a time met heaven, was the venue he preferred. The new would
never be built, and if it were built, abortion mills and other temples
of paganism would deface and disgrace it. "In trying to construct
perfection in their own image," he would write years later, "to institute an earthly paradise, men only succeeded in underlining their
own imperfection; their earthly paradise is seen to be a heavenly
hell."

The old Muggeridge, the new Muggeridge—no clear, bright line
separated the two. The wit, the gift of satire, the sense of the absurd,
the dazzling literary style went to work in the service of new—rather,
newly clarified—objectives.

In his youth he had mocked Christianity; he became, in old age,
one if its foremost champions. Still he mocked: this time trendy clergy
and bishops who bent over backward to please the world; defenders
of faithlessness, intent on squeezing all the juices out of the Christian revelation. His model of the faithful Christian was Mother
Teresa—victorious in her total surrender to God.

He declined for years to join any organized religious body: all
the while writing religious prose of great sublimity and fighting for
religious principles. He was conspicuous in his scorn for pornography and his hatred of abortion. "All I have cared about," he wrote in
Jesus Rediscovered, about twenty years ago, "is the living presence of
Christ; the life he lived, and the death he died, and the unique salvation he offers to a distracted world today."

He became, near the end, a Roman Catholic. Not much surprise
in this. He once asked me, conspiratorially, if I planned on going to
Rome. (No, I replied; or anyway not in the foreseeable future.) It
was clear he wanted a shove in the back.

The year of which I speak is 1977. My wife and I are visiting "St.
Mugg" at his home near Robertsbridge, in Sussex. He has fetched
us from the station. We greet his charming wife Kitty. We sit in the
sunlit living room and talk, talk, talk—about all that we have been

doing in England. We lunch at the kitchen table: ham for the visitors, yogurt for the vegetarian Muggeridges. We don "Wellies" and tramp about the premises. We take our leave with the same reluctance I know now in letting him go for good.

At all events, we know where he has gone, and we sense the longed-for communion he savors at last.

"So he crossed over," as Bunyan wrote of Mr. Valiant-For-Truth, "and all the trumpets sounded for him on the other side."

November 17, 1990

Walker Percy

While Walker Percy lived, our lunatic world could rejoice in the presence of one sane man; one author able to frame simply, humorously, the plight of the man or woman alone and disarmed in the twentieth century.

Ill? Walker Percy, America's foremost novelist, had been ill with cancer? I hadn't known. And anyway, how could this be? He was our physician. The world of the late twentieth century was his patient; in his graceful Southern way, he drew up his chair alongside our bed, took our temperature, chatted softly, comically, and scribbled prescriptions for—what?

What indeed? That was the thing about Walker Percy, who forty-odd years ago actually scrapped a promising medical career when he fell ill with pulmonary tuberculosis. Whatever did he want us to do about our vexations, our maladies?

We knew from his novels, commencing with *The Moviegoer* in 1962 and ending with *The Thanatos Syndrome* in 1988, what he *didn't* want us to do—namely, conform ourselves to a world gone bonkers, a world morally disconnected, a world in which the old guideposts have been hewn down for scrap lumber.

Modernity was the disease. The good man in the late twentieth century was as out of place as an Eskimo in the Mojave.

Money could never inoculate against the moral bacteria that assumed a virulent shape under Walker Percy's microscope. Money—far too much of it—was if anything part of the problem. How the modern world loved money! And how distracted was the modern world: no ideals or dogmas to animate it, save the dogma of Success; a TV world, the images of the small screen more alive, more real than life itself; a worn-out world with a death wish, yearning for extinction.

Walker Percy's novels take place in the modern South—chiefly Louisiana, where the author lived—but not the South of romance. No magnolias perfume the air. The smell is of the oil refineries that dwell cheek by jowl with the mansions of the long-dead planters. The Old South has gone. The New South is as nutty as the North.

Religion itself has failed—or, rather, the search for religious certainty has taken off and gone down strange and unreliable paths. The saints and ascetics of old have been replaced by pompadoured preachers of worldly success.

Walker Percy's central characters are losers, strays, even a little nuts themselves. They never get rich and famous: usually the opposite. Yet, on closer viewing, these "failures" prove to be the only genuine successes. The Greek chorus in *The Thanatos Syndrome* is a crazy —or not so crazy—old priest who perches atop a firewatch tower, observing modernity with more understanding than the groundbound.

Father Smith, distractible, unprepossessing, a modern St. Simeon Stylites, tells us what we hate to hear—that we've given up on God; that, indeed, we've come close to making gods of ourselves. *The Thanatos Syndrome* is a wonderful sendup of that twentieth-century heresy, the quest for worldly perfection.

Pretty bleak, yes? Pretty bleak, no. Partly because no other twentieth-century writer, not Evelyn Waugh himself, is funnier than

Walker Percy, partly because Mr. Percy is a Christian—a Christian existentialist—and true Christianity is joy; not the Christianity of the marketplace but that of sacrament, sacrifice, and submission.

Well, what *do* we do then to satisfy Dr. Percy? "Live a life," I think he says somewhere. Not a difficult prescription, you think, until you begin ruminating on what life is like in the late twentieth century.

I think what Walker Percy is saying is, hunker down. The storms blow, but for those who seek it, there is peace. Fall in love. Marry. Live quietly. Go to Mass. Pray. The storm will pass, and the sun will shine. There is something in this of the monastic; not the marriage part, obviously, but still something very old and un-twentieth century—self-abnegation and denial.

At least I *think* this is what Walker Percy whispers in my ear. You see, I had wanted more: his next novel and the next and the next. I had thought he might yet make it all clear, but maybe he had it clear enough for present purposes. Live a life, a twentieth-century life. Do what can be done—no more, no less.

May 12, 1990

Evelyn Wood

So passes Evelyn Wood, inventor of speed-reading for the masses. God rest her soul, as He very well may, in view of the satisfactions she provided generations of speed-reading students: the power over paper and the ability to chew up English prose faster than a Waring Blender purees tomatoes.

Wood's theory was that the faster you read, "the better off you are." Finish one book and you can start another. And another. And another. This was why John F. Kennedy famously sent his staff to Evelyn Wood classes. If you're going to push paper, Kennedy reasoned, you might as well push it fast and in mounting quantities. That was the way to get things done.

The Kennedy mythos still enveloped the Evelyn Wood studios when I signed up for the course nearly twenty-five years ago. If knowledge was power, we Evelyn Wood students had only to help ourselves. What excuse could there be for not racing, muscles taut and straining, through the *Syntopicon* and the Durants' histories? Whereas average readers dawdle along at two or three hundred words a minute, Evelyn Wood students read fourteen hundred, sixteen hundred, two thousand words a minute. So a Maserati performs when passing a Honda Civic.

Any literary Maserati from the Wood school should be able to race through entire libraries, taking in the sense of the thing faster and retaining it longer than the Honda folk, who poke along in the traditional way, reading left to right, sometimes lip-reading, sometimes repeating.

The Evelyn Wood Method is to read straight down the middle of the page, the eyes guided by a downward-sweeping right hand. Forget words, grammar, structure and so on. It's the thought that counts. Everything else can take care of itself.

And so, in class, we swept away Camus's *The Stranger*. Likewise Hemingway's *The Old Man and the Sea* and much else besides. Knowledge and understanding were ours.

But reality dawned. I wrote then, as now, a newspaper column. I bethought myself that one of my columns was meat for about ten seconds of an Evelyn Wood reader's precious time. That, of course, meant my own time as well!

Yet, ten seconds was not at all what it took to produce a column. The task of researching, writing, crossing out, restoring, experimenting, and perfecting could go on all day. Strolls to the window, telephone conversations, lunch—these too had to be factored into the creative process. I was to throw one of my columns to an Evelyn Wood reader? Someone capable of draining it like Dracula at work on a Transylvanian maiden? A reader willing to ignore my similes, vocabulary choices, and grace notes? Even so.

I discovered myself to be a Honda Civic: irretrievably so. In the spirit of economy, I completed the Wood course, for which I had paid up front. I tried out my new techniques on Wood's other prey— the likes of Jane Austen and Bill Buckley. Even in impetuous youth, I should have known better. Reading the Evelyn Wood way turned out to be no fun at all.

The only thing better than good English writing is—I can't think of anything. You don't just pour it pureed over your potatoes. You savor it as if it were a fine chardonnay. What on Earth does it matter if you stop and repeat a phrase, roll it around on your tongue, dart a few lines ahead, and then suddenly come back and reread it? If the phrase is good enough, you are supposed to stop and rejoice in it. A reading rate of two thousand words a minute? It depends on what you mean by reading—shopping for information at full tilt or sitting enraptured at the feet of a story-teller.

I would not for one instant submit that Wood and her popular method ruined reading. Television has taken a far mightier whack at this historical pastime. But remove the sensual pleasure from reading, as does the Evelyn Wood Method, and you convert it into a strictly utilitarian function, like running the bath water. What have you got? Not half as much as the Maserati crowd might think.

August 31, 1995

Rowena Newman Wilks

Row upon row of family members, friends and admirers sat piously, patiently as Rowena Newman Wilks was memorialized and laid to rest in Denton, Texas, aged ninety-one.

Among the mourners: a pundit, thinner of hair and shorter of sight than when he sat, second row from the windows, first desk, in Mrs. Wilks's sophomore literature class at Corsicana High School.

This was—well, let me put it thus: Richard Nixon was vice president, and Elvis was inarguably alive and shaking. The KN root beer stand was where the action was on Saturday night. Nobody had ever heard of a pizza.

The pundit was at the funeral to honor a teacher and friend—or was it friend and teacher? Rowena Newman Wilks was both. It went with the territory.

The territory was public education—an institution that in modern times causes the strong to tremble. Not so in pre-pizza days. As a community, we cherished our public schools. Did they not boast teachers like Rowena Newman Wilks, who could get you to love reading about a dry old stick like Silas Marner and a bleeding piece of earth called Julius Caesar?

The pundit's mature conclusion—Rowena Newman Wilks, with eyes atwinkle, would brand it a cliché—is that great teachers are born, not made. God gives them to us. It is for us, at that sublime juncture, to brighten when they approach, lay aside intrusive thoughts, and listen, listen, listen. Of course. no student does that *all* the time, but it's the ideal.

Rowena Newman Wilks was a great teacher—certainly the most influential the pundit ever had prior to his departure for college. What made her a great and influential teacher? And how would she fit in today? The pundit scratches his head—a more useful pastime than dabbing damp eyes.

What made her great? Zeal and love—a dynamite combination. There is, first of all, love of learning; then there is zeal to communicate that learning; but for what purpose? Love, care, concern for students—all those little blank slates with their entire futures before them. If a classroom does not make the resident authority feel responsible, what will? A savings and loan office?

These are the human factors. Education bureaucrats think education is all about programs and techniques, and about the money that pays for them. It is not. It is about love. Generalized or particularized, who cares? Rowena Newman Wilks loved her pupils as individuals, because that was the kind of person she was, but if she had cherished them only as Platonic ideals, they would have received not a whit less of her enthusiasm and uplift.

Those whom Teacher loves she chastens. Sorry about that. Discipline there has to be, and order. And plain hard work. Rowena Newman Wilks, one of the most benevolent people the pundit ever has known, expected work. Her pupils had to memorize—an extraordinarily unfashionable undertaking today, when children are expected chiefly to Express Themselves.

There was no vogue in the 1950s for denigrating Western civilization's treasure trove of classics. One didn't apologize for pouring Shakespeare and George Eliot into minds unexposed to the great sub-Saharan revolutionary feminist treatises, whatever they were. These days, love of the Western classics is punished, in education school, by thumb screws and the strappado. Rowena, with a name straight out of Sir Walter Scott, wouldn't have understood at all.

But then she was deeply old-fashioned, as is the pundit who sat at her feet (actually at her right hand, or a little northeast thereof) for a magical year when love and zeal had their way with an entire classroom.

The pundit knows the world has moved on since Elvis was alive and Julius Caesar was dead. Yet he knows the world was in many ways better off then: not least in the scope it afforded love and zeal, and in the honor it paid them both. The Lady Rowena, Sir Walter's Saxon princess, is no fairer to think on than her namesake with the twinkling eyes and a love that enfolded the world—or at least that portion lodged at a given hour between radiators and blackboard.

April 28, 1994

IV

The Tragic Sense

"TRAGIC." WELL. Life is many things, beginning with complex, full of odd turnings, with vistas in every direction—forward, back, up, down, sideways. The political obsession blocks these vistas sometimes. I mention here a few of them.

A Hole in the Head

As I've been saying these last two weeks, I feel fine for a man with a brand-new hole in his head. And, by the way, acoustic tumors are the pits.

Acoustic whats? The newly minted medical authority clears his throat and speaks from personal experience.

Acoustic tumors are brain tumors, only not in the brain, but adjacent to it. Such a tumor—or neuroma—starts in the internal auditory canal and ultimately oozes out into the cerebellopontine angle, where it has no conceivable business.

As the tumor presses on the various nerves, dire things happen, such as your wife's saying you are ignoring her when she talks to you—though it's plain she has mush in her mouth. Next, you notice that, having consumed only a Dr Pepper, you are wobbling as though you had polished off a pitcher of martinis. These are not encouraging developments.

Hence, you consult the doctor, who prescribes an MRI, which produces a finely detailed image of this thing you never heard of before, which, you are plausibly informed, must come out.

My own acoustic tumor came out on February 7. The surgery,

eight hours long, was spectacularly successful. The four-centimeter tumor, though tenacious as a New York panhandler, yielded in due course. Everything went right that should have gone right. In only four days, the patient went home, where his good wife and family coddled him and he read English church history and Southern fiction.

After effects? Loss of hearing in the right ear was the predestined consequence of the surgery. At least this affords me standing to make a politically incorrect remark: I am deaf as a stump in the right ear! Already, the left ear is compensating both for this deficiency and for the attendant loss of balance.

End of medical lesson—and yet not quite the end. When a man talks about His Operation, there should be a purpose. Two commend themselves to me.

First, the world-beating quality of U.S. medicine. We just get better and better, no thanks to the Clintons. Thirty years ago, when this particular kind of surgery was new, the mortality rate was one in three. Dr. William E. House of Los Angeles, who pioneered the present surgery, labored ingeniously and successfully to perfect it, so that today virtually no one dies of it. Did House do so because the government cracked the whip over him? Yeah. Sure. The same way my own two surgeons—Dr. Fred D. Owens, the neurotologist, and Dr. Sam Finn, the neurologist who performed with sublime efficiency and professionalism—stood around waiting for federal orders. Drs. Owens and Finn are fleshly monuments to the glories of private medicine.

There is this, too: Medicine thrashes about in no intellectual or moral vacuum. To go through brain surgery is to know something of this.

The ear, the ear—look at it, would you? Whittaker Chambers observed in *Witness* that his religious conversion began when, observing the elaborate whorls of his infant daughter's ear, he reflected that chance and accident could never have contrived such a wonder. Nor is this to mention the unseen wonders behind the ear—the mastoid, the eustachian tube, the nerves conveying facial movement, taste, hearing, balance; all working in splendid concert. Accidental? Circumstantial? The ear should knock any mere materialist off his feet. Perhaps even to his knees.

Who is the real doctor? It can only be the Author of all this wonder, whom we know as God. How lonely the materialist must be, faced with the crumbling of a material body whose fitness he has taken for granted. He may find it hard to mutter, "Thy kingdom come, thy will be done." Yet no other prayer so neatly answers the purpose of composing mind and body for the facing of calamity. Again and again, it is borne in on me: A good God who has made all things from ears to mountaintops means only good for His creatures—and yearns for them to ask it be given.

And so it came to pass in at least one woefully deficient, cantankerous life: the goodness of God displayed in the miracle of healing. There is no other way to look at it. There is no other way to want to.

February 27, 1995

The Yard Man

To our homestead, the yard-care season has come again. Which brings vividly to mind a cherished childhood ambition—not so much as to notice the yard-care season; not to touch rake or shovel or weeder but rather to farm the work out to those with more of a taste for stooping and scooping.

The ambition, though unrealized, is worth cherishing a few seasons more. However, the ambition's author is at something of a moral disadvantage. He is in favor of all the homely virtues and sentiments connected with backyard labor. He is foursquare for the joys of running winter-white fingers through spring-black soil. He swears by the importance of contact with things eternal and immutable.

Growing, creating, cultivating, enlarging on the possibilities of the real and the earthy—to all these imperatives, he bends the knee. It is when he has to bend both of his knees and hunker down in the Johnson grass that finally he demurs.

It is easily more satisfying to praise the outdoor virtues than to practice them. Praising can be accomplished from a chair, outside or indoors. Practicing requires rising from the chair, flexing the nearest muscles, and starting to spade up the Good Earth.

In no time at all, work makes hash of philosophy. Take mowing, a pastime slightly more diverting than rowing a Roman galley. Upon a postcard-blue Saturday morning, the sun just warming to its work, bees buzzing in the honeysuckle, and a stillness hanging over the peaceful earth, out comes the lawn mower.

Immediately discordance sets in. The bees fly off, stillness shatters violently into a thousand fragments. You see?

Still worse is the can't get-aheadedness of yard work. The lawn, once mown, will be mown all over again the next postcard-blue Saturday morning. Every day, the eyes take nervous note of grass blades marginally higher than the day before.

So with hedges: Slash them to ribbons, and in a few weeks, the job will need doing all over again. So with the pulling of spring weeds, the raking of autumn leaves. Yard work is not for the restless; it is for those with long vistas of patient hours stretching before them.

Or is that yard work's real virtue, all mystical visions of Mother Earth laid to the side. Could yard work be Good For Us—including those of us who shrink from it—in the sense of reining in natural impatience, imparting a sense of processes that go on irrespective of anything mortal? Er, um, well, maybe.

Look at it this way: The yard worker is a realist of the most uncompromising sort. He knows what can be achieved, yes, and what can't be, try though he might. He'd never do in twentieth-century politics or sociology. No gauzy hopes of future perfection for our friend of the grubby fingers and grass-stained blue jeans. The Johnson grass chokes out notions of this sort.

Our friend knows the nature of things—how grass will grow and weeds spring up and leaves scatter themselves on the driveway, not because he wants them to, but—blast, darn, heckfire—just because they do and there's not a blessed thing he can do about it.

Armed with hard, sharp knowledge of this sort, the yard worker refuses any temptation to utopianism. Paradise-on-the-Patio, the Brotherhood of Men and Grub Worms—these he knows for fantasy. On he plugs, doing his best, knowing that even the best is inadequate.

One gets to wondering. When society started going gravely wrong, in the 1960s, was it partly because non-yard worker theoreticians started grub-worming their way into power? How much do the Clintons know about yard work? Would they know a dandelion from a boxwood? Has the Clinton Cabinet a theory of compost?

Suspicions on these scores are strong. But so, on any postcard-blue spring day, are consolations. The reluctant yard man understands something in addition to the tenacity of Johnson grass. He understands that, in the great scheme of things, which he senses more than sees, aching back and sore fingers count for something after all.

His ear takes in, while the lawn mower whirrs away, the perverse harmony of a perverse—but, oh, so necessary—instrument.

April 1, 1993

Who's in Control?

Thoughts about life and its fragility flood the mind. "Flood"? Shows you the appeal of aqueous images during a sure-enough drought.

In the early 1990s, the clouds dripped fatness—to quote the Psalmist. No longer. Nowadays a good cloud is hard to find. With the glee that bad-news bearers always experience, the media assure us We Are In For It.

What, no rain? In the 1990s, this could qualify as a violation of basic constitutional rights. Why doesn't someone headquartered inside the Washington Beltway press a button, throw a switch—make it rain?

The inescapable reason: There are matters beyond human, not to mention governmental, control. Droughts, floods—these things happen. Nature, as we continue to call those forces external to the human body, changes moods: pampering one moment, punishing the next. And without reference to human desires or deserts.

The rhythm of drought-fatness-drought is built into Southwestern life. You don't fight it; you endure it. It helps, a little at least, to have lived through the 1950s—"the time it never rained," as Elmer Kelton titled his fine novel about the period.

No one over fifty needs corroboration for such memories. Texas, in the 1950s, burned to a cinder. As now, crops withered, and cattle died. Not a few Texans went through the whole period without air-conditioning. Sometimes a water-cooled fan in the main bedroom blew through the house; otherwise there was the open window, where a passing breeze might be lured inside and held for ransom

To get really cool, you plunked down nine cents at the Palace Theatre and feasted your eyes on *Three Coins in the Fountain* or *House of Wax*. You sat in the shade a lot. On the worst nights, all hope of sleep renounced, the neighbors drifted outdoors, there to exchange consolations and news.

Then for some reason the drouth—as we spelled it in those days—finally broke. The time it never rained became, in the spring of '57, the time it never quit raining. This new state of affairs we silently appropriated, as we had the old. It was how things were.

And still are? Maybe, just maybe. Because, even when it does rain, the marginality of human measures and defenses is impressed on us. Hard.

Here we sit in Dallas, on a calm Saturday morning. Winds blow through at one hundred miles an hour, rain falls, power lines topple. Whereupon, throughout the community, refrigerators cease; massive air-conditioning units shut down. Houses and businesses fall dark. Gasoline pumps can't pump. Restaurants can't serve. Picture shows can't show. Our life of conveniences comes to a stop.

Little but waiting and wondering remains for the victims. The power that civilization gained over nature, through electricity, is forfeit. To benefit from electricity you have to have it. And when you don't. . . .

The power and pride of modernity, together with its accomplishments, started to die with the sinking of the "unsinkable" *Titanic* in 1912. Year by year, the process has escalated. The fragility, the conditionality of human life grows plainer. Yes, you can have this, do this, go here, go there. If. . . .

Man, the measure of all things (as Protagoras boasted)? Ha! Icebergs, snow, wind, rain, bleak unsparing sunshine; the inscrutable ways of God, as our fathers referred to them—you never know when or how long. Mechanical contrivances are defenses against nature. None is a reliable substitute.

What do you do when it doesn't rain; or when the lights go out and stay out? The old answer is . . . you endure, knowing that hardship, hard as it gets, passes away. Our fathers found lessons of this sort in the Bible, and in history. Neither consolation appeals profoundly to moderns, who, with their computers and power plants and government agencies, know both more and less than the old folks did. Maybe we'll see how long that spirit persists; because, as we Texans say, it ain't gettin' no cooler around here!

June 3, 1996

Reunion

So. Everybody is ga-ga to hear about my thirtieth high school reunion? That's what I was expecting. Ahem.

Corsicana High School's class of 1959 was duly reunited the other day, and one heck of a good time was had by all. There was meeting and greeting and hugging and kissing, all correctly chaperoned by spouses.

As is customary on such occasions, we bathed in nostalgia—the time Johnny Humphries painted "Srs. '59" on the gym roof; cokes (not coke) at the Little Steak House and root beer at the KN; *Macbeth* and *Canterbury Tales* in Miss Anna Belle Kiber's room.

We registered at the old high school—now a middle school—and concluded that they don't build 'em like that any more. Afterward, at the country club, a jam box (the sound system had unaccountably failed) played "Earth Angel", "Donna", and "Silhouettes." The years melted away.

Nostalgia is an addictive drug. Mainlined, it can persuade you to a moral certainty that the time you grew up in was one of unexampled sweetness, and that, ever since, it's all been downhill.

There is no gainsaying that the world has changed since May 29, 1959, our graduation day. *Tempora mutantur*, as our much-beloved Latin teacher, Miss Frances Broadstreet, would have said. These—my classmates, my childhood friends and sweethearts—are as long in the tooth as am I. By two AM, we were drifting away from the breakfast at Punchy Dycus's house. In the old days, we'd have been out in our Chevys dragging Beaton Street.

Thirty years after graduation night, our class is knee-deep in grandchildren. A few classmates are deceased, a word that, on festive occasions, sounds more suitable than "Dead." No small number have changed marriage partners. The divorce rate, which our parents perceived only as a faraway rumble, hit our generation like a freight train.

The times have changed indeed. Elvis himself, I see from the tabloids in the supermarket, has a new granddaughter.

I stand up not to deplore—because there is no present purpose in deploring—but quietly and thankfully to exult. It is no sin or shame to attend a mega-high school in the feverish 1980s. I can speak only to the blessings of attending a small one in the 1950s. It may be that the characteristics of that time and place have not disappeared entirely. I hope not. They were good.

What were our great blessings? A peaceful world, a relatively stable social environment—and friendship. Not just friendship; rather, friendship that blossoms in the early morning hours without withering at noon—or even midafternoon, where we are now. It comes of—may I use an old-fashioned word?—community. Perhaps I am wrong, but I doubt there is as much old-fashioned community as there used to be.

Half of the class of '59 started school together in September 1947. Today we can't recall not knowing each other. Look at the old class pictures; there, in jumpers, cowboy shirts (and occasionally knickers), we stand—Johnny Hollingsworth, Larry Norwood, Joe B. Fortson, Patty Ferguson, Cassandra DuBose, Carol Jackson, Ed Willis, Mike Everheart. We still know well the contours of each other's faces.

How do you purchase this kind of continuity, this kind of enduringness? Alas, you don't purchase it. You live it. In the unfrenzied 1950s, a time quite unlike today, people came to live in a town and stayed there. They seldom moved. Often enough their grandparents lived there and were a presence on the juvenile horizon, particularly at Sunday dinner.

Neither great wealth nor great poverty was a source of discord. We knew no one terrifically rich or terrifically poor. Consumption was seldom conspicuous—a condition that manifestly no longer obtains in society.

Sinclair Lewis struck it rich running down the American small town, but the small towns have their strengths and resources as well as their narrowness and blind spots. Friendship blossoms where friends are continually thrown together and obliged to devise their own entertainment—dances, baseball, cruisin' around, etc.—as for generations was the case in small towns. I know from my own experience as a modern parent that entertainment is more prepackaged and diffuse today than yesterday. There is something for everybody, and it all costs money.

But there we were for a spell and a space: small-town America, the 1950s, and it was—different. Was it likewise better? In some ways, yes; in others, no. Let it go with "different."

And the fresh-faced, flat-topped children of that difference—the class of '59? Ah, look at us now. Graying, many of us; some trim, some stout; some happy and secure, others not; but friends in any event—because that's how it always was and, please God, always will be.

June 21, 1989

V

Letters to My Children

I HOPE IT IS IN PART a tribute to my exceptional children that the public birthday letters I have written to them—sometimes to their annoyance and embarrassment—have proved the most popular of all my columns: much more so than my musings on politicians. I think this actually has as much to do with the sense that children matter as it does with the excellence of these particular children. Politicians always claim to be building for our future. What can they build that is more memorable, more lovable (most of the time) than a single, discrete, God-given child.

DEAR WILL . . .

A Glorious Baby

Your father hears that the doctor, poking his head into the hospital room, referred to you as "a glorious baby." But of course you are, my little one. Was there ever any doubt of this?

Would that you could contemplate the wonder of you. This is difficult, I admit. You have not fully cultivated yet that open-eyed curiosity that will come in due course. You love sleeping. If your parents did not know themselves to be brilliant conversationalists, they might suppose you to be bored with their company. You drop off during the most scintillating remarks.

Ah, well. A wonder you are. Those tiny fingers, hardly thicker than a strand of spaghetti but able to grip a parental thumb and hang on for dear life! Those miniature eyelashes, those Lilliputian lips! My son, you are an eight-pound, eight-ounce miracle. I know no other way of expressing it.

There are those—you will find this out as you grow sadder and wiser—who say that man is a mass of molecules that unite randomly, only to break apart randomly when we reach old age. They lie, my son. We are all of us God's creations. "It is He hath made us and not we ourselves." They are words you will learn to sing once you are able to open the Book of Common Prayer. And they are everlastingly true.

Could random molecules have made those sleepy eyes, formed the lovely, delicate curls of those ears? Not for a moment! God did these things. And how beautifully he did them, too!

I should not be surprised if you wondered who on earth you were. Well, I shall tell you a bit about yourself. You burst onto the world scene just before ten PM on June 12, in the year of grace, 1978. You were flailing your arms and bellowing. My son, you bellow magnificently. I would stack you up against a full chorus of operatic bellowers. Yours is a right baritone that should grow truly spacious with age.

Your mother esteems you accordingly: She is an opera lover, as well as a linguist and a gourmet cook. Your father is a gourmet eater.

You are, just for the record, the fourth of your line within five generations to bear the name "William Polk." It belonged originally to your great-great-grandfather, who as a youngster rode with Nathan Bedford Forrest's Seventh Tennessee cavalry, the outfit that got there "fustest with the mostest." He came to Texas following the War for Southern Independence (as your family prefers to call it) and died in 1908. Your Grandfather Murchison was named for him, and your father inherited the name in due course.

And you!—you are "the Third." The weight of tradition is therefore upon you. I do not think it will prove a heavy weight. It is better, far better, my son, to know who you are and where you have come from than to live as though there had been no yesterday.

Those who deny yesterday are the people who stir up most of the trouble in the world. They think no one ever had an intelligent thought or notion prior to, oh, late 1977. You will know better, my son. The three Roman numerals—so chaste and upright!—at the end of your name will remind you.

And what of the world you live in? You must think it terribly blue and white—which, to be sure, it is, when viewed from the depths of a bassinet. There is more to it than that, as your eager eyes and groping fingers will discover in good time.

There is, for example, a yard you are sure to like, a yard fringed with beauty; your mother being, if I may say so, a terrific gardener. To her a drooping day lily is a spectacle more horrifying than the latest Act of Congress. She is a lover of loveliness, your mother. It will be hard for you to escape her beneficent influence, her sense of the importance of gracefulness and dignity and courtesy—all the things that lubricate daily existence and are lamentably out of fashion today.

In worldly goods, you are fixed well enough, I suppose. Let me see: You have heaps of diapers (which is fortunate, let me tell you), gobs of blankets, a menagerie of stuffed animals, a bathtub shaped like a frog and a music box that plays Brahms's "Lullaby." What more, my son, could mortal infant desire?

Real animals? No, there are none of those at the moment, I'm afraid. And no bellicose brothers or solicitous sisters either. You are the first—the beginning, only think of it!—of a whole generation.

How do you like this thought my little one? It is awesome, is it not? The first, the forerunner, the trailblazer! This is enough, perhaps, to make you tremble in your tiny socks.

Do not be awed, though. Others have been first. The mess that they have made of matters is hardly worth dwelling upon. Soon enough you will see what your father is talking of. Suck in the meantime that exquisite thumb of yours—so astonishingly small, so astonishingly new!—and treat life like the sun-splashed thing of beauty it can be for those young in body and in heart. Those like yourself, my fortunate son.

June 20, 1978

One Year Old?

There is among grownups, as you will some day discover from first-hand experience, a basic confusion regarding the likes of you.

Grownups, if I may explain, cannot tell a boy baby from a girl baby. To the grownup eye, you look just alike, especially in this unisex era, when a girl baby is as likely to turn up in coveralls as in a smart pink dress. Why, you yourself, in earlier times, were mistaken for a girl.

As if you could imagine such a thing now! For on this, your first birthday, my son, there is no doubt at all as to what you are. You are a boy.

Yes, a squirming, wriggling, shrieking, sofa-climbing, spoon-waving, food-throwing, mud-encrusted boy.

How different things are now from the days when you lay placidly in your bassinet. Well, all right, you never did anything exactly placidly. But as you have grown in wisdom and in stature, so have you grown in energy. My word, there is no keeping you down!

May I divulge one of your favorite pastimes? It is being held upside down, before being flung upward into the stratosphere and caught under the arms as you come down squealing with delight.

Of late, you have been learning to ride piggyback, though I must say, your behavior on these rides leaves much to be desired. You like to bat your parents over the head as you gallop along. You even yank your father's spectacles from his nose. For heaven's sake! Do you want him to run into a tree?

Your behavior on most other occasions is no less—well, let's be charitable about it—high-spirited. You are growing up already to be just like King Henry II, the father of Richard Lionheart, who would never sit down at the table. Standing up on the chair seat, you spin from side to side, never content just to sit sedately and put your six teeth to work. Some day, you will discover stand-up cocktail buffets and realize that you have been eating thus for a long time.

But enough of so messy a subject. There are pleasanter things to talk about than mealtime, such as climbing. Climbing is great fun, is it not? It must be. You do enough of it. Stairs, sofas, knees, whatever seemingly affords a more exalted view—there on its slopes you are to be found, scaling your little Everests like a sun-suited Hillary.

It is no wonder you love being flung into the air. Heights are what you like—altitudes from which to survey an increasingly familiar world.

As yet, you are a hands-and-knees explorer. Oh, you walk well enough when holding on to a parental hand. Still, you lack the hang of stepping out by yourself; which lack, by the way, your parents are inclined to count as a temporary blessing. You are enough of a traveling man as it is, without the knack of propelling yourself, on two plump little legs, out the front door and across the lawn.

And what of the more cerebral pastimes? What of reading and conversation? Well, here, too, you progress, though less markedly, perhaps, than in the physical realm.

At any rate, you no longer rend a magazine in twain when you pick it up. You are given now to thoughtful thumbing of its pages and to reflection on its colorful pictures. The other day, we went through the *National Geographic*, and you were much taken with pictures of an archaeological dig in Tidewater Virginia. Or so it seemed to me.

Keep it up, and we will be delving into Boswell.

I will grant that, as downright gabby as you are, some progress in vocabulary development is indicated first. How often, after all, in the masterpieces of world literature, does the word "bah-bah" turn up? Very infrequently, I can tell you. This is notwithstanding that a good, refreshing sip of "bah-bah" does indeed hit the spot at meal time.

Derivatives of "Ma-Ma" and "Da-Da" turn up with somewhat greater regularity. But I will be frank with you, my son. You are going to have to learn to distinguish between the two. I assure you they are not the same, even though you sometimes treat them so.

The other day, just when we thought you had the distinction down pat, we were strolling around the back yard. You turned to the stone cherub that ornaments our bird bath and addressed it fondly as "Da-Da." There is evidently more work to be done.

But still your progress in just one year has been astounding—from small lump of pink flesh to large armload of boy. You are on the way, my growing, thriving, seam-bursting son. Your father, as you might by now have surmised, is proud of you.

June 12, 1979

One of Life's Landmarks

What does it mean to be six years old—as are you, on this very special day? Why, six means to have two loose teeth and a plastic chicken-liver container full of doodle-bugs. What more, I ask, partly in envy, could youth desire?

Six years is one of life's great landmarks, as I'm sure you surmise. Brother John, at age three, certainly surmises it; witness how he runs around after his venerable sibling, copying all he says and does.

Behind now are kindergarten, and Mrs. Parker's well-loved class. Ahead looms the Real World—the first grade. Lots of readin', 'ritin', frettin', and workin', and I regret to tell you, after a lifetime of experience, that it only gets more so. Of course, that's almost three months down the road. Plenty of time, here at the onset of summer, to contemplate the things that *really* matter—like doodlebugs.

How breathless was your telephone call the other day. "Can you believe," you demanded, "that I've caught fourteen doodlebugs in one day?" No, actually, your father couldn't believe it. You are the Frank Buck of doodlebuggery. You bring 'em back alive.

Nice cage, too, that old chicken-liver container, full of soil and black ants for company or food, I forget which. Let us hope our doodlebugs outlast the previous star attraction of your zoological exhibit—the moth you put in a mayonnaise jar.

Come to think of it, your goldfish didn't fare very well, either: Fred, Fred ii, and such other Freds as came along before you concluded that fish were not your thing after all.

Meantime, your mother and I count ourselves thankful that our wits were about us when the MacIntire boys offered you a baby hamster, and we said, er, ah, thanks, but no, thanks, wouldn't dream of depriving you. Doodlebugs are one thing; rodents, even cute, cuddly ones, are something else again.

Tell you what: Maybe, if we are lucky, the lightning bugs will return this summer. For six-year-olds, these electrified varmints are just the ticket, fun to catch and even more fun to wave around in a jar. I speak from deep experience of lighting bugs.

Meanwhile, back to loose teeth. Behold, I show you a mystery: the way a tooth drops out, leaving a gap just the right size for exploring with the tongue; in time, the gap will fill with—a whole new tooth! If this is not a miracle, I have never seen, or heard of, a miracle.

Actually, at Age Six, miracles come with regularity. Six is a time of marvelously expanding capacities, such as reading words—real words!—and beating the throw to first base for a good, clean single.

On the first count, I declare you to be doing very well indeed. To be sure, I should probably apologize to you because you don't yet read Dickens or conjugate French verbs while programming an i b m computer.

That sort of thing is the vogue right now among parents who see childhood as nothing more or less than the doorway to adulthood. Your father, an unabashed Old Fogey, says to this view of things: Phooey! As it is, you will spend almost your whole lifetime committing adulthood. Why rush it?

Better right now anyway to develop your throwing arm. My boy, it is not the world that presently needs your invaluable help; it is the Gold Mustangs. Among Park Cities-North Dallas YMCA Tee-ball teams, we Mustangs are in sad shape: halfway through the season, and still winless. Lots of runs (including four by you!) but clearly not enough.

It is not for lack of hustling; we have lots of that. Nor for lack of imaginative coaching; which, being one of your five coaches, I feel amply qualified to say.

Our day will come. Indeed, many days will come; days of all sorts, shapes and lengths. If that's how it is when you are in middle age—and it is—how much more so when you are six, and every sunrise brings new wonders and surprises. Your father has not been six since the year Truman whipped Dewey, but he thinks watching you, he wouldn't mind being so again.

June 12, 1984

Marked by Decades

Double digit aging—that's what we're into these days.

I recollect my own tenth birthday. Tenth birthdays are always occasions. This is because—as my own father pointed out to me, and I duly point out to you, oh, My Best Beloved—it is no small thing to begin writing your age with two numerals instead of just one. You will find it becomes a lifetime habit.

Likewise, as you may have noticed by now, life in general is marked by decades—the '50s, the '60s, the '70s, the '80s. Decades are fine promontories for forward and backward viewing.

Looking backward, I find only wispy traces of the Will who came expostulating into our midst back in June of 1978. The expostulating—the lawyering, we have come to call it—goes on. But eight pounds has become sixty-plus. Instead of diapers, there are blazers and neckties. There are dances now, and sports competitions. There are strange and provocative creatures with long hair. They are called girls, and as you and many of your classmates have observed, they are Different.

Yes, it is something to be ten—halfway between the bassinet and your junior year at the University of, where else, Texas. Your father is inclined to cherish the present moment. Fifth-graders are notoriously cheaper to feed, clothe, and educate than are college juniors.

So are they cheaper to move around from place to place. You wonder why I talk so admiringly of the shiny yellow unicycle you won in the school raffle? It is in part because I am charmed by the sight of a boy and a wheel flying down the street; the boy rocks to and fro, arms outstretched, like a June bug on a matchstick.

You may have sensed a second reason I like to tout unicycles—or for that matter garden-variety bikes. It is that I am grateful for any excuse to turn aside talk of Porsches and Ferraris and the other supermobiles beloved of ten-, eleven-, and twelve-year-olds.

What would you do with a Ferrari if I bought you one—drive around town at sixty MPH, peeping through the steering wheel? You would straightaway get picked up, and rightly so. Aren't you glad, this being the case, I have other uses for the money—like traveling around the world twenty or thirty times, or endowing a home for motherless milk cows.

It is all a case no doubt of different strokes for different folks— ten-year-olds and parents of, well, a certain age. Your father owns up to other intergenerational differences. Your father's favorite physical pastime, at age ten, was chasing crooks and bad guys with a cap pistol. Yours is turning flips, chinning, handstanding, executing push-ups, swinging this way and that on rings high in the atmosphere. Who do you think you are, Burt Lancaster? And please don't ask who Burt Lancaster is.

Your forebears, when they took the athletic field, never exactly brought the professional scouts swarming round. But, oh, what a gymnastics nut our ten-year-old has turned into, not altogether un-expectedly. I thought I could see it coming years ago—the way you scampered up the attic stairs before you were completely proficient at walking; the way, indeed, you wanted to climb everything in sight. It is related to the desire always to be on the move, which desire is of course part of boyhood and also, in intensified degree, of Will-hood. We are what we are. You too, My Best Beloved.

How you sit still long enough to play the violin in school is a matter of some theoretical interest. It occurs to me that at least in violin-playing the right arm gets a good workout. I am confident Mozart never begrudged any performer the varied satisfactions of playing his music. Your mother and I hope merely that you will play on and on, if not necessarily in the philharmonic. Music is one of the nicest things in the world, nicer even than unicycles, and tough ten-year-olds need it, so there!

Well, then, what are we gonna do this summer—Summer Number Ten? Swim, do handstands, ride the unicycle, go to camp, read *Treasure Island*, and mark the passage of a decade? Yes, that, too.

Tempus fugit—meaning, gosh, how'd such a little fellow get so big? And how much bigger can he get? Lots bigger, and wiser, and more accomplished, and experienced, and thoughtful—with a little luck, a bunch of prayer and all the rest of that good stuff.

June 11, 1988

The Big Day

Sixteen of these rather public birthday salutations! You know very well what that kind of landmark signifies and portends. A couple of days distant from The Big Day Itself, I will suggest, nonetheless, what it signifies and portends.

First of all, some permanent alterations of style. This dawned upon your father as he sat down to write. In previous epistles, there has been a certain, what shall I call it, verticality—a looking-downness inherent in, and appropriate to, the relationship of father to son. I must say, my more-than-half-grown boy, verticality is a tougher reach than it used to be.

Here's you, and here's me, communicating these days essentially at eye level. An inch, or thereabouts, your six-foot father still has on you, but that's not much. Moreover, it's probably not going to last long. It could well be that the next time we do this *I'll* be looking up, and *you'll* be looking down. That's some switch!

And it's not just a matter of feet and inches but of something immeasurably—pun definitely intended—more urgent: a kind of meeting of the minds, as well as the eyes.

The relationship of father to son is necessarily tutorial, but at a certain stage it becomes less didactic, more conversational. There is more room for the exchange and interplay of ideas, real ideas. Ideas, I can tell you, don't figure notably in burpings and bottle-warmings— disgusting things that sixteen-year-olds don't want to be reminded about, so let that pass.

The point is, at age sixteen it's different. Your father wouldn't necessarily have recruited you, at pre-sixteen, to assist him in covering the Democratic State Convention a few days ago, not to mention the upcoming Republican Convention. But a gift for writing, an eye for detail, and a burgeoning interest in, heaven help us, politics make you eminently suitable for keeping watch on our main political actors. And on anyone else you might fancy writing about in future, I strongly suspect.

Your father has not the least intention of shanghaiing you into journalism, which craft he has pursued these thirty years; on the other hand, if you find that's what you like, well, there are more discreditable professions—serial killing, for instance.

Of course, there's another aspect to this whole age sixteen business. We call it The Car. Which car? As far as you're concerned, any car with an ignition and four wheels. With sixteen comes eligibility for full drivers license, a.k.a. the teen-age Emancipation Proclamation. No more strollers, no more tricycles, no more bicycles with training wheels. Cars are what sixteen-year-olds crave.

We sigh heavily, your mother and I, and await the insurance tab. And the tab is just for starters. Handing your sixteen-year-old the keys to a mechanical monster, saying, 'bye, have a nice time, check in with us in two hours, then listening to vrooom, vrooom, and watching as the tail lights disappear from sight—is that what we have geared up for all these years?

A moment's pause, some chewing of lower lips, and the answer becomes as clear as most things get in this transitory life. The answer is, gulp, yes. For exactly this we have geared up, and for much else also, so that blue jeans might replace rompers and real teeth crowd out baby ones—and cars, real cars, with stick shifts and bucket seats, take the place of tricycles, irretrievably and forever. The Car takes you home, and also it leads you away.

Not yet, though, sorry to tell you. Two more years of high school lie athwart the path to the wider independence, and before that a semi-lengthy summer. Time for working; time for sleeping late and consuming enough calories to throw the average middle-aged parent into a coma; time for some family travel and for looking over a few college campuses; time for, yes, all right—for driving. Vrooom, vrooom. That's life at sixteen, and don't we all know it!

June 6, 1994

Parting Words

Well, Kid, I guess this is it. Eighteen years these epistolary meditations have gone on in public: ever since, to be exact, your triumphant debut in the world, courtesy of Almighty God and Dr. W. Kemp

Strother. Tomorrow, high school graduation: pomp, circumstance, exhortations, and tears.

And that's it for these communications. Word of honor. No full-fledged citizen of this great republic—a distinction you achieve three weeks hence, on your eighteenth birthday—wishes his life advertised in the fashion we have made customary here. I offer no promises concerning matrimony and grandchildren. In any case, that sort of thing is well down the road. Got to get you through college first.

We've been on a journey, that's for sure. Through the '70s. Through the '80s. Halfway through the '90s. Through "Good Night, Moon" and YMCA soccer. Through "Star Wars" parties and swimming lessons, through traffic tickets and church confirmation and guitar practice and junior-senior proms and—oh, I don't know, what is this anyway, a newspaper column or a biography?

Eighteen years! Your dad and your mom—the former drooping with age, the latter blooming and vibrant as always—salute you. As would Brother John, I'm sure, if he weren't busy itemizing his aspirations for domination of the household once you're truly gone.

It's useless to point out how much we all have changed since the year of grace 1978. Which of us more so than you—a squalling bundle of intermittent joy in those sleepless, hungry days, all grown up now into what I am proud to acknowledge as manhood? Productive manhood, I add with delight. Your grades, your scholastic achievements are a source of endless joy to us—not to mention your personal rectitude and common sense. All are attributes that should, as commencement speakers are wont to say, Stand You in Good Stead as You Go Out Into the World.

What, all these years, has been the point of such public and one-sided conversations as we have carried on? Well, why do people promenade baby carriages? Because, where their children are concerned, parents are instinctive exhibitionists.

Your father is as shameless as any of his fellow dads. As you grew in wisdom and stature, it seemed to him only right—permissible anyway—to show you off. And to inflict on you the fatherly view of life. Ask and ye shall receive, or don't ask—you get it just the same.

But we're past that, aren't we—all that instructional stuff? The life you lead, at all-but-eighteen, is your own, in important particulars, at least, such as where to go to college and whom to date and what time to go to bed.

It's not that moms and dads have fewer uplifting ideas than of old! We just can't count on their being received with other than a tolerant smile. Why, I wouldn't presume to tell you what political candidates to vote for. Though, of course, if you asked . . .

Your dad and mom happily reflect that circumstance in the near term will keep our lives intertwined: holidays, vacations, homecomings, and such like. But always the gap must widen, lives diverging like the limbs of the mulberry tree that shaded your bedroom so many summers ago.

Exactly! Why had I not previously thought of it? Tree limbs. A family is a tree. The tree has roots and limbs, all different, all unique, all part of the same great organism.

Limbs are uniquely themselves—part and yet not part of whatever larger limb they spring from. However they grow, the tree endures: lengthening, spreading as the seasons pass, grander and grander, a blessing (one may hope) to the environment.

This week, the limb of the Murchison tree with the name of Will diverges unmistakably. To grow—where? We'll see soon enough. Mom and Dad have a hunch. The direction will be upward, the movement graceful and regular. You're doing great, O Best Beloved. Our tree is your tree, and yours ours, now and always.

May 21, 1996

. . . WITH LOVE,
DAD

DEAR JOHN ...

Brotherly Love

Your mother thanks you, your brother thanks you and I—your doting father—thank you.

For what? Well, what do you suppose?—for finally making the scene, two weeks subsequent to your Estimated Time of Arrival. Aw, never mind: We gladly held your reservation. Come on in and pull up a bassinet.

As Charlie Chan would say, you are Number Two Son, your brother Will having staked out seniority three years ago next June 12. But I would not have you think this accident of the calendar consigns to second-class citizenship such a work of art as you.

You are utterly first-class—"Grade A," in the delicious phrase of your doctor. If this is so, what a gourmet omelet you constitute, all nine pounds, six ounces of you!

It is time, I suppose, to say a word about your circumstances. Fathers do not long command their sons' undivided attention, so let me command yours while I may.

First, as to names. You are John Alexander Murchison—the First. You ask how we came to call you such. Both Christian names are tributes to various great- and great-great grandfathers.

The name "John" in particular has kicked around our family since the days when, fresh from Scotland's wind-beaten coasts, we struck roots deep into American soil. So you see: You begin life with a backward nod, as well as a forward one. This is only right and sensible. The most dislocated people in our dislocated century are those with poor memories, or worse, no memories whatsoever.

I have said the century is dislocated, and so it is. Would you believe that, only days before your arrival, someone tried to assassinate the pope? The morning your father helped convey you home from the hospital, he read a magazine article suggesting that the economy's general crumminess makes house-buying impossible for most people.

There is hope, to be sure. Now is not the time to preach politics, but America seems by way of recovering its equilibrium after long years of crazy excess.

In any case, your father is unable to think of a time in history when all was hunky-dory. By your presence, you grace this particular time. Perhaps you will even help redeem it. That is the sort of thing fathers universally like to believe of their children.

For the moment, never mind the Stream of History. Just watch out for your brother. In the efflorescence of Not-Quite-Three, he is greased lightning; irresistible force and immovable object rolled into one; a flurry of arms, legs, and expostulations.

But I have good news: He loves you. Twice he came to the hospital to see you through the glass. Do you recall? And when at last you arrived home, unbidden he threw his arms around you and kissed you. What did you think? That a hurricane had swept you up and away? Not to worry: That was only Will.

So it was Will, concerned and big-brotherly, who wound up your music box the minute you began crying, hoping to pour consoling noises into your ear. He said "Don't cry, John." You did anyway, but shall we not credit him with trying?

On the whole, I think, you will find big brothers to be a useful commodity: a little bossy sometimes, but, ah, the things they can teach little brothers! As a big brother myself, I am constrained to admit that the things they teach are not in every case the things fathers prefer to have taught.

With your advent, my son John, the household takes on a maler complexion than ever before: Three men to one very womanly woman, your mother. Let us try not to overwhelm her, then. Let us say "please," and "thank you" and "won't you have some first?"

However, I am not worried about your mother. What is wonderful about women such as she (actually everything is, but this is what I have specially in mind) is their skill at smoothing down rough corners, softening the high-speed collisions in which runaway wills are eternally involved.

You see, what we are, the four of us, is a family—that mysterious melding of human flesh and spirit, no part able to exist alone, exclusive of the rest. I have read that families are seriously unfashionable these days—like wide-lapeled sports coats. But confidentially I do not believe a word of it.

Families, as you, my son, will learn in good time, are marvelous, God-given structures for the living of life. You are thrice—yea, ten times and a thousand times—welcome to ours.

May 26, 1981

His Royal Twoness

One thing about it: As you cuddle and bounce into your third year of citizenship in the human fraternity, strangers may find it slightly easier to know what variety of human you are, the boy or girl.

What I mean to say is, you have had a birthday haircut. Well, sort of a haircut—the kind that gentle-fingered mothers give to little boys blond of hair and sweet of face and manner: scissors nipping grudgingly, maternal tears falling almost as fast as golden curls.

Not that you have been turned into a U.S. Marine bootcamper. It seems to me that the effect of these motherly ministrations has been to uncover the bottoms, respectively, of your ears and neck.

Your father, in case you wonder, had nothing to do with any of this. He is no enemy of curls, which he regards as atmospherically Victorian. Indeed, give him leave to interject that, harrrumph, when Victoria was queen, the world was on average a better place than it's been since she died.

So much for politics, economics, religion, and culture. What about two-year-old boys? Here the world progresses. The Victorian era lacked you, my John: much to its detriment, I might add.

What is Age Two all about? Quite a lot of things actually. One of which is mastering the art of conversation. Here at last you appear to be on your way. There was a time when we wondered about this. Really we did.

Brother Will—who, as you know, is crowding Age Five—came into the world reciting the Declaration of Independence and negotiating for changes in bath temperature and bedtime.

Not so Brother John, a young man of comparatively few words. But, then, as we have discerned, O John, you are a doer, not a talker.

Your way is not to ask: It is to grab a parental pants leg and head it in the direction of whatever-you-want. Parental hands, when they can be seized and appropriated, are more useful still.

Of late your vocabulary has been expanding rapidly. It is hardly Churchillian, but it serves. I am interested, among other things, to see you developing a proper respect for private property. Your cherished and perpetually grimy blanket is not "blanket"; it is, flatly, affirmatively, "mine." I sense a free-enterpriser in the making.

Linguistic breadth will come in any case, because you are a lover of books. I do not lightly use the word "lover." You love to feel books, love to handle them, to carry (and even sling) them around and, of course, to have them read to you, which is where parents occasionally come in handy. Will, whom you so like to follow about and copy in all things, likes books, too, but with you the instinct is, well, more instinctual.

Are you likely to become that socially despised commodity, the bookworm? I should hope so. Bookworms are merely people who like to find out about a lot of interesting things. Nor have I noticed that holding a book ever ruined anyone's pitching arm.

Your love of literature, my son, is exceeded only, if at all, by your love of good cooking. Oh, all right—any kind of cooking, so long as it's filling, which, at our house, it commonly is. Fat? I suppose we couldn't fairly call you that. But what a tummy, even so—too expansive for clothes that Will was wearing at age three! No use protesting to the world that you groove on bean sprouts and other nourishing matter. Hot dogs, chicken pot pies, and frozen pizza are your passion. Obviously.

At this juncture your father wishes to venture a subjective judgment. He has been looking at human faces for four decades, and never has he seen a smilier one than yours, your Royal Twoness, alight as it is with the joy of life and fellowship. Maybe it is the way you are—which I suspect is the truth of the matter.

What is the old song? Stay as sweet as you are. Yes, and enjoy being Two.

May 19, 1983

Declarations of Independence

When in the course of human events, it becomes necessary that four-year-olds should assume among the powers of the earth that separate and equal station to which—aw, skip it, My Best Beloved.

What need you Mr. Jefferson's eloquence? In the independence department you are progressing gorgeously as you enter your fifth year on this planet.

Let us recall last Sunday. It was warm and humid—a Houston-New Orleans kind of day up here in North Texas, and you were pulling off your church clothes. We looked in your closet. You pointed to a sweat suit. Your father—me—said, "No, that's too hot, let's put on some shorts."

You said, "No, I want my sweat suit." I said, "Shorts." You said, "Sweat suit." You won.

All Sunday afternoon, as the humidity turned adults into pools of moisture, you ginned around in a sweat suit, looking cool as a cucumber. I think you looked cool on purpose. To have done otherwise would have been—well, to back down on principles fiercely cherished, fervently asserted.

We are learning as a family, John Alexander, that principles are your stock in trade. Even wacky ones.

Like, for instance, putting on your T-shirts backward. Give me, if you can, one good reason for walking around with a backward T-shirt, especially when observant parents communicate that backwardness to you.

Yes, and why go resolutely about the house with right shoe on left foot and left shoe on right foot? Is there some detached, analytical reason for doing so?

I doubt it seriously. I think it is all part of being four years old—and a new, exuberant, self-aware, self-examining human being, who is more than just the extension of somebody else's personality.

You are declaring, my fiery four-year-old, your human independence. Well, to be sure, not your *total* independence. That would be a horrid thing.

Were you totally sovereign, who would fix your bologna sandwiches? Who would read you *The Little House* and play Go Fish with you? Even at age four, you see, there are many worse things than dependency. I understand, all the same, the need for sovereignty. Number Two brothers—I mean, of course, chronologically, not qualitatively—are at a disadvantage. They wear Older Brother's clothes; they walk, figuratively, in Older Brother's footsteps.

Your own older brother, Will, is six, going lickety-split on seven—a soccer player, a student of Dr. Seuss. From so great an eminence he is bound to look all-knowing, all-powerful to beings below. It is no wonder you so often copy his tastes, his wants, his very words.

No wonder either that from time to time you decide to be nobody else but John. That may be one reason you spurn the nicknames I tend to hang on you, declaring with firmness (not to say indignation), "I'm just plain John."

John you are, my best beloved. I know this, because it is John, not Will, who demands, "Throw me over your shoulder!" Which I do, to the creaking of middle-aged bones.

It is John, not Will, who cries, "Swing me around!" I grasp your wrists, and around we go, 'til the both of us drop from dizziness. Whereupon you want more.

Oh, yes, you are your very own person! If, for example, you were your father, you would lean against the sweet gum tree 'til your head stopped reeling; then you would sit down on the porch.

Not John of the backward T-shirts, John of the reversed running shoes. The same John, who is wont, long after tuck-in time, to issue forth from his room, checking his parents' remonstrations with, "Mommy, Daddy, I love you." That John suits us splendidly—as do they all, every last one of them.

May 16, 1985

Holding Hands

I can tell—oh, how clearly I see it—that we stand here poised on the edge. Somethin's happenin'!

On the way to the soccer game a few evenings ago, your father reached for your hand, prompting you to rejoin, with all the righteous indignation of Practically Eight: "Dad, that's what babies do, hold hands."

But, then, the next weekend, at the Indian Guides campout, as we clambered around the Arbuckle Mountains, I counted, once, twice, thrice, the occasion when you reached for Dad's hand. Dad with pleasure took the hand offered him. Over the ridges and through the valleys we went, laughing all the way. There are times when it is no fun being autonomous: graduated and diplomaed from babydom and dependence.

Now you have passed into the full splendor of Eight Whole Entire Years Old. We are in for another time of transition, I can tell. We have had such times before; I can always smell them coming.

Oh, My Best Beloved, you are, of all stars in our individualistic family firmament, the most independent-minded, the least quiescent. No, I did *not* say disobedient. We naturally have some of that, too, from time to time, but that is not really what I am talking about. I am talking about all the marching you do, to a drummer whose cadences the rest of us rarely detect.

Your father is fascinated by the inspirations that come upon you. Back to that nature hike in the Arbuckles. There we went, amid the post oaks and cedars, beneath the gray-blue Oklahoma sky. Firewheels sparked at our feet. Still waters glimmered, as did your eyes.

The hike over, you disclosed what was turning you on. Not the firewheels or the junipers, rather, an idea—the idea for a Nintendo game. Nintendo, I must explain for the benefit of the adults in the audience, is an electronic game, in which heroes battle dragons and vampires across the television screen, the usual objective being to rescue some princess or another. It is what eight-year-olds like to do these days. I would not have thought the Arbuckle Mountains would put Nintendo into your mind, but then I am often wrong, particularly about eight-year-old minds.

Off you dashed, drawing pad in hand, scribbling for the next hour your inspirations for a game about—what?—campers being captured and a hero dispatched to rescue them. Something like that.

Ah, well, not everybody grooves on firewheels—and, may I add that not every eight-year-old designs Nintendo games for a hobby.

The sparkle of creativity, Best Beloved, is ever about you. What a fertile little mind: forever designing games, and if not games, then neighborhood clubs, and if not clubs, then birthday parties. It takes away the parental breath. Sketch paper we find everywhere—on the floor, in chairs, on the back seat of the car, under your covers. Did little Amadeus Mozart cover his father's house with sonatas and symphonies? He could have created no bigger paper blizzard mess than you, best beloved.

The thing is, we usually don't know what to do with all these priceless sketches—save them for your archives (which no doubt you will one day establish at Harvard), or toss them in the trash for neatness' sake. What a frightening state of affairs, not knowing what to take seriously and what to write off. Future biographers may have harsh things to say about your mom and dad and their phobia concerning litter.

One thing John Alexander Murchison has not lost, at Age Eight, is his native sweetness. Best beloved, you remain what you always have been—a terrific hugger; given to occasional shows of temperament—moments when the spark hits the dry tinder; yet these, too, burn out, the smoke lifts, and soon enough all is well.

And now Eight Years! You will have to forgive your father's continuous marveling at this fact of nature, but it seems so short a time ago since Age Eight Minutes. A lot of water has flowed beneath this blond-headed, snaggle-toothed bridge, and it saddens no less than gladdens your parents' hearts.

What shall we do in this year ahead—while Boy and Dad, on those two spontaneous occasions, still hold hands? Get two front teeth back, for starters. Design more Nintendo games. Play soccer. Read more *Arabian Nights* and *Winnie the Pooh*. Learn how to pick up socks, and what to do with them. Make up your bed. Get into it on time.

I see I am becoming tedious. Birthday boys—especially independent-minded birthday boys—do not cotton to that venerable institution, the parental lecture. Anyway, there's endless time for lecturing. The present occasion calls for celebrating, which, with your gracious permission, we now shall do.

May 20, 1989

You? Ten?

Off we go! Up, up and away! I mean this literally as well as figuratively.

Off we go, you and Dad, leavin' on a jet plane, in partial celebration of your tenth birthday—an event of some aeronautical significance in and of itself.

That is how tenth birthdays are and should be—soaring, high-flying. We adults mark lives in decades: tens, twenties, thirties, forties (gulp), and so on. A decade is a platform on which to stand, gazing backward and forward at the same time. That is just what I think we will do, oh, best beloved.

Backward, to begin with. Well, how in the world! You? Ten?

Why, it was just the other day, yet here you are, lithe, long-limbed and loquacious: a very different commodity from the armful of pink flesh and squawls that was you, ten years ago.

This is called life, and it is wonderful. Grow we all must. What if you were ten years old and still wore teddy-bear jammies? This would not do. Nonetheless, as you belly up to the next decade, your parents, sentimental slobs at heart, acknowledge sadly that the next anniversary decade is twenty—and that all decades pass at precisely the same rate of speed, and, hey, where's my handkerchief, anyway?

The boy soon to fly off with Dad to the Rio Grande area, where Dad will address some lawyers, is a boy of wondrous gifts and aptitudes. Not a football player or first baseman and yet physically alive in a way I have rarely seen.

Always in motion—that's John; always planning, plotting, cutting, pasting, drawing, drafting, writing, and otherwise making quick work of whole forests cultivated, I suppose, for his own personal use. Above all, creating, making what didn't use to be but now, suddenly, is, thanks to John's insights and exertions.

John-at-Rest is a phenomenon observed exclusively in the still watches when the lights are out and small bodies replenish themselves for the next day's go-round.

The Creations of John is a bracing topic for a card catalog: games, stories, narratives, poems, pictures, sketches, designs. You are a Renaissance Boy. Remember the time I sat down at the typewriter and you dictated a script of the home movie you planned to make about Count Dracula?

That was the Dracula phase: old-hat now. I suppose it is Mega Man presently. Or Roald Dahl, the World's Greatest Writer, right?

Or—I don't know—it's probably all changed since I saw you this morning. Please jot it down and let me know.

Creativity is very often messy, like your room, to get down to brass tacks: these being the *only* objects I haven't helped you pick up off the floor lately!

The other morning before school, if you recall, we couldn't find your missing recorder for school music class, search as we might; but, oh, the artifacts our excavations did uncover! Socks, pencils, drawings, paper stars, T-shirts, marbles, crayons, rubber bands, two pairs of underwear, a paper clip, *Nintendo Power*, *Boys' Life*, five Dr. Pepper cans destined for the recycling bin—I pause for breath. The wonder was, the room had just been cleaned!

I pray you become a rich as well as famous artist. Or novelist. Or screen-writer. Or whatever. You will need to pay a valet to follow you around, picking up shoelaces and paper clips.

Anyway, my best beloved, the happiest possible birthday from the people who supply the paper and pencils you use up at such blinding speed.

A great age is ten; great possibilities lie before you. But I hear the clock ticking above the festive noise. You are moving ahead, best beloved. How nice that you are moving with style, agility, and growing confidence in your capacity to be you—you and you alone; the wholly lovable if messy being with whom we, your family, joyfully share past, present, and future.

May 18, 1991

Sweet Sixteen?

"Sweet sixteen," I believe the expression goes. In your case, ah . . . um . . . er . . .

Bashful, blushing, swooning, eyes-cast-downish, sugar-on-your-tongue—nope, must be somebody else the teller was talking about.

That you are kind and generous and thoughtful and all those

other good things remains true, and for it, your parents rejoice as this, your epochal birthday, Number Sixteen, draws nigh.

But this picture has a frame: a large, showy, and—I am sure this pleases you most of all—unconventional one.

The truth is, you have never reveled in convention. No social straitjackets for John; no how-to-do-it manual. How to do it? Why, the way *you* want to—consistent always with The Great Tradition of the West (yeah, yeah, right, Dad).

You thought we hadn't noticed all this? Not likely. Who, at age eight, wanted his room painted bright red? Who demanded a futon instead of a plain old bed?

But such are the rights and prerogatives appertaining to Age Sixteen. The adult authority figures under your roof will not intervene any more than is necessary—consistent always with The Great Tradition of the West.

As you know, we began this custom of the public birthday salute many years ago—sixteen, come to think of it—back when there was no chance of your offering objection. Dad would propound some well-seasoned wisdom, and you, unable to read, would burble happily. Burble. I wish. Could we try it again sometime? No? I see — that would mean accepting the interventions of adult authority figures (hereinafter "AAFs").

Well, speaking as one AAF, congratulations on the way life is going. You didn't think I would say that? Shows how little the rising generation knows about AAFs. The likes of us don't care about heel-clicking hosannas. How dull! How dehumanized!

Discovery is what we like. And, yes, what a voyage of discovery you are launched on now: cars, books, journalism, architecture, poetry, Spanish. No mean flotilla for buoying and bearing a sixteen-year-old into the larger life.

Need I add, the "more expensive life"? Car insurance! Aaarghhh! And then college. But that's two years down the road. Let us rejoice in the meantime at the quality of your interests. How unspeakably delightful for a bookworm dad to find a son stretched on what, in baby days, we called the tummy, book propped open, eyes fixed on magical words. And a summer reading list that encompasses Steinbeck, Orwell, Cervantes. I believe I may have died and gone to heaven.

And a published poet—such you became this month with the publication of the high school literary magazine. And such I rejoice to see living under our roof. Maybe I will slip into your stack the lyrical Mr. Yeats, to be discovered some warm afternoon and, if that works, Kipling (for the surging rhythms, not the imperial vision at which you, in your present mood, would turn up your nose).

The creative urge, the artistic urge, is upon you, if the word of an AAF may be trusted. But it has always been upon you. This is nothing new. The forms are what is new: in the old days, designs for Nintendo games; today, designs for houses. (For you have chosen architecture as your professional interest? I understand that to be the case.)

Down like a old barn goes the family reputation for conservatism as the bare, smooth, modern designs pour from your pen. Well, why not modern (though you yourself dwell, futon and all, in a chimnied saltbox house)?

Adventure, adventure! Change, change! Sixteen was made for it. You are made for sixteen. In consequence, all that your AAFs (who love you dearly) can do is sigh, felicitate you warmly, and assert again The Great Tradition of the West. Which Tradition generously accommodates creators of the irrepressible, over-the-top variety. Know any such? Please don't give 'em our address. One is about our quota at the moment.

May 12, 1997

. . . WITH LOVE,

DAD

VI

The Holidays

OVER THE YEARS, I have felt obliged, but also privileged, to put down on paper some thoughts about the core meaning of the days we set aside for public observance. This obligation seems to me more and more necessary as we Americans blithely come to regard holidays—or holy-days—as mere days off from work. Which they are. But isn't there more? Much more?

CHRISTMAS

1995

As usual on Christmas Eve, churches will be swamped, partly by people who don't patronize churches any other time of year. These, as usual, will ooh and ahh over carols, candles, banked poinsettias, and the congregation's upward surge on the first note of Handel's "Hallelujah Chorus."

Bless these folk, you have to say. Better to be in church once a year than never. On the other hand, there are profounder reasons for observing the birth of God's Son. These reasons shine out from the faces of a group of worshipers at a Dallas Episcopal parish with which I am acquainted. These particular faces are not white—they are ebony, like a Victorian cameo. The frames to which the faces are attached are long, lithe, and lean—the frames of Sudanese refugees.

From what have these refugees taken refuge in North Texas? From oppression? Yes. There is a lot of that going around. But, in the case of the Sudanese, the oppression is of a character we rarely envision today. The Sudanese are refugees for the sake of the Gospel—victims of frank persecution by their country's Islamic fundamentalist regime.

The story of Christ's birth is not to them, shall we say, a seasonal tale—a happy story to read when garlands festoon the mantle and chill winds blow outside. The story is transformational. You hear it, and if, with all your heart, you believe its truth, why, everything thereafter is different. The story is more than story. It is Gospel—Good News. Unto us is born this day in the city of David a Savior, which is Christ the Lord. . . .

This is a business much more serious than poinsettias, more serious even than Handel! The kind of business that can drive men, women, and children out of their ancient homeland and into a world unfamiliar to them—it is that sort. It reconciles them to the loss of jobs, possessions, and culture. Because, when all's said, the Gospel is meat and drink to those who embrace it. The rest is pumpkin pie: sweet but dispensable.

Out of nowhere, seemingly, the Sudanese turned up one Sunday recently at the Episcopal Church of the Holy Cross in Dallas' Oak Lawn section. Their refugee housing was relatively near. Anglicans all, they sought and found the sacramental, prayer-book worship to which they were habituated in the Sudan.

The Sudanese came with hands outstretched—to receive not a wad of dollar bills but the Body of Christ in the sacrament. "Not one came here asking for help," says Father Henry Pendergrass, Holy Cross's rector. "They asked for a church."

A church they found. Holy Cross' congregation, with one heart and mind, took them in: objecting only, as one member put it, that "I don't like to think of them as 'the Sudanese.' I think of them as Peter and Philip and so on. . . ."

The objection proved definitive. Into the Body of Christ, 4052 Herschel St. branch, each refugee has been tenderly incorporated. The three or four dozen Sudanese who attend Holy Cross have been joined by a handful of Ghanans and Liberians.

Will the Sudan ever see its lost sons and daughters again? Much depends on whether the free world rouses itself against the bigots who, in Allah's name, forbid the building of churches and flog priests rash enough to administer communion wine. So far, the outside world has hardly noticed the war against Sudanese Christianity.

Meanwhile, on Christmas Eve, at least one altar rail I know of, the hands of African Christians will reach out reverently for the sacrament as if there were no more important gift on earth — better than twenty-four-karat jewelry, better than a new Lexus.

Actually, as these particular Christians see it, there *isn't* anything better than the Bread of Life. They shame the aesthetic Christians, the social Christians, so comfortable and cultivated and decorous.

"The Sudanese"—as Holy Cross Church refuses proudly to call them—know much more than the name of the child for whom angels sang at Bethlehem. They know his love; they know his power.

1993

The *Wall Street Journal* shed a little Christmas joy the other day, revealing that Americans regard government with the flinty-eyed scorn they normally reserve for telephone solicitors at dinnertime.

Of course it's possible to take such news, if you call it news, in another sense entirely—as evidence not of corrosive cynicism but rather of maturity: good tidings of great joy, which shall be to all people.

What is Christmas about, at one level of understanding, if not the futility of the secular enterprise: kings, courts, parliaments, congresses, laws, regulations, codes, the whole shmear? "O put not your trust in princes or in any child of man," the Psalmist enjoins.

Government? Ancient Judea had it in spades—the Roman kind of government; the most meticulous, the fairest, the most efficient in the history of the world up to that time. Perhaps that is not saying much by modern standards, but by the standards of the first century AD, it is saying a great deal.

Even by contrast with Israel's and Judah's home-grown monarchies, Roman rule had its sunny characteristics. There was order, there was comparative peace—it was nothing like the chaos and dissension under the kings whom God had raised up reluctantly to supplant the judges. Even the judges hadn't worked out that well. Samuel's own sons "turned aside after lucre, and took bribes, and perverted judgment." Why, you might suppose they were congressmen—if that didn't sound like more of the cynicism the *Journal*'s reporters find so unedifying.

Where was it getting anyone? The judges had given way to kings, the kings to foreign invaders, the invaders to the meticulous Romans—who made the chariots run on time. As far in the future as human eyes could see loomed magistrates and decrees, and human desire pitted against human desire.

Whereupon God upset the apple cart—or, as the Scriptures eventually would have it, turned the world upside down. The most extraordinary personage in world history showed up in a stable, of all places, surrounded by shepherds, all of low-born riffraff. The birth of Jesus Christ is rebuke to the pretensions of all those princes and princelings we are bidden not to trust overmuch. Who are they, these petty potentates with the large titles, against the Son of God? What is their power against his?

Such questions, asked in a late twentieth-century context, have a distinctly post-Victorian odor. The twentieth century keeps nervous distance from the Son of God: afraid to renounce him entirely (what if he's really who he said he was?) and afraid to embrace him (who needs politicians and public officials if this world turns out not to be the ultimate world, but something intermediate?).

The power machines of the late twentieth century seemingly exist for their own sakes, churning and churning—and with what result? One problem (e.g., the communist bloc) disappears. New ones (e.g., wanton crime and family breakdown) rise to the fore. Some power! We put our trust in princes; invariably, the princes strike out.

All strike out but the Prince of Peace, whose kingdom, as he himself explained, is not of this world. The late twentieth century, hugely materialistic though groping toward the spiritual, has no idea what to do with a prince disdainful of worldly power and disrespectful toward its uses.

Jesus, the Babe of Bethlehem, Messiah, King of Kings and Lord of Lords, is quite a morsel for the 1990s to digest: dead yet alive, absent yet present, supremely powerful yet tender. What's his foreign policy? ("Go ye therefore, and teach all nations....") How does he stand on welfare reform? ("Blessed are the poor....") On crime? (Whosoever "is angry with his brother without a cause shall be in danger of the judgment....") The secular world knows nothing else like it. What it does know, it neither admires nor trusts. As the Babe of Bethlehem extends once more a tiny finger ready for grasping, the world holds back in anxiety.

So many worldly temptations yielded to! So many chances for divine communion passed up! What of this latest? What of the silent and holy night now falling?

1992

Happy winter holiday, to use the public school vernacular, and don't forget to visit the shopping center of your choice. Because what are winter holidays all about anyway if not easing the educational grind and gratifying the merchants?

Bemoaning the paganization of Christmas is no new pastime, that's for sure. When I was young, advertisements this time of year urged us to "put Christ back in Christmas." Just as now, there are warnings that commercialism is fatally warping this sacred occasion.

Still, the paganization process hadn't made much headway. Christmas was Christmas, at school as elsewhere. We eagerly inquired of each other, "What are you getting for Christmas?"—not knowing how controversial an occasion we were endorsing.

In choir programs—held, I confess, on public property—we belted out Christmas carols with gusto. Such naive little twits were we that, while singing "Christ the Savior is born," we failed to notice the American system collapsing in upon itself. We thought the birth of Jesus a fine, wholesome thing worth celebrating.

Well, times do change. That era's children, having grown up, have erected protective barriers around their own kids—"winter holidays" and such like. This is lest innocent minds should encounter, unprepared, the concept of a virgin birth, in a manger visited by the unlikely combination of angels, shepherds, and wise men, drawn there every one by a God bent on the redemption of his people. A recent school choir concert we attended was almost wholly unholy. There were the merest passing references to herald angels, holy infants tender and mild, and other such otherworldly concepts.

The abandonment of Christianity—its doctrines, its morals—proceeds with the sly encouragement of the cultural elite. A noted British convert to atheism, the novelist-biographer A.N. Wilson, has written a new book on that decrepit topic, the Jesus of history. According to Wilson, the story of Jesus's birth in a stable comes from "the deep world of folklore." As for the baby's subsequent career—harrumph! "I found it impossible to believe that a first century Galilean holy man had at any time of his life believed himself to be the Second Person of the Trinity."

I find it impossible to believe A.N. Wilson knows the society he is addressing: one where personal assertions enjoy at least as much status as the multi-generational witness of Augustine, Aquinas, Luther, Calvin, Wesley, Newman, Bonhoeffer, Lewis, Muggeridge.

The really odd thing, perhaps, amid the "winter holiday" preposterousness, is finding so many wishing us a Merry Christmas anyway. It is no small thing to buck your own society's fashion trends: which, if you please, is exactly what Christianity's founder did. The grown-up babe of Bethlehem kicked over more than the money changers' tables; he overturned common expectations as to the inanity of life and the immutability of the political order. He did this through, among other things, startling declarations: "Come unto me all ye that travail and are heavy laden. . . ." "I am the Good Shepherd. . . ." "I am the Resurrection and the Life. . . ." The faith he founded became the abiding counter-culture, a perpetual thorn-in-the-flesh to the proud and the indifferent.

All this was still to come that night at the very stable A.N. Wilson derides as mythical. Nonetheless, something world-changing was afoot. A star shone, angels sang, in due course shepherds and kings came calling, and nothing afterward was the same, or ever will be again. The Father had reached out in incomprehensible love to his own creations. The mighty were put down from their seats, the humble and meek exalted.

Nothing is sillier than modern society's attempt to fob off Christmas as just a picturesque interval in the school year, a make-or-break moment for retailers. For one thing, it's no use. You might as well try to housebreak a tiger as turn Christmas, that ultra-revolutionary feast, into something as sweet as spun sugar, as easily laid aside as another one of Aunt Minnie's hand-painted neckties.

THANKSGIVING

1995

Thanksgiving, otherwise an occasion for families and feasting, sends us spinning backward in time. We go back, if only for a moment, to our origins—to men and women on the slippery edge of civilization, scrambling for a toehold.

It is no bad thing to look back, if only between the grace and the cranberry sauce. We need to see where we began. It helps us appraise where we are now and where we may be headed.

The civilization of the Pilgrim Fathers, as we used to call them—I suppose the politically punctilious today would add "Mothers"—was unimaginably simple by modern standards. Between the settlers and God, there was hardly anything. Certainly not possessions! The Fathers and Mothers had brought few enough of these with them. Material temptations were not what you would call omnipresent in the American wilderness.

Nor was there much government to speak of. It was common, once upon a time, to note in Thanksgiving disquisitions written by patriotic editorialists how the settlers had adopted early on a kind of scheme for economic distribution. This scheme served them poorly. Instead of abundance, it produced dearth—instead of enterprise came sloth. The Pilgrims dropped it quickly. This demonstrated, we were assured, the abiding futility of socialistic fantasies.

The fascination that the Pilgrims have for us today is the fascination of Eden—everything in its original state, man's despoiling hand barely laid upon creation.

Edens never last. Certainly, the first one didn't. Nor could the Pilgrims' own, given that vast size and potentialities. It's helpful, nonetheless, to remember what life was like, stripped down to the essentials. To remember indeed that there *were* such things as essentials.

What were they? First in priority and power was God—the God in whose name the Pilgrims had voyaged here in the first place. His authority spoke for itself. Indeed, it was written down in a book, with signature phrases such as: "Thou shalt love the Lord thy God with all thy heart and with all thy soul and with thy might." There were explicit commandments. Good Pilgrims hand-stitched them on canvas. The society of which they were a part tried, with varying degrees of earnestness, to live by them. Church, where God was worshipped, was as natural as food and drink.

As for government, it existed for specific ends, as stipulated in the Mayflower Compact: "our better Ordering and Preservation" and the "advancement of the Christian Faith and the Honour of our King and Country."

It would be silly to say we can recapture the Pilgrim vision. It would be even sillier to say that no effort to recapture it is warranted. The Pilgrim basics were good, and they worked. God at the top, human appetites much lower down on the totem pole, and human relations as matters for private, instead of governmental, adjustment— there was symmetry here.

Such symmetry we do not find in modern life, what with God off to the side, appetite central to daily concerns, and government self-selected as the principal arbiter in human affairs.

We are, as I have observed already, a different kind of society, yet a society rethinking its assumptions. The turmoil in Washington over welfare and the federal budget is part of that rethinking—likewise the unsteady migration back to the churches and the revival of concern for moral matters.

The backward glance on Thanksgiving Day shows us not just how it was but also how—in spirit at any rate—it could be again. "Could be" isn't "will be." To talk about permeative religious faith and obligation is fine—and hand-tying. Start talking about powers higher than the human heart and there is no predicting what worldly aims one ends up surrendering.

But at our elbows this day sit the Pilgrims. I would not wonder if we heard them whispering to us, telling of the essentials. Lesson One: How to live as a strong, free people, worshipful of God and respectful of His intentions. Lesson Two: Well . . . maybe that can wait till dessert?

1991

So here once more we sit, trying to psych ourselves up for Thanksgiving while journalistic crapehangers decorate the premises—a sick economy, AIDS, crime, drugs, teenage sex, health care costs, Congress, crummy schools, political correctness, the greenhouse effect, know-it-all newspaper columnists.

It is time for talking, so to speak, turkey. Enough gloom and doom. Let us rejoice. Let us give thanks.

Nobody wishes to downplay the afflictions of the present day, least of all those who have lost their jobs or fallen sick with AIDS. At this point, nonetheless, I feel constrained to share a great historical truth, an insight of purest gold.

A lady of keen observational powers said it best: "If it's not one 'dee' thing, it's another." (Ladies of this lady's generation commonly say "dee" instead of the now-ordinary word for which "dee" stands.)

After a quarter of a century or so in the newspaper business, I note with glowing clarity the truth of this insight. There are no earthly paradises, and if we ever stumbled into one such, we wouldn't be able to stay awake for all the snoring going on. Part of the fun of life is trying to fix the multitudinous things that go wrong every day. I do not know why this is so, but so it seems.

Whatever we may suppose from the supermarket best sellers, there are no golden ages. The gleam we see is from brass: highly rubbed but subject to tarnish.

The early American republic was good—if you lived past birth. Europe, pre-1914, was good; then came 1914.

Together with my still sprightly contemporaries, I look back fondly on the late 1950s and early 1960s; but somebody around then must have done something wrong, because the Ringo-Paul-Jack-'n'-Jackie-Julie Andrews-Temptations-Goldwater 1960s, so mellow, so alive, dissolved into the Chicago Seven–Woodstock 1960s of putrid memory. The 1980s were similarly mixed—Ronald Reagan on the plus side, Congress on the negative.

The thing to remember, my friends, is that Thanksgiving is not about shouting, hip, hip, hurray, we've got it made! If it were, never a morsel of turkey would cross our lips, because never do we have it made.

Thanksgiving is about gratitude for what we do have—and hope for what we'd like. These are modest objectives. They do not look to the Complete, Final, and Irreversible Reformation of Society and Humankind. They look to hearts (are they loving?) and homes (are the payments current?).

The modern secularization of Thanksgiving—its rebirth as National Pigout Day—has raised our sights in a perverse sense. We expect more than we used to: in which expectation government has played a part, with its repeated promise to be our best friend. Expecting the world, we feel disappointment at receiving sometimes a handful of dust. The religious Thanksgivings of yore were occasions for celebrating dependence; often enough these days, we memorialize impatience, restlessness, and, supremely, appetite.

The time has come to stand back, if we can. Let us count our blessings, this Thanksgiving of 1991. These are considerable.

The shadow of nuclear warfare—to borrow a cliche from the Ringo-Julie-Jackie days—has passed. It no longer seems likely that our world may blow itself apart before the pecan pie reaches us. The economy, though sluggish, moves forward. Interest rates are the lowest in years, even if uncertainty is high. The good times don't roll forever, but they keep coming back.

The current set of Washington politicians leaves plenty to be desired, but at worst this encourages us to put less faith in Washington politicians, who have mucked up so many things. Crime, drugs, bad schools, family disintegration—these are calamities. And yet calamities awaken extraordinary responses from ordinary people. Who knows that this will not be one of those times?

All this, if we wanted, we could call whistling past the graveyard. I prefer to call it doing the best we can, playing the hand dealt us, turning our eyes from golden ages, past or future, to the present moment, in which alone we are called on to act.

For the chance to do our best, let us be grateful. Let us give thanks.

COLUMBUS DAY

1992

A jury of Scarsdale, New York, seventh-graders, in a classroom court-martial, has tried and convicted Christopher Columbus. He's a villain, a wretch, an exterminator of Native Americans.

Handcuffing Columbus at this late date is problematical, but events like the Scarsdale trial speak alarmingly of what is happening here in the New World. The apostles of political correctness (PC), still charged up despite all the indignation they have rightly excited, have launched a frontal assault on our traditions. Frankly, they don't care who gets run over or ground down, just so the end result is that Malcolm X, Sojourner Truth, and Sitting Bull emerge as our main national folk heroes. Speaking of bull . . .

The five-hundredth anniversary of Columbus's epochal voyage evoked from the PCers the expected brainless caterwauling, not just on college campuses but also, startlingly, in elementary and secondary schools. According to the *New York Times*, "Students across the nation are learning everything from skepticism to contempt for the explorer's exploits. At a Brooklyn high school . . . a 17-year-old debater pilloried Columbus as a pitiful fraud who cheated his sailors and lied about his discoveries." In a play, Greenwich Village fourth-graders mocked him as "a bewildered fool obsessed by gold." In other words, students are having their brains washed.

A sense of the ridiculous helps one cope with tidings of this sort. I mean, look—seventh-graders judging a world-changing explorer? Chill out. Yet it's not the kids who should most worry us; it's the adults in their lives, pouring half-truths and outright lies into impressionable ears.

An assault on Western civilization goes forth in the classrooms of Western civilization. This paradox can be accounted for only in terms of our own negligence and guilt.

We feel guilty in proportion as we regard—falsely—our tradition as having less to do with liberty and opportunity than with exploitation and racism. We are negligent insofar as we suffer paid pedagogues to retail these half-baked notions to our children.

The problem at the college level has been recognized and addressed in first-rate books like Dinesh D'Souza's *Illiberal Education* and Charles Sykes's *The Hollow Men*. We should not lazily assume the PC infection has been quarantined on campuses such as Yale, Dartmouth, and Duke. The cultural elite cast a wide net.

A newly issued report by Lynne Cheney, head of the National Endowment for the Humanities, finds that, "The aim of education, as many on our campuses see it, is no longer truth, but political transformation—of students and society." She takes alarmed note even of movies and museum exhibitions that lie about the American past.

A frequent theme is what bad guys our explorers were, starting with Columbus. Why didn't they just leave this wonderful land to its original inhabitants? I don't know. Why is the sky blue instead of green? Why do birds fly rather than hopscotch? A more time-wasting exercise than the repeal of reality I just can't think of. Nor is there a more dishonest enterprise than deliberately low-keying a dominant good (the West's promotion of liberty, moral responsibility, and tolerance) so as to play up a tributary evil (the exploitation of the Indians).

What do we do? Cheney accurately sees a need for transformation of the present PC climate in colleges and universities. Among other things, she calls on college trustees to begin actively representing "the concerns of the larger society," making plain that "what happens on our campuses is of importance to all of us."

Hooray for that. Yet parents cannot abdicate to higher-ups their basic responsibility for the shaping of character, the imparting of truth. If you live with a seventh-grader who regards Columbus as one of history's rascals, there's been a patent failure somewhere along the line to communicate the truth to him. This failure should be addressed promptly before he helps convict Moses of complicity in drowning Third World charioteers.

These are extraordinary, upside-down times. We're like Columbus: We don't know quite where we are going. Likely to Davey Jones's Locker, unless the wide-awake among us are ready to reef, tack, and steer.

1991

To the familiar query, "Is nothing sacred?" a troubling answer asserts itself: Nope. Nothing I've noticed lately is sacred.

Least of all—as everyone has noticed lately—the memory of Christopher Columbus, which came under furious assault during anniversary observances we used to regard as staid and routine.

The National Italian American Foundation reports indignantly that Columbus statues were defaced in New York City and Washington, D.C. Demonstrators disrupted Columbus Day parades in various cities, including Denver and Los Angeles. We all know why Native American activists, and their well-wishers, have declared Columbus a slime bag and, worse, and exploiter and colonialist. They appear to wish the Niña, Pinta, and Santa Maria had been swallowed up in the Bermuda Triangle.

This is not an essay about the Columbus controversy of which we have all heard much more than we care to. It is an essay about how typical, how characteristic, is the Columbus controversy today, when heroes of all sorts are suspect. Though Columbus is a Political Correctness victim, his present plight goes beyond this. Actually we don't like anybody any more. We trash our heroes with fluency and abandon. Norman Schwarzkopf is about the only American who commands anything like general esteem. It will be interesting to see how long he survives the spotlights' withering glare.

The best-seller lists abound in books that demolish or impair the reputations of famous people, Kitty Kelly's pseudo-biography of Nancy Reagan being the obvious example. It is all a far cry from Plutarch's approach.

Everybody should read Plutarch, if possible in the majestic seventeenth-century translation by John Dryden. Plutarch's idea was to hold up for admiration the great men of ancient time, both Greek and Roman. The reader was summoned to emulate their virtues (and eschew their vices).

Today we wouldn't want to know Caesar's tactics in Gaul. We'd want to know what he was doing with the kitchen maid—or, spicier yet, one of the handsome legionnaires—when Calpurnia's back was turned.

Why the radically different approach today? Part of the trouble is technical, stemming from the sheer volume of biographical information available for digesting. "No man is a hero to his valet," the old saying goes. The valet knows too much, as do we moderns, potentially, about everyone, including Supreme Court nominees.

There is of course the question of what you do with what you know: what weight you give vices as against virtues. I am not talking of suppression; I am talking of perspective.

The way the biographer deploys his material ties in with his view of great men—indeed, of greatness itself. This is the problem today. A meanness of spirit is abroad in the land. Ordinary people seem eaten up with envy and cynicism.

Our refusal to acknowledge greatness has to do most of all with our smallness. People who succeed in one endeavor or another are resented and distrusted because they make us question our own accomplishments or lack thereof. So we chortle over their defects, their shortcomings, their broken marriages and drinking problems. Was Robert Frost, the poet, a curmudgeon and domestic tyrant? (Yes, says one biographer.) Just what you'd expect from someone who'd write all those famous poems. Why, it sometimes becomes clear that they are no better than we are, these celebrities, just luckier.

What a lot of sourpusses we are turning ourselves into, down on humanity, down on—by extension—ourselves, inasmuch as we are part of humanity; ready to believe the worst of our fellow man, particularly when the man in question has managed to distinguish himself.

Sneering at heroes doesn't prevent truly heroic types from doing what they find themselves called on and able to do. What sneering does is broaden the gap that exists already between heroes and the rest of us. It lowers the whole tone of society; lowers our sight form the mountaintops to the sewers. Some people, I admit, just love sewers. Heroes don't: which helps a lot to explain their heroism.

VII

Episcopalians and Others

THE "LITTLE PLATOON" to which I belong, ecclesiastically speaking, is the Episcopal Church: which church I love much more than many readers believe, given how frequently I fault its leadership and the drift of its theology. The truth is, I use my branch of the one, holy, catholic, and apostolic church as a figure of speech for Christianity itself. Within our own Gothic walls are to be seen the same tensions, strifes, joys, hopes, and so on found in most modern American religions. I stand ready at the same time to be corrected—brought up short and sharp—by the church's Lord if my evaluations prove wrong or wrong-headed.

What's Happenin' Now?

Why, from time to time, do I write of the Episcopalians? Because, as the saying goes, I are one, but also because the Episcopal Church brilliantly exemplifies the ambiguities in American religion today.

"Exemplifies the ambiguities"—what sociological mumbo jumbo, but having written it, I kind of like it. Big, gray institutions tend to talk like that; after a time, they begin to look and smell like it. American churches, almost across the board, are becoming big and gray. Name me a church or denomination, from the Southern Baptist to the Roman Catholic, which is untenanted by politicians, bureaucrats, sociologists, mega-thinkers, trend watchers, poll takers, and such like.

Back to my beloved (honest, I mean it!) Episcopalians, who wound up their general convention in Phoenix, unable to say, one way or the other, whether homosexual practice violates the moral law; unable to say, without great scratching of heads and carefully nuanced studies, whether there is a moral law; unable to affirm, as a portion of that maybe-existent, maybe non-existent law, the standard of sexual chastity for clergy. For clergy! I beg you, chew on that for a moment.

On the ordination of homosexuals, which turned out to be the central issue in Phoenix, the convention wouldn't say yes and it wouldn't say no; it wouldn't say stop and it wouldn't say go. Shall I tell you what it did? It sat with a sheepish smile on its face, hands spread wide in—yes—ambiguity. The convention voted to study the matter three years longer, on the off-chance that three thousand years of moral teaching might yet be shown up as false and stale.

One deputy or bishop, I forget which, alluded in debate to the church's "emerging theology." I guess it's like watching a fax emerge from the machine. We rip and read it. What's the latest word?

Various bishops, including talk-show superstar John Shelby Spong of Newark, New Jersey, are feeling anything but ambiguous on this matter. They have had their own show of hands, and the moral law, as applied to the practice of homosexuality, seems to be null and void. Starting almost immediately, nine bishops plan to ordain practicing homosexuals to the priesthood, so there, nyaaah, nyaaah.

I feel called at this point to say what a loving and lovable church the Episcopal Church, even today, can be when it tries—as much so, in many places, as when circuit-riding frontier bishops braved Indians and tornadoes to bring a young nation the treasures of the faith. Lord, what wonderful days!—days before the powerful and the glorious lowered their gaze from heaven and began passing political resolutions.

If political resolutions were pimento cheese sandwiches, the Phoenix convention could have fed the multitudes. Bishops and deputies were as busy as George Bush (a fellow Episcopalian) when it came to solving the world's problems. Energy, racism, environment, health care, recycling, Iraq, the Kurds, the Shiites, the Palestinians, you name it, the convention had an answer.

I was observing the House of Bishops when a resolution on the banking system came up. Hey, interposed the bishop of Texas, we're not experts in banking law. A fellow bishop fired back: We don't have to be experts to identify with inner-city folk who need better banking services. The resolution, duly passed, will be forgotten with the rest. What counts is feeling in tune with the world and its enumerated concerns.

Three more years and another general convention can solve the rest of America's problems, if any. It may not be a placid three years. The number of Episcopalians, unsurprisingly, has dropped by a third from a few decades ago. The national church, strapped for cash, is planning budget cuts and layoffs. (All that paper for resolutions costs money.) A traditionalist fellowship, the Episcopal Synod of America, accuses the church of embracing "two religions" and worshipping "two gods"; it adds with heavy significance that its members will start ministering "throughout the nation and by all means" to orthodox people.

It was hot in Phoenix—up to 110 degrees. One Episcopalian I spoke with said, uh-huh, and if the church doesn't change, it's going to get a lot hotter. He hoped I knew what he meant. I did.

July 24, 1991

Theological Taxidermy

The Episcopal Church of the 1980s is a theological taxidermy shop. It can be depended on to stuff and mount in the window whatever societal trend seems most up-to-the-minute. Some years it's politics. This year it's sex.

The church meets next month in Detroit, with at least two sexy subjects before it. One is the attempted castration of the church's liturgy.

The Methodists will know what I am talking about. Their own church, adopting a new hymnal earlier this spring, took care to prune away as much "sexist" language as possible. "He's," "Him's," and "His's" were cast into hellfire. What liberal Protestants hope to end up with is a unisex God who speaks in sweet, piping tones and leaves earthlings mostly alone.

In which regard the Episcopalians have made less headway than the Wesleyans. A proposed "alternative" service due to come before the Episcopal General Convention would eliminate much, though not all, "sexist" language in the *Book of Common Prayer.*

Nobody would yet be forced to use the new services—yet. They are a beginning, a point of departure. By way of example, the revisers suggest an alternative to the *Gloria Patri,* whose historic form is "Glory be to the Father, and to the Son, and to the Holy Ghost." How do you like "Honor and glory to God, and to God's eternal Word, and to God's Holy Spirit."? Where does this send you—to your knees, or to the restroom?

The notion behind "inclusive language," as the above is called, is that the male-chauvinist imagery of scripture and church history enslaves modern women. The revisers tell us that "the metaphor 'Lord' is often seen as a term of masculine domination in our society." The revisers do not tell us who sees the term as such—or why it is seen so only now, after two thousand years when no one gave a thought to the sociological significance of pronouns.

On the other hand, you have to remember that religion, 1980s style, is a make-it-up-as-you-go-along proposition. Witness a recent attempt by advanced circles inside Episcopaldom to overhaul the historic Christian moral understanding.

A new sex-education curriculum for Episcopal schools and parishes seeks to do away with the idea of "sex as guilt." The curriculum asserts that sex is "a Christian sacrament"—making one wonder if the curriculum was written by clergymen or by a P R firm, hired to double attendance at Mass.

From the perspective of the task force that wrote the curriculum, Christians are behind the times in refusing to condone gay sex and other "non-traditional relationships."

Sexuality: A Divine Gift isn't a rousing call to strike off ancient shackles. No such call is necessary. The task force stacks the theological deck as deftly as a riverboat cardsharper.

Although students of S A D G won't learn much about the fundamentals of Christian morality, they'll receive a thorough indoctrination in the need to cast off old stigmas against gay sex (this in the age of A I D S) and unwedded bliss.

The traditional Christian family receives scant mention in the curriculum, but, among resource materials, Deryck Claderwood's *Lovemaking: Heterosexual, Bisexual, and Homosexual* goes on and on about, well, just what you'd expect.

A recommended film strip, *About Your Sexuality*, explicitly depicts matters and practices I am constrained from mentioning in a family newspaper. Ah, religious education! It's sure not what it used to be.

S A D G is one of the saddest productions to issue from any modern church body. One is glad to say that it has been condemned by various bishops: the more passionately perhaps because of fallout from the Diocese of Newark's recent vote to "affirm" loving gay relationships.

The national church, having commissioned S A D G, has taken to pretending that it's all just for cerebral discussion, folks, nothing to get alarmed about, pay no attention to that couple behind the curtain. This is blather. The task force invites us to admire, not the old morality, but a whole new species: just such a species as you might expect from the flabbergasted keepers of a 2.8 million-member flock that lost 340,000 sheep in 1986 alone.

The Episcopal Church not so long ago took its cues from On High. Today—lest the knowing and worldly-wise laugh at such unaffected spirituality—it genuflects to theological authorities like *Ms* magazine and the National Organization for Women.

Have you ever seen a coiffed and bejeweled dowagger in a mini-skirt? Then you have seen—metaphysically—the Episcopal Church of the 1980s, rolling its eyes, rouging its lips, praying that some chic passer-by will notice and speak an approving word.

June 8, 1988

Drawing Conclusions

John Shelby Spong, the Episcopal Church's only quasi-Buddhist bishop—I think—is distressed and distraught. Robert Williams, the practicing homosexual Bishop Spong recently ordained to the priesthood, is not the role model the bishop had supposed.

Sexual orientation, you will readily understand, wasn't the problem. Mr. Williams was ordained not in spite of but *because of* his gay lifestyle. Bishop Spong—a broad-minded prelate who worshiped last year at a Buddhist temple and found it good—had wanted to make a statement about homosexuality and why the church should accept it. What if his own church didn't (or at least tried not to) ordain practicing gay people? The bishop of Newark would do it anyway, so there!

The bishop did it, amid choruses of protest that have not yet subsided. A few weeks later, Mr. Williams, at a homosexual-rights symposium in a Detroit Episcopal church, spoke disparagingly about monogamy and celibacy. He called them "unnatural" and unnecessary; he said he knew no monogamous people.

Mr. Williams didn't leave it quite there. He was asked: How could Mother Teresa possibly benefit from a sexual relationship? He replied: Mother Teresa would be better off "getting laid." I'm sorry, but that's what he said.

There were coast-to-coast gasps when the news got out. Even Bishop Spong was appalled. He promptly suspended Mr. Williams from priestly functions and obtained his dismissal as director of the diocesan ministry to gays and lesbians.

What was the matter? Mr. Williams had come out for infidelity. "Monogamy in committed relationships," homosexual or hetero-sexual, is the bishop's position. Bishop Spong wanted an apology.

As Artie Johnson used to say, ve-ry in-ter-esting. Bishop Spong can go further than the church wants to go; Father Williams can't go further than Bishop Spong wants to go. It's fine for Bishop Spong, in a recent book, to challenge St. Paul on homosexuality and women's rights. Mr. Williams can't advocate promiscuity. On his own premise—historic-equals-outdated—how can Bishop Spong know promiscuity is bad?

The real question, of course, is, how do Christians these days know anything with certainty? Religion is in flux, thanks to the official teachers of religion, many of them questing spirits who can't believe truths can be true for more than twenty years at a stretch. Sex, not sin, is what these clerics most like to talk about. Well, isn't that what Phil Donahue likes most to talk about?

On the doctrinal level, the Virgin Birth, the bodily Resurrection of Christ, and the Trinity are steadily being marginalized. In vari-ous seminaries, the Bible is taught as a human document, a product of its time and place. Small wonder the mainline denominations are shrinking numerically. Oakland A's fans seem more committed to their side than some bishops and clergy to theirs.

Spongian liberals de-religionize religion. Religion is, for them, a sort of dress-up branch of politics, heavy on plebiscites and per-sonal revelations. That Bishop Spong could worship in a Buddhist temple, and afterward call for cessation of Christian missions, shows how far things have gone.

"Affirm" is these people's favorite word. They want to "affirm" everybody, whatever he does or thinks (unless, of course, he thinks Scripture divinely inspired or the Virgin Birth a necessary and wholesome doctrine).

The faltering of religious faith is the most conspicuous sign of Western decay, just as the upsurge of religion in the Eastern Bloc is the most conspicuous sign of that region's ongoing recovery from darkness and oppression. Westerners just might consent to be caught dead in church—at their own funerals. Growing numbers of Poles, Russians, Ukrainians, Romanians, and so on, throng the churches of the East.

Maybe the East will yet save the West: a heartening prospect, because right now Westerners—the legatees of Augustine, Aquinas, Luther, and Bach—can't decide what they believe. Or why. Or whether belief is just another name for bigotry.

It is probably no accident that we have a pope from out of the East. In fact, when you look closely, many strange and wondrous events turn out not to be accidents at all—though I wouldn't trouble Bishop John Spong with such a non-affirming thought.

February 3, 1990

Politicos at Prayer?

As America's oldest Christian body—the Episcopal Church—strives to commit suicide, absurdities multiply.

Late in February, a bishop is to be tried in Wilmington, Delaware, for ordaining an active homosexual to the priesthood. His acquittal is almost a foregone conclusion, inasmuch as the majority of the fellow bishops judging him likewise favor ordaining homosexuals.

In Washington, D.C., on February 4, a woman bishop means to

force her way into a parish that doesn't recognize women as priests, far less as bishops. That doesn't bother the Right Reverend Jane Holmes Dixon, who represents a movement—the gender feminist movement—fonder of grinding down opponents than of extending the hand of charity.

When Bishop Walter Righter says, "Hey, what's chastity got to do with ministry?"; when Bishop Dixon (at the Church of Ascension and St. Agnes) bulls her way to the altar and says, "Here I am," the Church's human dimension blots out its divine one.

And that's just the Episcopal Church. My own, I have to confess. The other "mainline" bodies—Methodists, Presbyterians and so on—offer up on a daily basis similar instances of unconcern for evangelism and the salvation of souls.

During the height of the federal budget battle, a deputation from the National Council of Churches waited on President Clinton, urging him to "be strong for the task" of resisting Republican budget-cutters. The council was horrified to find that "government priorities serve military interests at the expense of family life." By protecting American Christian families from foreign enemies? The council didn't say. It didn't have to. The National Council of Churches is the Democratic Party at prayer.

But hope flowers. Honest. A redemptive project burgeons: one in which American churches may engage themselves, politically and socially, and still advance the gospel.

The National Association of Evangelicals would have American Christians combat religious persecution in foreign lands.

Persecution? Like death and imprisonment for the sake of the gospel of Jesus

Christ? Something very like that. A number of nations, including communist ones like China and Vietnam, are harsh on Christians. So are hard-line Islamic countries—including allegedly friendly Saudi Arabia, where Christian services are banned, even though mosques flourish throughout America. The evangelicals are belatedly taking a leaf from the book of U.S. Jewish activists who, stoutly and commendably, kept the heat on the Soviet Union during the 1970s and 1980s. Whenever Soviet Jews were jailed or denied exit permits, their American brethren raised a holy tumult with their own government. In the early 1970s, under sustained Jewish pressure, Congress made U.S.-Soviet trade conditional on freedom of emigration for Soviet Jews.

What the Jews did with superb zeal and industry, Christians mostly neglected. Christian efforts to help Soviet Christians were mild and limited. The evangelicals, understanding perhaps how a great chance was lost, are seeking to enlist the Clinton administration's aid in succoring their co-religionists. One wouldn't be surprised to see some kind of aid materialize. An administration berated for its moral standing, or lack of it, could benefit from taking an explicitly moral stance. We may once more see U.S. trade and aid linked to the human-rights practices of the recipients.

If nothing else—and much else ought to result from so necessary a project—the defense of foreign Christians might recall some U. S. Christians from their devotion to trendy secular politics.

What's the central issue in religion anyway—forcing welfare politics and gender feminism into the religious mainstream? Or is it the spread and defense of the Good News?

Far too many American Christians think the only news worth hearing, and responding to, comes on at 5:30 PM every night: politics, budget debates, new cultural "styles." The evangelicals are giving these folk an electric shock. Don't worry—all the pain is inner, and anyhow, it's well-earned.

January 29, 1996

Transcending Doctrine

A strange shoal, homosexuality, on which to crack up a whole church. But the twentieth century is a strange time. You never can tell.

Disapproved in Scripture and disallowed in Christian moral teaching, homosexuality is accumulating power within the major Protestant denominations. The clearest evidence of that power is the recent judgment by an Episcopal court that sodomy constitutes no barrier to priestly ordination.

The court, in other words, finds homosexuality no different in substance than heterosexuality: six of one, half a dozen of the other; you say po-tay-to, I say po-tah-to.

The court, whose members are bishops, had been asked by seventy-six brother bishops to find that another of their number—Walter C. Righter—had transcended doctrine and good order when he ordained a practicing homosexual. The request, issued in the form of a "presentment" against Righter, galvanized and titillated not just the Episcopal Church, but American Christianity.

One could call it the last stand of orthodoxy—moral and theological—within the church. If Episcopalians couldn't figure out that homosexual practice ran counter to two thousand years of Christian teaching, then what precisely *could* they figure out?

The bishop-judges came down squarely on the side of "what's-the-big-deal?" This they did while claiming they were not passing judgment on the rightness or wrongness of homosexuality. Of course, that is exactly what they were doing: judging the moral irrelevance of a man's, or a woman's, bed partner. The judges said, in essence: If it feels good, do it.

The next logical step is a formal vote—which will likely take place at the church's General Convention next year—to declare sexuality a morally neutral undertaking. The vote, when it comes, will split the church and cause moral traditionalists to take their patronage elsewhere while turning the Episcopal Church, once a vital and not-unpowerful institution, into a kooky backwater—albeit a backwater with classy buildings and great music.

What is it about sex? How did it get to be a wedge issue in religion? If Christians fall to fighting among themselves, you might suppose it would be over key doctrines that abut the question of salvation. Ah, but maybe that's what we're rubbing up against here in this matter of sex. Sex, to the twentieth century, *is* salvation: salvation here, salvation now. The relationship with the human body, visible and pleasure-giving, rather than the relationship with God, unseen and formidable, is at the center of modern concerns. Salvation, in religious terms, is down the road. In worldly terms, you have only to reach your hand across the bed.

Sexual preoccupation is the logical hallmark of a society that, if it hasn't entirely forgotten God, seems to have forgotten what he wants—which makes the churches' collaboration in these amnesiac proceedings altogether baffling.

The bishop-judges of the Episcopal Church, rather than interpose a religious standard against worldly preferences, adopt the world's preferences as their own. Thereby they raise a question: What is the point of a church that doesn't think like a church or talk like a church? Is it doing anything a Washington, D.C.–based agitation committee couldn't accomplish with, very likely, greater expertise and professionalism?

The sad thing about the Episcopal Church is that it used to attend to religion with quiet dignity and a certain pizzazz that influenced other believing bodies. It doesn't do that now. It throws itself with gusto into secular battles, generally taking the side you would think a church would walk miles to avoid taking.

That's just it: The Episcopal Church is a new kind of church, with—evidently—a new mission in religious circles, that mission being to reshape the whole Christian understanding along more tolerant and broad-minded lines.

As an Episcopalian, I should know. I watch this stuff with pain and anxiety. Nowadays, when someone asks me, "Are you still an Episcopalian?" I have a ready answer.

"Yes, very still."

May 16, 1996

Domesticating God

PHILADELPHIA—To overwhelm and engulf a church solemnly committed for centuries to the Christian essentials requires some moxie, and also some raw power. Twentieth-century secularism is up to the job. The Episcopal Church's Seventy-Second General Convention last week was an almost unmitigated disaster for orthodox Christianity. But, oh, what it did for secularism—the creed of man without God (or, at best, God nicely domesticated, made to keep His autocratic and patriarchalist nose out of human affairs).

Where to begin? Maybe with the decision to stuff women's ordination—a novelty of the past twenty years—down the throats of dioceses and parishes disposed, in line with Scripture and tradition, to regard the all-male priesthood as other than a sexist imposition.

You can't get thrown out of the church for disbelieving the Trinity or the Bodily Resurrection of Christ, but you surely can get squashed for denying career aspirations.

The General Convention, on its last day, apologized to gays and lesbians for years of rejection and maltreatment by the Church. But, asked to endorse a statement by Third World bishops affirming the authority of Holy Scripture as to sexual morality, bishops and deputies politely buried the statement in committee.

The next General Convention, three years hence, is dead certain to give gays and lesbians what they discreetly refrained from pressing too aggressively this year—permission to have their unions blessed by the church. This is at least because the church's new presiding bishop, Frank T. Griswold III, enthusiastically (if generally) favors the whole feminist-gay rights agenda.

The Church, one liberal bishop boasted, is engaged in a new Reformation.

Well, OK. If that's what churches are in business for—namely, giving an ecclesiastical tinge to the secular world's agenda—one has to admit that the Episcopal Church has fulfilled its calling.

If, on the other hand, churches exist to reshape human concerns and responses along heavenly lines, you'd have to call the Episcopal General Convention a bust.

A predictable one, perhaps. What mainstream modern church these days is doing its old job with consistency and conviction, that job being to oppose, rather than affirm, the world and the flesh?

My kingdom is not of this world, said the church's Founder. Couldn't prove it by most modern churches, whose agenda has less to do with individual sin and redemption than with political and cultural and economic theories.

By the same token, most modern mainstream churches are fading. Prior to the Episcopal Church's stately descent into political and cultural uplift, beginning some thirty years ago, there were 3.6 million Episcopalians. Guess how many there are now. About 2.4 million.

Ah, well. Do old-style Episcopalians believe what they say they believe—to wit, that God runs the show, and not the Democratic Party, or the Republican Party, or the National Organization of Women, or the Chamber of Commerce? Actually quite a few do.

A division of the house is in the offing: not a schism, please; more a backing away, a disengagement, a mutual distancing of the sort now going forth in different forms and at different paces throughout modern Christianity.

Bible-believing Episcopalians are bunching up even now as the secularists celebrate their Philadelphia triumphs—much good those triumphs will do them. As the Bible-believers do so, they will find comfort and moral support along the whole range of an American Christianity divided over the question who's really in charge here? God? Man? Nobody?

A new Reformation probably *is* in prospect: not the kind at all that the jubilant secularists of Philadelphia are jubilantly forecasting.

July 29, 1997

Death Wish

America's liberal Protestant churches—Episcopal, Methodist, Presbyterian, Lutheran, etc.—are working overtime at reversing the growth and achievements of the past few centuries. If they haven't fully succeeded in wiping themselves out, look what reverse evangelism has accomplished in three decades. Membership rolls in the so-called "mainline" churches are a fifth to a third of what they were in the 1960s.

The Methodists, once admired for their personable vitality, have been losing one thousand members a week. There are presently more Mormons in the United States than Presbyterians or Episcopalians. As the exodus grows, the remnant grays. Three-fifths of Methodist laymen are over fifty. Almost half of Presbyterian youth end up rejecting not just Presbyterianism but church affiliation of any kind.

What in God's name is going on here? Professor Thomas C. Reeves writes: "Americans are a practical people, and a great many of them fail to be convinced that the mainline churches are worth their time. Liberal Protestantism, in its determined policy of accommodation with the secular world, has succeeded in making itself dispensable."

In *The Empty Church: The Crisis of Liberal Christianity*, published by Free Press, Reeves puzzles over this phenomenon. If it weren't for the singing, you might not be able to tell some liberal worship services from a Planned Parenthood meeting or a Pat Schroeder rally. Reeves taxes the liberals with throwing out the Christian essentials—the stuff of the Creeds, all those "I believe . . . —while substituting personal expression, liberation, the higher consciousness: a social gospel, in short."

Gallup polls assert that fewer than half of American Christians can name the four gospels but that 56 percent of Lutherans and 49 percent of Methodists believe in UFOs.

Mainline Christianity, Reeves writes, "has been watered down and is at ease with basic secular premises about personal conduct and the meaning of life."

The mainline churches, from which American religion chiefly takes its tone, have agendas all right—but not necessarily religious agendas concerned with the old mainstays of repentance, faith, and salvation.

"It is all too often presumed," says Reeves, "that God is wholly and merely . . . nice." What we have, in consequence, is "Consumer Christianity." Pick and choose your favorite doctrines—if any.

Liberal Protestantism becomes as a result "a sort of sanctimonious echo of National Public Radio or the left wing of the Democratic Party." It favors feminism, homosexuality, and the liberal political agenda.

A special court made up of bishops in Reeves's own church, the Episcopal, couldn't manage last spring to lay blame on a colleague—a fellow teacher of the faith—who had ordained a practicing homosexual. Historic Christian moral norms, so far as the bishops seem concerned, have the permanence of a TV schedule, the authority of a birthday card.

Significantly, while the mainline churches wane, the harder-core bodies—Roman Catholics and evangelical Protestants—generally wax.

The Romans may have as many liberationist types as the Episcopalians, and the electronic quasi-music of the evangelical fringes may send Bach-lovers up the wall. Still, the religious content you get at such venues bestows a kind of marketplace cachet. Like Microsoft, like Nike, these concerns know what they were set up to do. So they do it.

Reeves, a best-selling biographer of John F. Kennedy and professor of history at the University of Wisconsin-Parkside, suggests that the mainliners can come back if they try hard. Well, it happened to Lazarus. On the other hand, Lazarus had divine help. The mainline churches will need that in spades if they are to ditch gush-and-goo theology, retrieve a sense of mission and take into the world the unimpaired, uncluttered gospel of the politically incorrect Savior who said, "No man cometh unto the Father, but by me." The odd thing is, the mainliners used to do exactly this; then many quit. See where it got them?

September 23, 1996

Evangelicals and Catholics Together

Roman Catholics and evangelical Protestants the other day dropped a sledgehammer hint concerning the shape of the twenty-first century. They threw their arms around each other—figuratively at least—and said henceforth in these troublous times they want to stand together, small differences being less important than large similarities.

It would have seemed to our recent forbears the oddest, most unlikely of alliances—like the Dallas Cowboys and Washington Redskins pricking arteries in order to make themselves blood brothers. Catholics and Protestants, in the olden time, just didn't get along.

These men of God who rose up—thirty-nine of them, ranging from Charles Colson to New York City's John Cardinal O'Connor—pledged fraternity and solidarity on key questions such as abortion, school choice, and the revival of respect for moral standards.

Mind, no such lofty declaration can bind the various churches to which the signers belong. At the same time, the churches in question are unlikely to burn the signers at the stake. Anything but.

Amid the worst cultural crisis of modern times, Catholics and evangelicals are discovering how much they have in common, and how much their agreement matters to the world.

The cultural crisis has worked this remarkable transformation: the stunning drop-off in standards of personal behavior and achievement; the disintegration of the family; the escalating disregard for life itself, whether reflected in the crime reports or the statistics on abortion and euthanasia.

These cataclysms have been raining down on us for a good thirty years. All the while, the so-called "mainstream" churches have nodded their heads agreeably, as if nothing could be more logical than the collapse of the old social order founded on Judeo-Christian conviction.

Left-wing churchmen, starting in the nineteenth century, conceived it their duty to put aside all the old "fairy tales" about virgin births and saviors crucified and resurrected. This, so that the full range of human social problems could be addressed: grievances rectified right here on earth, before our very eyes, with the assistance of smart young clergymen who saw little good in presuming on the patience of an invisible God.

Historic notions of sin and redemption dropped below the theological horizon. We were all of us, it appeared, simply wonderful folks, save when evil capitalists, racist cops, unsympathetic teachers, or cold and paternalistic fathers intervened to warp our personalities. Well, at least there was a ready answer: government. More money for schools, more rights for criminals, more tolerance for the expression of Alternative Viewpoints would save us.

We notice of course how neatly we have been saved.

But did all clergy simper and preen themselves in this fatuous way? Not all—the Romans and evangelicals much less so than the "mainstreamers." The former held up their veneration for historic teaching, the latter their adherence to the Holy Scriptures. Increasingly, they found themselves collaborating in the defense of common principles—respect for God-created life; the sanctity of the family; personal honor and responsibility.

The signers of the Roman-evangelical document see themselves as joined at the theological hip, whether or not separated by intellectual distinctions (e.g., the Pope's charter of authority) that bear less and less on the condition of the modern world. Both sides agree on enough—not least their alarm at what goes on in the world—that there seems no point in quarreling and every point in working together.

We are going to see more and more of this as we move into the twenty-first century: "fundamentalists" of all sorts—and what's wrong with fundamentals, by the way? Aren't they better than non-essentials?—arrayed against theological vagrants who ought to have gone into social work instead of religion, who increasingly stand exposed as irrelevant to the purposes of moral recovery.

The next century, paradoxically, looks not just more dangerous but more and more and more hopeful.

April 11, 1994

Why They Fear the Religious Right

Members of the "religious right" can't say the summer of 1994 has been 100 percent awful; no one has yet fingered a Christian activist as the Simpson-Goldman slasher.

That may be just around the corner. The possibilities for half-way intelligent commentary on religious conservatives seem to have collapsed. Into La-La Land we stroll, there to encounter, among others, Anthony Lewis, warning *New York Times* readers that "the leaders of the Christian right . . . want to substitute their vision of a religious polity" for our "secular" system. "It will be an intolerant America," Lewis admonishes, "if they have their way: something like a Christian version of the Ayatollah Khomeini's Iran."

Meanwhile, a new Interfaith Alliance, organized to combat this outbreak of bigotry, sees "religious extremism" as an attack on valued traditions like the school breakfast program. A letter writer to the *Dallas Morning News* reminds readers that early American leaders, whom these awful Christians venerate, "burned 'witches'" and "hanged Quakers." (Historical footnote: Salem *hanged* nineteen "witches" and pressed Giles Corey with stones; nobody "hanged Quakers"—but, then, considering the state of modern education, it's nice to know someone has *heard* of the Quakers.)

What do you say to these people? No, no, no, won't suffice. For one thing, there certainly are some kooks on the "religious right," even as there are kooks on the secular left. Religion is amply qualified to understand this. The doctrine of Original Sin explains why human beings misbehave and misunderstand at the best of times.

The religious right scares the daylights out of the secular left. A newsman of my acquaintance—*not* a religious-right type—interviewed some self-styled "moderates" at the Texas Republican convention. He found them "as paranoid as the John Birchers used to be."

Paranoid regarding what? Regarding the likelihood, as they saw it, that religious rightists would ban abortion, restore school prayer and make life, well, more religious than it is. Heavens to Betsy! Take this country lurching back to the 1950s? To the dispensation we'd lived with more or less since the country got started? Oh, what a Terrible Menace!

Where do the folk biting their nails over the religious right suppose it emerged from anyway? Did the preachers, for lack of anything better to do, just decide one Sunday to take over America?

Here's what happened. The "religious right"—defined as that loose coalition of ordinary, tax-paying, law-abiding Americans concerned with the manifest social problems this country faces—said to the people they now offend so flagrantly: Whoooooa!

Hardly any one doubts that our social dislocations are greater and more grievous than was the case thirty years ago. Murder, divorce, child abuse, AIDS, illegitimacy, illiteracy—all have increased sharply since the early 1960s. They are the consequence, each and every one, not of moral tightening but of moral loosening. Live it up! we've been enjoined. If one considers the consequences of this advice, can one truthfully say to the exponents of re-tightening, "You're all a bunch of nuts!"?

The oddest thing in the world is the idea of hermetically sealing off religion from contact with the secular world. It never works, for one thing. Morality, at bottom, depends on religious conviction. No religion, no seat of authority. Who says kindness or generosity is the right way? This editorial, that speech? Get outta here! Nobody tells Number One what to do.

Those who affect terror at the approaching tread of the religious right need to ask themselves what they are really afraid of. Active persecution or just the restoration of a sense, now lost, of right and wrong: on which sense civilization depends utterly and forever? It will be nice to talk of such matters when our secular saviors calm down enough to see what they're defending—the mess, muddle, and malignity of the 1990s.

July 18, 1994

VIII

Watching Our Mouth,
Minding Our Manners

I AM AN UNREGENERATE OLD FOGEY. I like manners and decent language. The Present Age doesn't. Well, there we are. Nothing I can do but interpose the values with which I grew up—values I believe retain their heft and pungency—against those of the time in which I now live. It's frequently a thankless job, but somebody has to do it!

Hath the Mouth of the Lord Spoken It?

The National Council of Churches last month gave birth to a revised Revised Standard Version of the Bible. A bible for a new day; updated, ready to rock and roll.

Scholarship has marched on since the original RSV came out in 1952; likewise, social sensibilities have changed. Feminists, for instance, object to the use of "man" and "mankind" as social generics. Better "One does not live by bread alone" than "Man does not live by bread alone." Anyway, the former is now what the Good Book says. Doubters and troglodytes will please get with the program.

Various other linguistic changes reflect modern social mores, such as they are. The most beguiling, maybe, has to do with St. Paul's account of his tribulations in Second Corinthians. "Once I was stoned," the RSV has the apostle declare. One (in the current parlance) can see the problem, though the full context of chapter eleven makes it clear the apostle had not, in fact, attended a rock concert. Primly the revisers tidy up with "Once I received a stoning."

The new RSV, for all the changes it enjoins, is not the event the original one was. The original was meant to supplant the beloved King James Version, whose supporters erupted in fury at the notion of tampering with words obviously dictated by God! Modern language versions have since that time become commonplace. Even old war horses like your servant own and consult them. Whatever their stylistic defects, they are occasionally clearer than the King James of 1611.

But, oh, the style, and, oh, the language! And, oh, the loss! Are we better off today with seamless modern English than with the "verbal archaisms" of the seventeenth century? I somehow doubt it.

A modern writer shouldn't make this known, but modern writers aren't as proficient as their forbears. More than one viewer of PBS's *The Civil War* talked rapturously to me about the beautiful English in letters written by soldiers and other ordinary people.

Were these folk more literally gifted than we? I think not. Their advantage was that, as they wrote, they drew unconsciously from a well of English such as we in modern times have allowed to silt up: dignified, poetic, leisurely, frequently inspired. The King James Version floated on the very surface of the well.

Among our ancestors, Bible-reading was as normal as eating. Our ancestors masticated and digested the KJV's sublime poetry, its lofty cadences. Yea, though I walk through the valley of the Shadow of Death. . . . He that believeth in me, though he were dead, yet shall he live. . . . And, behold, the veil of the temple was rent in twain from the top to the bottom.

Speaking of "twain," I remember fondly of the pronouncement of an acerbic Episcopal priest from Savannah, Georgia, talking of what revision had done to the six-winged seraphim in Isaiah, chapter six. "With twain [said the KJV] he covered his face, and with twain he covered his feet, and with twain he did fly."

Father R. went on, his voice hardening. "What do they say now? 'With two he flew!' I submit to you that 'with two he flew' is *ludicrous!*" He won't get an argument from me.

The KJV—perhaps the only completely successful enterprise ever performed by committee—emerged in one of the great periods of English literature. Shakespeare was still alive, and Bunyan's, Dryden's, and Milton's achievements lay ahead.

John Bunyan wrote self-consciously plain prose, but see him send Mr. Valiant-For-Truth off across the River Jordan: "My sword I give to him that shall succeed me in my pilgrimage, and my courage and skill to him that can get it. My marks and scars I carry with me, to be a witness for me, that I have fought his battles who now will be my rewarder. So he passed over, and all the trumpets sounded for him on the other side." Words of one syllable, mostly, yet this necklace of zircons, so beautifully strung together, glitters like diamonds.

No one talks like that any more, we are constantly reminded. I won't argue about that either. I would argue, possibly, that we might talk—and write—better were we not told that no one talks like that any more.

Even conservatives sometimes dismiss the King James Version. I myself laid it aside for a while in favor of the New English; I have lately taken it back up, with renewed appreciation of its splendors. Splendors of any kind are hard to come by in the age of George Bush, Dick Darman, Dan Rather, Joseph Biden, and Luther whatever-his-name-is who beat the obscenity rap in Florida.

October 27, 1990

Dead Language

The West is going through some, forgive me, heavy stuff, here in the twentieth century's twilight years. The West's great universities have become psychiatric couches. Doctor, oh, doctor, can you help? We can't stand our forefathers, who robbed and oppressed weaker cultures. Patriarchalist laws and moral codes, smokestacks, deforestations, voyages of discovery (Columbus-bashing is the new gig)—what a mess Western culture has made!

A new term of opprobrium has entered the lexicon: "DWMS." Dead white males. Like Bach and Shakespeare, University students increasingly are taught to ignore or, if that's not feasible, to despise the breed. Western literature and civilization courses are being turned inside out with a view to down-playing the West and exalting the thought of folkways of Asia and Africa. Ted Turner, a guru of Right-think, has banned the word "foreign" on his cable network's broadcasts, yes, and in private conversation among employees.

Thus I stare in some befuddlement at the *New York Times* headline: "Latin Redux: A Dead Language Finds New life." Latin? New life? Enrollment in Latin classes has been up sharply? Latin teachers tracked down like eighteen-point bucks by school districts unable to match pedagogical supply with student demand? Thank you, Lord.

There are hard-headed reasons for the revival. Latin illuminates, it broadens. The, I guess we'd say, relevance of Latin, a language deader than Elvis, is the structure. By studying Latin, we find out what makes English tick—or, in these fallen times, not tick.

It is more than a matter of vocabulary—"aqua" yields "aquatic," "magna", "magnify", and so on. It is, oh, so much more than recognizing, when we see them, antebellum and e pluribus unum. Latin is structured, ordered, symmetrical: every word in its place and a place for every word. As we read Latin, we come to fathom, and even to value, structure, order, symmetry.

Such concepts as these are unfashionable because they bind and restrain. In these twilight times we want nothing bound, nothing restrained. We want it, you know, loose.

Appreciation of Latin goes hand in hand, the *Times* tells us, with appreciation of Roman culture. This may be the most curious aspect of the Latin revival. By modern standards, the Romans were the pits. "Patriarchal" comes from "pater," father. Daddy ran the show in ancient Rome. "Senate" is from "senex," elderly. Rome deferred to the wisdom of age—and of the ages.

There was a generous, public-spirited sternness in Roman culture, hard to appreciate in a modern culture that puts appetite and self-gratification on adjacent pedestals. The prized Roman virtues were *virtus* (strength), *gravitas* (moral seriousness), and *pietas* (piety). Man! What did these birds do on Saturday night for fun?

The Roman concept of duty and responsibility was likewise lofty. Cincinnatus, elected dictator, left the furrow he had been plowing, defeated the invading enemy, handed back the authority he had wielded, and returned to his furrows. "Then up spake brave Horatius [Lord Macaulay says], the captain of the gate./'To every man upon this earth death cometh soon or late/And what death could be better than facing fearful odds/For the ashes of his fathers and the temple of his gods?'"

"Family values," as we might call them today, resonated in Rome. The matron Cornelia, besought by nosy friends to bring out her jewels, instead brought forth her children. "These are my jewels," quoth she. Cornelia, you poor, sweet dope—how're you going to make president of IBM that way?

During the French Revolution, Edmund Burke predicted that men and women, severed from their roots and traditions, would flit about like "flies of a summer." Righter and righter he seems.

It goes without saying that we long ago parted company with the Greeks and the Romans. Today, intellectuals and other busybodies stand before the divorce court protesting their society's lingering attachment to the mores and thought patterns of the Renaissance, the Reformation, the Enlightenment, whatever else preceded Phil Donahue.

Then, mirabile dictu, we look around, and there aren't enough Latin teachers in America to satisfy the demand for instruction in a dead tongue and culture we thought nobody'd ever want to bother with again! I'm jiggered if I know what—if anything—it all means, but it couldn't be bad, could it?

October 12, 1991

What I Like About the South

What we had in North Texas the other day was a norther except that we didn't call it a norther. Following the lead of our weather prognosticators, we called it a "cold front."

This discrepancy dawned on me as I sat before the fireplace, glancing over a periodical mailed by a chicken-fried organization to which I belong, the Southern League. The League encourages Southerners in the exercise of their indefeasible right to be Southern, never mind Northern reproaches and sneers.

To this praiseworthy end, a certain James E. Kibler Jr. of Whitmire, South Carolina, exhorts Southerners to speak like Southerners rather than, well, non-Southerners. He'd rather we not just blend in but stand out. "I believe," says Brother Kibler, "we have the capability to assemble lists of . . . Southern words and expressions toward the goal of creating a respected Southern idiom and way of speaking."

"Re-creating," it might be more accurate to say. We had the idiom once. We just mislaid it—doubtless while watching television.

A pertinent example would be "norther." I am not sure what Alabamans and Tennesseeans call these blasts of air that roll down from the frozen Northland, but Texans formerly called them "northers." We have not done so for years—though "norther" is easily more shivery and evocative than "cold front." Nor is there any meteorological substitute for "blue norther"—the species of "front" that, while bearing down on us, imparts to the sky the hue of a Sunday-go-to-meeting suit.

Brother Kibler is full of recommendations to restore distinctiveness in Southern speech. One proposal is that we drop "lunch" and recommence calling the mid-day meal "dinner." The evening repast would once again become "supper."

Johnnie! Susie! Come to supper! The music of iron skillets, the flitting of lightning bugs, is in that antique invocation. Supper, in the South, was the light meal: cereal or sandwiches, sometimes bacon and eggs. No culinary folderol, anyway. All of that belonged to the mid-day repast known as dinner, when the whole family turned up, from office or school, to feast in solidarity on meat loaf and turnip greens.

Brother Kibler's linguistic preferences fly in the face of drastic changes in Southern society since World War II. We hardly breakfast at all these days. We "lunch" at our desks on vending-machine salads. In the evening, the business day behind us, we finally "dine"— if we dine at all. The language of the older South is the language of the small towns in which most Southerners grew up. Gone with the wind! The culture of the towns, and sometimes the towns themselves, have disappeared.

But Brother Kibler is right: The old way of speaking has charm and value. Language is a part of being. To talk one way is to be something that people who talk differently are not. This means the lords of language sometimes meet with defiance when they mandate change. Brought up saying "ice box" rather than "refrigerator," I would not now dream of speaking otherwise. I am frozen in solidarity with the past, on this question anyway.

Particular customs can also command defiant affirmation. A well-educated Texas woman I know relates how, in the old days, her equally well-educated mother, whenever a black cat crossed her path, would spit and say "damn."

It's a good old custom, the woman still insists—not for any theological purpose it serves, but rather as a tiny, feeble thread linking generations. The more such threads we break heedlessly, the more isolated we become in a society seemingly bent on annihilating memory itself. We're not supposed to love the past; we're supposed to hate it. Modernity drums this message into us relentlessly.

Thus, the woman of whom I speak, whenever a black cat crosses her path, spits and says "damn." "Damn" to the cat, "damn" to modernity, and "damn" to all who say it doesn't matter what you say. That's the spirit! One day, she and I and our families will have to sit down and talk about all such matters. Over supper.

March 11, 1996

Cautionary Words

"Language is being dragooned into the service of a fashionable political orthodoxy," writes *New York Times* television critic Walter Goodman, taking off from a new *Dictionary of Cautionary Words* issued by the University of Missouri School of Journalism.

Mr. Goodman describes the dictionary as a "prophylactic guide to writing, its avowed purpose to sensitize reporters and editors to usages that members of minority groups may find offensive." Language with formerly neutral connotations is to be supplanted with deliberately prejudicial language.

Thus, "housing project" becomes "subsidized housing"; "elderly" gives way to "senior citizen." Goodbye, "invalids"; hello, "people with disabilities." "Handicapped" is verboten.

"Illegal aliens" have been wondrously transformed; now they are "undocumented residents."

No gratuitous physical descriptions, please, such as "blonde and blue-eyed," or, in the interest of equal treatment, "beefcake" and "hunk." (Quick, name one man offended by this extraordinarily flattering usages. Better yet, capture him so he can be psychoanalyzed.)

Careful with "articulate," which "can be considered offensive when referring to a minority, particularly a black person, and his or her ability to handle the English language. The usage suggests that 'those people' are not considered well-educated, articulate and the like."

Nor should we brush too swiftly past "his or her," as used in the previous paragraph. "His" without "her," "man" as shorthand for "men and women"—these have become grave offenses to woman-kind. Or so we're routinely instructed.

President Bush, in his State of the Union address, tried to toe-dance around the difficulty. He ended up falling off the stage, gram-matically speaking. "If anyone tells you America's best days are behind her," the president said, "they're looking the wrong way." I guaran-tee you they didn't teach "they" for "he" at Yale in the 1940s, though today they may. Some ideologically attuned speech writer stuck that banalism into the speech text.

Happy talk does have its limits. I experience them all the time. The media introduce my fellow Scottish-Americans into the lumpy broth they call "Anglos"—Americans of English descent. Why, mon, we're as English as strudel. Did we not lay low the English tyrants in Bannockburn in 1314? We want our linguistic rights! I guess we're just not articulate enough to claim them without help.

The language "reform" movement is intensely political; but be-low the ideological stratum is something even creepier and more unusual. It is the presumption that everybody—at least every politi-cally approved everybody—should feel terrr-iff-ick (as I once heard a motivational speaker exclaim) about himself. Yes, and about her-self. And, further, that you and I are responsible for making this happen.

We're to wrap our conversation, our letters, our newspapers, our sermons and speeches in linguistic cellophane. The president of the United States makes a deliberate grammatical blunder, and churches recast their liturgies—yea, the very words of Holy Scripture—to eliminate offensive male imagery.

Woe and alas. No law or Supreme Court decision proclaims it as a basic American right to feel terrific every day. A sense of true self-worth proceeds far more from what is inside the head and the heart than from what reaches the ears and eyes. Society can pat us on the head all day long, whisper to us sweet, neutral, inclusive, well-balanced nothings. In the end, we feel terrr-iff-ick to the extent we comport ourselves with dignity, honor, and charity, according to the great codes that until recent times regulated behavior.

These nowadays aren't the codes that count. The word-twisters at the University of Missouri are codifying the new rules by which we're to live. Down from the mountain come the tablets, smoking-hot. (Is it OK to use "smoking" without an "anti" in front?)

Bow low. The tolerance of the word-twisters extends only so far; it will not stretch to those for whom language is a great unifying, instead of a fragmenting, force. Dr. Johnson, thou shouldst be living at this hour. Or, again, maybe not.

February 6, 1991

Cover Your Ears

Two post-game, nationally televised expletives from Dallas Cowboy players. Two from the Pittsburgh Steelers. The Super Bowl isn't likely to remind us of a Jane Austen movie. But, oh, how the obscenity flap reminds us of life as it used to be.

Does that sound weepy, nostalgic, arthritic? I am #!&% sorry about that. In certain urgent respects, life was better in the old days. Football players, for one thing, didn't drag out their locker-room vocabularies to entertain old ladies and preschoolers.

Had the Cowboys of Tom Landry's day talked publicly in the manner of Michael Irvin and Nate Newton this past Sunday, would you care to guess their fates? Deacon Tom would have come down on the offenders like an avenging angel. The anatomical features they used for sitting would have been sore for weeks. Note, please, that Jerry Jones, ringmaster of the Cowboy circus, kissed off the whole furor with "No action is warranted." What a class act is our Jerry!

True, in other, more civilized quarters, outrage and decision are aimed at the perpetrators. William Bennett, our leading cultural critic, told *USA Today* that the episodes demonstrate how locker-room language has gone mainstream. It isn't "the end of the world," Bennett said. "It's one more notch. . . . Civilizations don't collapse all at once, they do it one degree at a time."

If the offending cretins didn't resemble Sherman tanks, one would enjoy taking them by the shoulders and shaking them—and Jerry, their enabler-in-chief, with them. But alas!—if you'll pardon a passé interjection—shaking them wouldn't do all that much good. Where do football players get the idea they can turn the air blue with expletives? Why, they get it from society at large. Alas! Alack! Jerry isn't their only enabler.

Yes, I know all too well—this sounds like tear-stained twentieth-century liberalism. "We're *alllllll* guilty! Sob! Choke!"

In a way, maybe we *are* all guilty. Society as a whole has raised the linguistic portcullis, admitting to ordinary discourse expressions that thirty years ago would have been firmly barred.

Thirty years ago! My moss-encrusted memory calls up the early-1960s flap over the Jimmy Dean song "Big John." Jimmy had employed in his lyrics a four-letter word signifying the place of eternal torment. The hand of censorship descended. Jimmy dubbed in More Suitable Language. There were things one could say in private but not public, and "hell" was one of them. Earlier, David O. Selznick had had to obtain special permission for Clark Gable, in *Gone With the Wind*, to tell Scarlett, "Frankly, my dear, I don't give a damn." In the 1960s, that line still brought titillated murmurs from the audience.

Modern vocabularies are, you might say, less refined. We are into self-expression these days. Norms and standards are for old movies and old minds. Irvin-Newton-like language saturates television, which may be one reason the players feel free to indulge in such language while performing for the cameras. How much worse do they talk on *NYPD Blue*? You can sit in nice restaurants and hear fellow diners say things for which Gary Cooper would have called them to account but that now you let go because—who'd understand? Bennett is right: Civilizationally, we're collapsing by degrees.

One hates to reinvent the wheel, but the case against bad language in public clearly needs restating. The case is that such language embarrasses and degrades. The embarrassed are those who, if they enjoyed the atmosphere of a locker room, would take up permanent residence in one. The degraded are those who see the language of the locker room as normal, everyday, no big deal at all.

What are we anyway, a bunch of apes? One hopes that isn't our destiny, but one never knows. Act like an ape, with disdain for others and with unabashed joy in the more squalid features of life, and pretty soon, you turn into an ape.

Where's Tom Landry now that we need him? I know—he's covering his ears.

January 16, 1996

Anglo-Saxonisms on the Air

Voices of Enlightenment and Tolerance have been hollering bloody murder ever since the Federal Communications Commission announced a crackdown on the "raunch radio" phenomenon.

Anguished prophecies rend the air: First the federal government—which, in law at least, owns the air waves—tells disc jockeys to knock off their—these days—routine references to "sexual or excretory activities." Next thing you know, Ed Meese will be writing radio scripts. So much for the First Amendment.

One of the deejays in question, poor fellow, is almost hysterical over the prospect; he insists that he is the First Amendment. Would that he were a tenth as temperate and concise.

I can think of just one appropriate response to the flap over the FCC ruling: *#$@*$!!!

This is for two reasons. The first is that Dirt-talk hasn't a thing to do with liberty of speech, as understood by Messrs. Madison et al. The fundamental motive is to pull in a big drive-to-work audience and thereby jack up advertising rates.

So far, the strategy seems wildly successful. In Providence, Rhode Island (founded by the Rev. Roger Williams, 1636), Dirt-talk has doubled the eighteen-to-twenty-four-year-old male audience; ad rates have increased two-and-a-half times. Dirt-talk DJs earn as much as three hundred thousand dollars a year.

The FCC already possesses statutory power to regulate on-air language. The Supreme Court has concurred in that grant of power. The commission is doing no more than it has a right to do—and no less than it has a duty to do.

I'll tell you the major reason, though, that the FCC crackdown is welcome. In the matter of public language, it is time that somebody —anybody—drew a line in the sand, saying, thus far, no farther.

I confess to a rather old-fashioned preference. I liked it when people watched the way they talk. These days you can say anything to anybody. The 1960s—the godawful, godforsaken 1960s—did this to us, and we have not yet recovered. If anything, matters are worse now than they were twenty years ago, when there was still a certain coyness about the way barracks language was deployed outside the barracks.

The expressions the FCC wants to prohibit—and this is why the FCC has a hard row to hoe—are common coinage in public speaking, and even writing. You are as likely to hear them at the supermarket as on the 13th hole. When you take your elementary kids to a PG or PG-13 movie these days, you steel yourself for the half-dozen or so Anglo-Saxonisms you know are coming.

May I affirm that I have nothing against Bad Words per se? I learned all the crucial words in Boy Scouts—though I was a few years taking in their full import. There are occasions, linguistically speaking, for undoing the collar and giving vent to what is really and truly on one's mind. I maintain that the man who blows a twelve-inch putt, then exclaims, "Fudge!" is blessed with supernatural self-control.

No, the problem isn't dirty language; the problem is the everydayness and everywhereness of dirty language.

The counterculture of the 1960s introduced obscenities into normal conversation so as to shock the Establishment's tender, middle-class sensibilities. The job was facilitated by a parallel trend—militant, clenched-fisted feminism.

One longtime behavioral restraint was known as The Presence of Ladies: in which Presence gentlemen deliberately restrained from certain words and actions. Feminism, 1960s and 1970s style, laid this barrier flat. A lady who could get into med school or write a newspaper column had a right, buddy, an inalienable right, to use and hear spoken the full Anglo-Saxon vocabulary.

Swearing, to a certain kind of liberated soul, became what cigar-smoking had been to Gertrude Stein—a badge of equality.

Well, that's modernity, I guess. But I don't know that it's made modernity particularly pleasant. One finds there's a reason bad language used to be reserved for particular times and places; the reason is, it grates.

A particularly ironic effect is all the sexist patter, so demeaning to women in general, that has become part of the "raunch radio" format.

The target audience of Houston's station KLOL—which invites listeners to call in while making "love" (yes, you've heard me right)—is males, ages eighteen to thirty-five. My guess is that these drooling cretins do not care whether the women on whom they eavesdrop are professors of French history or welfare queens.

I do not often cheer for the federal bureaucracy. On the "raunch radio" matter, I make an exception. Go to it, guys. Get the #^%$*@!!!

April 29, 1987

The Language of a Generation

In civil libertarian quarters it is averred that the banning of the 2 Live Crew album *As Nasty as They Wanna Be*, and the subsequent arrest of two band members for performing songs from the album, amounts to censorship and repression.

Oh! How horrible! I figure in consequence to lose 1.67 seconds of sleep tonight. I would sleep much more poorly, knowing the constituted authorities in Florida were such wimps they couldn't find anything offensive about an album containing, by the count of a family advocacy group, eighty-seven descriptions of oral sex, 116 mentions of male and female genitalia, and other lyrical passages referring to male ejaculation.

That's not a violation of what the Supreme Court calls "community standards?" A community that wouldn't be offended and repelled by 2 Live Crew is a community most of us wouldn't care to live in.

Not that nobody appreciates *As Nasty As They Wanna Be*, which had sold 1.7 million copies at the time of the crackdown. But that doesn't mean the larger community—a community with the character to be offended by eighty-seven mentions of oral sex on one album—can't or shouldn't prosecute this sort of thing.

That's the topic for today. Aren't there any defenses anymore against pornography for fun and profit? My sense of the matter is that the average American feels bewildered about speaking up in these matters. He "knows in his hips," as Willmore Kendall, one of our ace political philosophers, used to say, that eighty-seven mentions of oral sex in one album—there's just something wrong with it, that's all.

Yet, if he does speak up, he feels nervous and apprehensive. The self-anointed defenders of any and all "speech" assail him as a fundamentalist: than which, apparently, there's no more degrading epithet in today's marketplace. Being called a fundamentalist is equivalent to being called a bum half a century ago (back when Cole Porter and Jerome Kern reigned in popular culture).

Name calling, of course, is free speech of the old sort—the assertion of opinion, even wrong-headed, degraded, degrading opinion. To speak his mind is every American's greatest privilege, next to the freedom to bow low to his Lord—or deny the existence of any lord whatever.

The debasement of free speech—a sublime concept—is among the sorrows and tragedies of modern life. And we've done it ourselves. Or we've stood by and watched it done.

Just about everything today is put forth as free speech. The burning of the American flag is free speech. A photograph of a crucifix submerged in urine is free speech. Eighty-seven references to oral sex are free speech. Webster's Reply to Hayne and the 2 Live Crew ballad *Me So Horny*—occupants of the same shelf in our intellectual and political life.

We are asked seriously to believe this rubbish. Fortunately, we don't have to. We enjoy free speech, do we not? Free speech gives us the right to call a lie a lie, and the assertion that oral-sex-lyrics are free speech is a dirty lie, a blasphemous lie.

Judge Jose Gonzalez of the federal district court in Miami found that *As Nasty As They Wanna Be* fails to meet the Supreme Court test for protection against obscenity prosecution. It violates community standards, lacks artistic, scientific, or political value, and gives patent offense.

We are informed by music-industry figures that all this is just part of black culture, and we should let well enough alone. What a load of condescending rubbish! What are we hearing here, that because a few black millionaires push pornography into he face of the black community, we're all supposed to relax and enjoy it?

The oddest stories get in the papers these days. Did you conceive, not many years ago, that a handful of cretins could create a sensation, and in such a way as this? Probably not. We used to suppose a certain amount of self-restraint on the part of citizens. Apparently we can't suppose it any longer, not when free speech is taken as meaning anything some jerk wants to do by way of self-expression.

How perfect for the Me Generation. Me First. *Me So Horny*, as the popular ballad goes. Me, me, me. Judges and prosecutors must feel like the Dutch boy, thumb stuck in the dike, but their duty is to clobber the merchandisers of obscenity before they drown us in filth.

Me, I've got a right to say so, and I just did.

June 20, 1990

No Consequences?

William Kennedy Smith is off the judicial hook, the beneficiary of that reasonable doubt we hear so much about in courtroom lore. But the relationship of men and women, which is what the Kennedy trial was all about, is the most confused in human history, full of ambiguities and doubts.

It was fascinating to see these ambiguities and doubts played out on television, our national peephole. We wouldn't have recognized them thirty years ago, before Woodstock, *Roe v. Wade*, Madonna, and Phil Donahue. That's because the old moral codes, concerning sexuality, retained a good deal of their original force.

The old codes, which the 1960s and 1970s slew, had a singular virtue: they let you know, male or female, where you stood. The codes defined rights and responsibilities: do this, don't do that. Naturally, not everyone observed the codes, but they were there anyway, and when all else failed we could return to them.

The codes—to speak just of the issue underlying the Willie Smith trial—recognized that sex outside marriage happened: always had, always would. *But*—for departures from the ideal there would be consequences, not all of them felicitous. One knew this, and—often —one took warning.

Today's Sexually Liberated Society is better described as the No Consequences Society. Happy as larks are we, flying, fluttering over the sexual landscape, nesting here, nesting there, chirping the song of freedom. Except something here is not quite right. Willie Smith isn't happy (save with the verdict). The accuser with the blurred-out face isn't happy. Anita Hill isn't happy. Clarence Thomas isn't happy. Nor Marla. Nor Ivana.

Honesty and openness, as contrasted with pretense and repression—these were supposed to govern our relationships. Somehow it hasn't worked out that way. Neither sex seems to know quite what to expect of the other one any more.

Wedding ring, ivy-covered cottage, happiness-ever-after? Such were the older expectations, discarded in the 1960s and 1970s as backwater bourgeois. The currently fashionable expectation—pleasure—is working out more poorly than had been predicted.

Pleasure? Whose pleasure? Why not mine first, yours second? The pleasure ethic denies mutual obligations. "He likes Ivana very much," a Donald Trump spokesman observed of The Master, "but it just wasn't working out"—"it" being the mutual undertaking called marriage. No pleasure in it for Donald, hence no obligation either.

Things get nastier. Here we are, everyone entitled to pleasure and eager to get it. Aren't misunderstandings likely to occur—such as how quickly John and Mary bed down and where and on whose initiative? The "date rape" furor ("He made me," "No, she wanted it") is as clear a mark of moral confusion as I know of. Similar confusion arises with regard to sexual harassment.

It's no wonder distrust and hostility between men and women, far from diminishing in the No Consequences Age, is growing. A Roper poll last year said that 54 percent of women, versus 41 percent in 1970, think "most men look at a woman and immediately think how it would be to go to bed with her." Maybe they do. Maybe the breakdown of the old codes encourages them to do so.

Carry this a little further. Feminist legal scholars, who argue that women are always at a disadvantage in a "patriarchal" society, likely regard the Willie Smith verdict as further evidence of the system's corruption. Andrea Dworkin, one of the best-known feminist radicals, urges creation of a separate legal system for women. How's this for bonding?

The old, lost moral codes didn't sunder and fragment; they united and reconciled. Reconciliation isn't exactly our long suit here in the 1990s. Ah, but don't we have fun?

Well? Don't we?

December 14, 1991

Shall We Dance?

"Never heard" of ballroom dancing!? What do they do out in Kalispell, Montana, hometown of Susan Beamis, Columbia '87, who is quoted to this dismal effect in the *New York Times*?

Read on, nevertheless, before surrendering to despair. Miss Beamis says ballroom dancing is "more fun than rock 'n' roll."

How could she know? Big dance coming up at Barnard College, you see. Student government—under the influence of a quart of I. W. Harper or else the Divine Afflatus—engages "Swing and Sway with Sammy Kaye" and his orchestra.

Uh-huh; but swing how? Sway which way? The student body of Barnard College hasn't a clue. Disco is all anybody does or knows these days.

Score one for the intellectual acuity of Barnard College student government. A room at the student center is engaged; a ballroom instructor is hired. Oh, the recondite skills that are imparted—starting with the box step. Slide, together, forward. Slide, together, back. Quick, quick, slow.

What is funny is—I am relying on the *Times's* account—everybody seems to get a kick out of the experience. Allison McDonald, Barnard '89 says, "This is better than disco dancing. You can be closer and more intimate. And you can tell who people came with."

Very well, she ought to have said "whom." Whom cares? She got the point about ballroom dancing, did Allison McDonald, Barnard '89, member of the rising generation. I would like to wring her hand. Thanks, oh, thanks, Allison, for Seeing.

Among mid-life's severest shocks—a good 9 on the Richter Scale—is learning that Kalispell, Montana, in addition to hundreds of Kalispells all over America, never heard of ballroom dancing.

Well, all right, Kalispell's *parents* have certainly heard of ballroom dancing. But that's different. Parents are notorious old fuds, custodians of all that is moldy and moth-ridden; they are to be taken with whole handfuls of salt.

If Kalispell, Montana, knows not the box step, I can guess why. Dancing reflects time and place. The grave minuet and the well-ordered eighteenth century are of a piece; likewise the square dance and the rumbustious, communitarian spirit of rural America.

You can see how ballroom dancing works against the zeitgeist, 1980s style. The rules, first of all. Step this way, step that; if you're not used to being told how to do, well, anything, you may wonder why someone should tell you how to make your way across a dance floor.

Ballroom dancing has, one is almost ashamed to say, Sexist Elements: men lead. And do the asking. And even the cutting in. Ellie Smeal, call your office.

How these indignities are handled in socially progressive venues I don't know. Maybe nuptial-style contracts: John to lead Rumba; Jane to lead Samba.

Of course, the main affront the zeitgeist receives from ballroom dancing is the coordination the whole enterprise requires, not to mention rewards—man to woman, woman to man, back and forth, 'round and around, ummm.

Coordination of effort isn't exactly the hallmark of the disco decade, what with everybody these days accustomed to doing his/her own thing—at work, at play, at home, on the dance floor.

The philosophers call this outlook "solipsism," but that's entirely too large a concept (and word) to intrude further into a discussion of ballroom dancing; the point anyway being that solipsism isn't necessarily a lot of fun. Not the way ballroom dancing is fun.

Around the time of the American Revolution, when I was being carted weekly to Miss Jewel Walker's Dance Studio, it was considered cool—and desirable, actually, to hold members of the opposite sex on the dance floor.

Here was a rare chance. In those bygone days, you would scarcely dare to approach Eudoxia Lightfoot on the schoolyard and drape your right arm around her waist. On the dance floor, nevertheless, you had to do just that—even as she had to rest her soft hand on your shoulder.

Then off you glided together—or, I should say, lurched. Side, together, forward; side, together, back: two heads, one shadow, which is about as poetic as I want to get concerning the terpsichorean feats of sixth-graders.

A little practice, and you had it down; you could look each other in the eye, carry on a conversation, get acquainted, maybe for the first time. In subsequent years, ballroom dancing and soft lights served purposes even more romantic. I hope I really don't have to explain that one.

Ballroom dancing, to say the truth, has never died out altogether. Old-fud parents still swing and sway, insofar as creaking forty-year-old joints permit. What has been lacking up to now is interest, and understanding, among the younger generation. "Never heard of ballroom dancing" in Kalispell, Montana! You see the magnitude of the problem.

In a lifetime of daily journalism, I have concluded that there is no such thing as a trend. A trend, any trend, is, at best, what happened day before yesterday, only nobody noticed till last night.

No one is suggesting that the fox-trot is back and disco gone with the wind. But to hear a modern college student call ballroom dancing "more fun than rock 'n' roll!" "Um-hmmm," I hear an inner voice say, smugly.

February 18, 1987

After You

I beg your pardon. May I pass on, please, the *Wall Street Journal*'s observation that courtesy is fast disappearing from our midst? Thank you.

The *Journal*'s dispiriting story makes me feel the need of talking thus. I want to do something like, oh, spread my overcoat for a bag woman to walk on; beg permission to light up the cigar I don't own or carry. Somebody, it is clear, needs to take action.

The *Journal* calls attention to a general degeneration of manners: "Small, everyday courtesies among Americans these days seem to have gone the way of finger bowls and hand fans—rarer in everyday usage than an 'After you, ma'am' on the New York subway system."

A San Francisco woman describes her reward for yielding use of a pay phone to a man she supposed would take less time than she herself needed. The man made call after call. When she asserted her own needs, he snarled, "I didn't think I had to ask *your* permission to use a public phone." A Pittsburgh legal secretary says she is dumbfounded on those rare occasions when doors are held open for her.

The South and the small towns seem to be exceptions. Elsewhere, dog gobbles dog.

Everyone has his own, least favorite aggravations. Mine are:

1) Drivers. Who are inexpressibly less polite than they were even five or six years ago. On the great arteries of commerce, no quarter is given. Cruise along in the right lane at the speed limit, and some lout honks at you. "Speed up, you—! Get the—over!" Then, a shrieking of rubber tires in the next lane; another blast of the horn; and the inevitable—what I never saw or heard of till age thirteen—an opprobrious hand gesture. Often the lout is young, but sometimes he is older than I am, which is to say, old enough to know better.

2) Theater audiences. Specifically, those members of same who stroll up to my aisle seat and look meaningfully at me. They want the seats on the other side of us, and I am delighted to oblige. What I am looking for is a short phrase—something on the order of "Excuse me, please." Nonetheless, I step out of the aisle to make room. Silence, utter silence, from their lordships and ladyships, trudging past my wife's knees. This happens all the time, and frankly it bugs the heck out of me. I am wont to mutter, when it happens, "That's quite all right. Feel free." They always do.

Yes, people are turning into a bunch of slobs, aren't they? And what are we going to do about it?

Recognize the problem first, I suppose. The syndicated columnist Miss Manners told the *Journal* this was being done. Said she: "We're a half step above rock bottom." Miss Manners's books, I hear, sell like hot cakes. Now if we can just get the buyers to *read* them!

But beyond that: Manners are not behavior so much as they are attitude—a spirit of courtesy and respect for others, manifesting itself in courteous behavior. You have to care about other people in order to treat them with sensitivity.

Bad manners are nothing new; what is new is the way modern society teaches us to care chiefly, if not exclusively, for ourselves. The idea—to borrow from the title of a notorious best-selling book— is looking out for Number One, which means in practice jumping with hobnailed boots on numbers two, three, and four.

Thomas Hobbes, in *Leviathan*, had a name for this sort of social competition: "the war of all against all." We might say today: the culture of me-first.

Me-first businessmen cheerfully knife each other in the struggle for promotion or market advantage. Likewise me-first politicians, for whom office-holding is a creed.

And what about my own trade? "Some Americans believe no one has worse manners than the press," says a related *Journal* story.

The story notes that, after the Challenger disaster, newsmen virtually took over a memorial Mass for Christa MacAuliffe. Glory and gain, it would seem, are the common goals of modern life.

What has happened? If I had to suggest one explanation, it would be the latter-day eclipse of Mom. Ever and always we have looked to Mom to set the basic social standards, hence the overall tone, of society. Mom's resources were fabled—a patient word of counsel first of all; that failing, The Switch.

Mom was Emily Post back before there were any Posts—or Smiths or Joneses either. She outlined and enforced the social norms. Fancy chuckling to Mom about how you had imposed on the woman in line behind you at the phone booth! Mom would inform you indignantly that you had done wrong. You were in the future to show a little more consideration for your fellow human beings.

The twentieth century has not been kind to Mom, which is one of the most grievous charges that can be pressed against the twentieth century. Divorce and desertion—the new social ethic—leave her frequently to run the home by herself. Or maybe she has to work all the time. It is notoriously hard to impart precepts over the telephone or on the run.

Whether my theory is right or wrong, it seems clear enough that, in the tutorial department, nobody is in firm, unquestioned charge any more. The time-honored social writs no longer run. "Thee" is out; "me" is in. If present trends are not reversed soon, the kindest word we may hear in the near future is, "Excuse me while I step on you."

March 18, 1987

Call Me Ishmael

The ball that Jimmy Carter got rolling eighteen years ago is traveling faster and faster. I wouldn't be surprised if, by this time, the whole game were lost. Maybe we'll never again have a United States president who doesn't go by his high-school yearbook name.

The 1996 election campaign makes plain that folksifying one's Christian name is now the standard practice among presidential candidates.

Jimmy Carter. *Bill* Clinton and *Al* Gore. But look who stands in the wings, waiting for Bill's job: Bob Dole, Phil Gramm, Pat Buchanan, Pete Wilson, Bob Dornan, Dick Lugar.

Just two Republican candidates have failed to folksify: Lamar Alexander—because there's no useful or accepted way to tone down "Lamar" (Mar? Lammy?)—and Alan Keyes. Whatever is wrong with Keyes that he thus stands on his dignity? Didn't anyone ever call him "Al"? No wonder he lost two U. S. Senate races in Maryland: no common touch.

With several of these candidates, it wasn't always thus. Against Jimmy Carter in 1976, Dole ran on a decidedly proper Republican ticket. The man at the top was Gerald, not Jerry, Ford; Dole was Robert. Gramm, when he broke into the *Wall Street Journal* in 1973 with a column on the energy crisis, was W. Philip Gramm. He retained this moniker for several years. At some point—I forget when exactly—he became Phil, just good ole Phil from over yonder a piece. This no doubt was fitting in a man whose speeches often tout the needs and insights of his friend Dickie Flatt. Similarly, Bob Dornan used to be Robert, and Buchanan was Patrick.

Informality is a notorious hallmark of American politics, but there used to be limits. Whereas we could talk about Teddy Roosevelt and Cal Coolidge, that was for purposes of cracker-barrel chit-chat. The country was actually run by Theodore and Calvin. Indeed, the former wore a silk hat, and the latter was photographed fishing in his business suit. Neither could have envisioned one of his successors jogging through downtown Washington in shorts and a baseball cap.

Personal dignity, albeit of a hearty democratic sort, went naturally with the office of president. The chief magistrate was your leader, not your pool-shooting pal. Some distance had to be kept, but not for the sake of snobbery—for the sake, rather, of mutual respect. A leader who eschews fake buddy-buddyisms shows higher respect for the individual voter than the leader who wants to compare T-shirt logos with him.

But then, people-to-people respect doesn't exactly abound in modern America. Boys let girls open their own car doors, airline passengers wear shorts and muscle shirts, motorists shoot "the bird" at whoever offends them, receptionists address visitors by their first names, and presidential candidates say, "Call me Bob/Phil/Bill/ Jimmy." So we do. With what effects?

It would be silly to suggest that what's in a name is—well, everything. A rose by any other name would smell as sweet—or foul, depending on your viewpoint—as Bill or Phil. What the candidate believes is what counts most of all, because what he believes normally determines what he does, once he is in office.

Still, it's pleasant to imagine that a real leader might lead us back toward a nicer sense of differentiation: not everything (for once) flat-out the same; some things in fact raised above other things, looking fresher and smelling better because of it. Differentiation is the human faculty least exercised today.

Why couldn't a President Bob Dole help us differentiate? Or even a President Bill Clinton? Presumably he could. But the Bob/ Bill business indicates he might not want to, having absorbed, or made his peace with, the culture of everybody-just-alike — the culture of muscle shirts at the airport.

If only Georgie Washington could have forseen what the twentieth century would bring! Or, again, what good luck he couldn't!

May 22, 1995

To Love My Fellow Man

The Rev. Jesse Jackson earned $209,358 last year—not bad for a preacher. And that's far from the most interesting item in the 1987 tax statement Mr. Jackson released recently.

Dipping a little deeper into the story, we find that Mr. Jackson and his wife Jacqueline contributed to charity the sum of $2,145— about 1 percent of the family income. Thank you, Rev. Rockefeller.

What *do* they teach at divinity school these days? The biblical tithe—as clerical shepherds once fondly reminded the sheep—is 10 percent of gross income. Maybe the Jackson family's missing 9 percent went to its favorite charity, the Jackson presidential quest.

Still, there's symmetry here. Jesse Jackson is one of those liberal/ collectivists who yearn to Share the Wealth. Other people's wealth.

Collectivists grow dewy-eyed over the plight of the destitute and downtrodden. Yea, brethren, let us reach out to these folk—with government check in hand!

Involuntary charity has been the cornerstone of liberal thought in America for the past half-century. Which makes sound practical sense. Grateful voters are loyal voters. As Franklin D. Roosevelt's lieutenant, Harry Hopkins, is reported to have said: "We will tax and tax, spend and spend, elect and elect."

Government, the Good Shepherd of the secular age, decides what portion of your daily bread you need not hand over in taxes. True, some of what you give the government goes for essential services, like ICBMs and lighthouses. The rest, alas, is political honey—set out to lure grateful voters.

Not so long ago, liberal politicians argued plausibly that "rich" taxpayers carried the poor upon their tuxedoed and sequined backs. Only the rich were much agitated over this state of affairs, and over the tax levels it necessitated.

Are things ever different today! The middle class pays most of the country's taxes, hence finances most of its social programs. Yes, in liberal/collectivist circles, the thirst to "share the wealth" is unslaked. The middle class stiff, thumbing through a sheaf of bills, is entitled to ask: "Wealth, what of wealth?"

And still we haven't gotten to the basic moral question involved here. Sir Walter Scott, in *The Heart of Midlothian*, speaks caustically of "that more impartial and wider principle of general benevolence, which we have sometimes seen pleaded as an excuse for assisting no individual whatever." Sir Walter, meet the Rev. Jesse Jackson.

Oh, how Mr. Jackson, and Jacksonian liberals, love people in the mass! More health care, more Social Security, more welfare, more farm aid—Mr. Jackson's for it. Even with the savings he'd realize from gutting defense, Mr. Jackson's program threatens to increase the federal deficit by three hundred billion dollars (a small portion of which he'd recapture, you'll be pleased to know, by raising taxes on corporations and the rich).

Because he so much loves "people" in the mass, individual people must not often invade Mr. Jackson's ideological radar screen. Individuals aren't the suffering, bleeding masses—they're this hungry man, this jobless woman, that crying child.

Always individuals, not crowds, were the objects and recipients of genuine charity, whose Latin root is *caritas*—love. Charitable giving is deductible under the tax code because Congress wanted to make attractive the helping of two, three, four, five people—not of thousands and millions. It is when thousands *do* help, that millions *get* helped.

One doubts that the average American taxpayer feels much *caritas* when money he has earned but never seen is poured by the government into programs he may regard as futile or wasteful.

Nor is it accurate to say that those who call for ever-bigger government programs are showing *caritas*. Only a tiny fragment of the money in question is their own; the rest is, or was, other people's. Where's the moral virtue in persuading the tax collector to pick your neighbor's pocket?

Charity begins at home, our grandmothers used to admonish us. In rarefied liberal circles, charity begins in Washington, D.C., or at the state capital, or city hall. The Rev. Jesse Jackson, by virtue of his title, is supposed to know better. If he truly does, why doesn't he show it?

May 11, 1988

Charity Begins at Home

The *New York Times* story about the recent national homebuilders' convention discusses all the things modern homeowners want. Or at least the things homebuilders think homeowners want, such as huge master baths with twin sinks; French doors with transoms; entertainment centers built into kitchen islands.

An accompanying picture of the New American Home for "thirtysomethings" depicts a glamorous two-story creation with columned front porch and 2,300 square feet, costing "just under $200,000."

Above this picture is a photograph of the American dream house, circa 1948. This one looks much like the house I lived in circa 1948. It is small, boxy: eight or nine hundred square feet. No thirtysomething would give it a second glance. It shows how times—and human expectations—have changed.

Twin bathroom sinks! Circa 1948, we did not even have twin bathrooms. We had one bathroom for five people. And two bedrooms. This today would count as serious deprivation. Definitely unthirtysomething, though my parents, in 1948, were both past thirty and comfortably established in life.

We called our house, purchased right after World War II, The Crackerbox. Houses were hard to find in those days, and we were delighted to have The Crackerbox. In any case it went with what would today be called "our lifestyle." The family had one car—a two-door black 1946 Ford, looking like a whale on wheels. There was no weekend lake house. The basic kitchen implement was a knife.

The Crackerbox served, but only just. Overcrowded, we bought a huge lot in 1950 and began constructing a home the month the Korean War broke out. This was some house: central heat, a garbage disposal and two bathrooms. However, only one sink per bathroom.

Expectations do keep rising. By modern standards, the 1950 house would probably qualify as a "starter" home, the Crackerbox as a lot-value write-off. What people need most of all today is closets and attics in which to stash the things designed to make life smoother. Heaps of things, piles of things. Things we couldn't possibly live without.

Listening carefully to conversation about Things is enlightening. The perception is abroad that, in Emerson's words, "Things are in the saddle and ride mankind"; that Things are not only expensive to buy but troublesome to get fixed. We are married to our Things, the complaint goes. Yet we spread wide our hands in puzzlement. What is there to do but buy? The Things we buy—car telephones, microwaves, compact disk players, etc.—make life go around.

There is much talk about The Simple Life. Some sound ready to climb atop St. Simeon Stylites's monkish pillar in the Syrian desert. Yet few actively move toward the simple life. I know people who have thrown out their televisions; I know none who have renounced air conditioning or automobiles.

Certainly, the Murchison boys have tossed out few of their innumerable possessions, however often I point to the doleful example of the Collier brothers, the famous recluses discovered dead in their New York apartment forty-five or forty-six years ago, amid mountains of accumulated refuse.

Concerning these matters, we seem fated to live in ambiguity. We want, yet feel uncomfortable for wanting. We accumulate and mutter about where we're going to put all the stuff. We complain about the repair industry's strangle-hold on our lives. We feel as though we were on a treadmill; to buy more and more, we work harder and harder.

The twentieth century, what's left of it, holds no larger challenge, perhaps, than learning how to cope with Thingdom.

One has the persistent feeling that life *was* in some sense easier to cope with in 1948. At least repair bills weren't so high. But daily life is no longer organized as it was organized back then, and there's naught to do except maybe look to our soul.

Perhaps it is not what we have, it is what we do with what we have. What *do* we do with our material possessions? Hug them, worship them, build lives around them? Or buy and use them with restraint, discarding them with no sense of loss or forfeiture? Fire up the microwave. How about some popcorn while we think?

January 27, 1990

IX

A Nation of Know-Nothings?

I COME FROM A FAMILY OF TEACHERS, to whom book-larnin' is important, not for its own sake, but for the sake of keeping us reasonably well elevated on the evolutionary ladder. In other words, education and civilization go together. We used to think this point is obvious. Not any more!

All Juiced Up

Don't tell the National *Education* Association about education. The NEA knows all about it.

Education, in the NEA lexicon, means boycotting Florida orange juice to protest Rush Limbaugh's verbal fireworks. Florida has a one million-dollar, six-month contract with Rush for promotion of orange juice. Better the juice producers should go belly-up than that a conservative broadcaster should profit from his observations.

Education, to the NEA, likewise means fighting California's proposal to cut off social services to immigrants. "California makes it a sin to be a child of a person who is seeking the American dream," protests a California teacher. Take that, all you Californians straining to balance the state budget.

Every July Fourth weekend, we have one of these ideological extravaganzas. The NEA's annual convention rolls around; the delegates just can't resist bashing Manifest Threats to Public Enlightenment such as the orange juice industry.

To these depths public education in our country has descended, nor are the prospects bright for rescue.

You say, what about all the rich, creative ideas for educational reform now bobbing on the surface of public discourse? What about school choice? What about vouchers? What about privatization, with outside groups contracting to run individual schools, with a contractual promise of improvement? All these ideas are exciting—to everyone but the NEA, which finds them hateful and loathsome and isn't going to put up with anybody trying to enact them.

The eye of the NEA—America's biggest labor union—isn't on educational betterment, save when betterment is construed directly and immediately as more government moola for schools.

Forbes has called the NEA "the worm in the American education apple. The public may be only dimly aware of it, but the union's growing power has exactly coincided with the dismal spectacle of rising spending on education producing deteriorating results." What makes the NEA so dangerous isn't sheer numbers but rather the hooks it has gotten into the federal government. The U.S. Education Department is a dreary enough business anyway; the NEA's constant involvement in federal education policy—through lobby work and lucrative contributions to federal candidates—makes matters drearier still.

Just now, the Congress is grappling with proposed changes to the Elementary and Secondary Education Act. The NEA's chalk-dust fingerprints are all over this legislation, which would vastly expand federal authority over education. For instance, federal oversight of curriculum content and student performance would increase; states would lose authority over the quality of school curricula and instructional materials. The House has passed the legislation already; the Senate takes it up soon, provided health care leaves time.

Federal control: Just what we've all be longing for. Just what we elected Bill Clinton to implement. But, never mind, federal control suits the educational establishment—at whose head is the NEA—just fine. Federal control means more federal bucks as well as regulations. It likewise shrinks the formidable challenge the NEA faces in trying to influence the policies of fifty separate states. How much easier, and more convenient, just to influence one national department of education!

The NEA's radicalism, and that of its allies in Congress, ill fits the public mood, which is one of disgust with powerful, unsympathetic elites. All the more reason to keep an eye on what the big educational union is up to.

Boycotting orange juice, indeed! This is education? This is academic prudence? A modest suggestion: Stick it to the NEA; go to the grocery store; load up on juice from Florida; drink it all. You can ward off common colds—if you believe that sort of thing—even while you render barren all the money spent on the big, loud convention of a big, loud, and deeply wrongheaded union.

July 7, 1994

History on the Quota System

Recent *New York Times* stories take note of efforts to rewrite history in order to accommodate ethnic and racial sensitivities.

Multicultural education means showing schoolchildren the accomplishments of women, blacks, Hispanics, Indians—and, one of these days, no doubt, gays and lesbians; anyone, in short, who sees himself as becalmed outside the White Male Mainstream.

California, as always, is in the lead. "California students," the *Times* says, "now learn that Mercy Otis Warren wrote political pamphlets during the American Revolution, Sacajawea was an Indian woman who guided Lewis and Clark's expedition in 1804-05, and Absalom Jones was a free black who established a network of black communities and African churches throughout the North in the early 1800s."

Meanwhile, according to another *Times* story, Hispanics demand that Hispanic contributions be highlighted. "Administrators in heavily Hispanic school districts have started to use recently published history books about Puerto Rican, Cuban-American, and Mexican-American explorers, Nobel Prize winners and leaders in education, arts and sports to supplement the regular textbooks."

What's going on here, you wonder, history or psychotherapy?

The latter, almost certainly. There is no other possible explanation for multicultural revisionism.

Modern education, it seems, must be tailored, not for society at large, but for particular sub-groups. Each sub-group decides what is relevant to its needs and purposes. The big picture tends to vanish. We see this happening in high-school and college English departments.

The history profession's enmeshment in multiculturalism goes back actually to the late 1960s, when black militants demanded academic exposition of the black experience. This led to the creation of Afro-American studies departments, patronized almost entirely by blacks. Dinesh d'Souza, in his bestselling book *Illiberal Education*, writes of the painful quest, among certain black writers, to demonstrate that black Africa was the fountainhead of world civilization.

There certainly is nothing wrong with broadening the perspective of the historical profession, a navel-regarding corps with a knack for making history—the most glorious subject in the world—as gripping as a cockroach race.

The fact remains: Multicultural history is a perverse and dangerous attempt to bend objective scholarship to political and sociological purposes.

The multiculturalists think they're raising our consciousness. Well, they're not. This grizzled old fogey learned about Sacajawea in the fourth grade. Fr. Hidalgo, the Mexican priest who raised the *grito* against Spanish rule in 1810—he figured in the Texas history texts of the benighted 1950s. White historians have seldom slighted ethnic and racial figures who marched in, or close to, the van of history.

Multiculturalists, nonetheless, denounce history as a white male conspiracy. Julius Caesar, Richard Coeur de Lion, Daniel Boone, George Washington, Tom Edison, Henry Ford—white males all. Yes, and are they to blame for it? And are history teachers to blame for highlighting their achievements?

There is only so much time during the school day. History teachers must make the best use of that time by teaching what matters most: how Rome fell, what the Middle Ages were like, how America was settled, who led the great wars, who invented this, that, and the other. White males? True, in large measure, Western history is what white males made it. So what? We cannot let the Edisons and Jeffersons fade into the wallpaper because of squeamish objections to their race and sex. Singling out "historical figures" for biological reasons alone is history on the quota system.

The United States, this lovely land, is the sum of the contributions of diverse folk from—literally—everywhere. Let us recognize and salute them all. What we must never do is turn American history into Psychology 101—I'm OK, you're OK, we're all OK: equally bedazzled by the irrelevant, equally unaware of what life is about and how it got the way it is.

August 8, 1991

Caring Less

Because the public schools in Corpus Christi, Texas, are tightening up on teacher attire, there are mumbles and rumbles. What, principals setting sartorial standards? Banning bluejeans? Sending teachers home to spruce up? The head of the local teachers' union comments: "I think we're moving headlong back to 1950."

Best news the resident cynic in these parts has heard in years. Back to 1950 education—ah, if only!

Yes, there is transparent danger in nostalgia. Tears of remembrance can cloud the vision until, in retrospect, everything about The Old Days seems to have been absolutely wonderful, and how come they ever changed? Niccolo Machiavelli—speaking of cynics—was on target when he commented that "men ever praise the olden time and find fault with the present."

But what about 1950, specifically? Let me, teacher; I remember it all. In the fall of 1950, Miss Jo Ann Dailey's fourth grade class at Robert E. Lee Elementary School was home base for, among others, a skinny, asthmatic kid with a burr haircut, name of Murchison.

What was it like? First of all, we worked hard, that being what was expected of us. Tests and homework were part of the rhythm of life. Second, there was no nonsense in class. Red-headed and fresh out of Baylor University, Miss Dailey (whom we supposed to be about a million years old) kept her young saplings decently pruned. Her weapon was the pinch, vigorously applied to the malefactor's forearm. The recipient of several pinches, I can testify to their efficacy. They hurt!

Today, an ACLU lawyer at our sides, we would haul her into court for child abuse. In 1950, our parents regarded Jo Ann Dailey as the appointed disciplinarian, who merited support in all instances.

My classmates and I, against the possibility that nostalgia might be overwhelming us, have compared our memories of that time. We all agree: Our parents *always* backed the teacher. "Don't come whining to me, young man (or young woman)" was the universal rebuke; "You do what Miss Dailey says, or we'll give you twice what you get from her."

Was Robert E. Lee Elementary perforce a disciplinary hell hole? It was nothing of the sort. It was a place of kindness and order; the latter attribute made possible the former. The two attributes, fused as one, undergirded the school's mission—there, as everywhere, the imparting of knowledge, the grooming of the gray cells.

What were we back then at Robert E. Lee, some kind of educational paradigm? Almost certainly not. By 1950, as is clear in 1994, educational standards were slipping. Post-World War II America, obsessed with the good life, was coming to emphasize personal fulfillment over against duty and service. Ahead, though shrouded in fog, loomed the depredations of the 1960s.

Back to 1950: What is the relevance here? The relevance is spirit—not externals like how we dressed (bluejeans and checked dresses) and how we learned (seated at rigid rows of desks), but internals such as respect and a sense of order and an affiliation with the purpose of the enterprise.

Whatever our other deficiencies, we cooperated voluntarily with the project at hand. A web of respect held us fast—respect for teachers and parents; respect for, or just meek acceptance of, the educational process and of the duties it imposed on us, such as homework and tests. It was not so much a different school system as a different age. Expectations were different. Standards were different.

Can we get all, or some, of that back? Not by crooking fingers or staging 1950s "sock hops." The central ingredient is care. Parents, teachers, and students must care, more or less in unison.

Care for what? For knowledge, for learning, and for the rights of others who would learn; for the dignity of the whole educational enterprise. Care was what we had in 1950, Robert E. Lee Elementary, Jo Ann Dailey's fourth grade. Teary-eyed nostalgics, take your business elsewhere. I talk of what was real.

September 8, 1994

The University as Public Utility

Welcome to the Wonderful World of Entertainment, where University of Texas head football coaches earn—I use the word advisedly—over six hundred thousand dollars a year. Which sum, the last time I looked, was nearly ten times the average pay of a full professor at said university.

What if we put it this way? By firing its head football coach, UT would free up enough cash to employ ten new teachers.

Come to think of it, the first half of that scenario just came true. UT dismissed the coach, John Mackovic, and will beat him through the streets for losing seven games this season.

Just don't expect the second half of the equation—the redirection of energies and money to academic purposes—to be realized soon. With each passing year, education and American universities have less and less to do with each other. Football is just part of the problem.

College sports were initiated for two basic purposes: 1) offering scope for wholesome, competitive play, and 2) linking the student body in common enterprises, such as swigging and cheering. None of this was to be regarded with excessive seriousness. Athletics wasn't the entree, it was dessert. It mattered who won, yeah, for about as long as it took to locate a post-game bar stool. At the heart of the academic enterprise remained . . . academics.

Or anyway somewhere near the heart. Nothing was ever quite as pure as it commonly looks through the misty lens of nostalgia. Overemphasis on sports ("Ya Gotta Be a Football Hero . . .") is an old, not a new, topic. Still, college sports hadn't until recent times been handed over completely to the outside world, which presently owns them in all but name.

College sports? Ain't no such no more, save maybe the squash team. We're not talking dinky little games in dinky stadiums, aimed at starry-eyed students and boozy alumni; we are talking big-time, all-the-time entertainment: dash and slash and splash. And cash.

The off-campus world wants bread and circus games, relayed via big-screen television? What, then, shall a modern administrator do? Give the customers what they want, that's what. This is what students and alumni have become—customers, stepping up to sift the wares, taking out or putting away their wallets. You pay the coach six hundred thousand if he can grab off a decent proportion of those customers; you fire him if he can't. College administrators, once considered among society's leaders, are generally, as at UT, wobbly-kneed people-pleasers, incapable of deciding anything, save in the commercial spirit.

The democratic marketplace drives modern higher education. Such, pardon the expression, is the bottom line.

And not an edifying line either. Modern universities, whose historic mission was the transmission of truth and wisdom, are public utilities, funded or regulated as such. Entertainment is a large part of it. Another part is what you might call the vocational-social element. The expectation is that universities will give students life and job skills. What apprentices used to do—learn a trade in a fixed number of years—is what college students now do, at vastly greater expense to their parents, I can tell you.

The affirmative-action debate illustrates another facet of the problem. Today's university sees itself not just as entertainer, not just as vocational counselor, but as social pacificator and facilitator.

"Black" and "women's" studies ornament the curriculum not because of any intellectual value they possess but because they show off the university's commitment to Expanded Opportunity. The public utility known as UT laments its failure to create a student body reflective of Texas's social, ah, diversity. But it's trying, it's trying.

What a mess! Would it have helped had UT not fired John Mackovic? Hardly. This deeply saddening matter transcends the entertainment value of college coaches. Still, the Mackovic affair is enough to make honorable coaches, of whom there are plenty, ask themselves quizzically, just what kind of a racket is this anyway?

December 2, 1997

Varsity Unlettered

Let us take this slowly, because statistics can be as slippery as bathtub soap. At more than one-third of Division 1-A colleges—those with the biggest sports programs—the graduation rate for basket-ball players was 0 to 20 percent. At another 23 institutions, no more than 40 percent of basketballers took degrees.

Football? Well, at fourteen colleges, as sunlight faded over gothic towers and choristers hummed *The Halls of Ivy*, 80 percent or more of the varsity slunk out of town, sheepskinless.

If we are shocked, that's the general idea. Congress is consider-ing a bill requiring colleges and universities to reveal how many ath-letes they actually graduate. The information generated by the Gen-eral Accounting Office of Congress at Senator Ted Kennedy's re-quest should move the bill along briskly.

Well, I dunno. I believe actually I have a certain sympathy for the athletic dropout who wants to get on with his career. Maybe he simply looks around the campus, saying to himself, "What am I do-ing here? What's all this got to do with me?" If we're going to pass legislation addressing the so-called dropout problem, let's make it read something like this:

"No person shall attend a college or university who, deep down in his heart, doesn't really want or need to.

"The penalty for breach of this statute shall be instant removal from campus and employment at a useful job at a decent rate of pay."

My own guess is that if such a law were on the books today, half to two-thirds of American collegians would be subject to arrest. Oh, these think they want to be at college, but, no, not really. Most are there because they think college is what society expects of them; in which they are largely right. On the other hand, society's expecta-tions are grandiose and inflated. Most people don't need college. They're bored there and can't wait to finish. It is not athletes alone; hordes of their fellow students are bored but dare not say so.

Once upon a time, the high school diploma served most people as the ticket to the larger life. (Earlier yet, skill and character sufficed.) The higher education industry took care of all that. It escalated the options. It helped persuade susceptible Americans that they needed a college degree to succeed and compete.

College is nice, but it takes time and money, especially the latter. Tuition has reached ludicrous levels—twenty thousand for four years at a *public* institution, four times that at "prestige" schools such as Harvard and Stanford. Shades of the James gang!

Often what the student gets in return is Marxist economics, history as the unbroken tale of Anglo oppression, and literature from which dead white males are increasingly siphoned in favor of live feminist thinkers and Central African poets.

Many students put up with this because you're supposed to have a college degree to get a job. It is an absurd conceit. Much so-called professional training consists of knowledge and skills that could be as easily, and perhaps more profitably, learned on the job.

Look at the law. Time was when the aspiring attorney "read law" in an experienced lawyer's office. Is the legal profession better respected today for the pompous degree ("juris doctor") and specialized knowledge the fledgling legal eagle takes away from law school?

Teachers are bored silly in most schools of education, whose curriculum is based on methodology, not content. You learn how to teach but not what to teach—or what to think of what you're teaching. Prospective politicians set forth on long voyages through schools of public affairs, where they learn sociology, civics, and psychology. An older generation, as the historian Samuel Eliot Morison has pointed out, learned from Plutarch, Demosthenes, and Thucydides.

Higher education isn't all that high anymore, it's awash in the narrow and the provincial, and the end can't be anywhere close—not with Congress getting ready to legislate. Maybe instead of commiserating with athletes who drop out of college—very possibly for intelligent, self-interested reasons, such as making two or three million dollars in the NBA or NFL—we should congratulate them for knowing where their true interests lie. Who knows they haven't got something to teach the rest of us?

September 13, 1989

So Who's This Shakespeare Guy?

You bet the "ebonics" fuss—still buzzing in our ears, thanks to the usual late-December news dearth—is about race. It's also about the uneasy feeling that our educational institutions are standing for less than ever before and certainly less than they ought to be.

Set up "black English" as a foreign language? Equally, why not let students at elite universities study "Thinking Queer" (Bowdoin College), "Literature and Sexualities" (Duke), "Avant Pop" (Indiana University), and "Genre: The Gangster Film" (Georgetown University)? Well, they do study it—if "study" isn't too rigorous a word in this context.

About the time ebonics inflated like a blow-up Santa, the National Alumni Forum issued a report documenting not only the foregoing offenses against good sense but one offense truly emblematic of our time. You might call this one the optionalizing of William Shakespeare.

The Forum's survey of seventy top-rated colleges and universities showed that "The abandonment of Shakespeare requirements is not merely a trend; it is now the norm. Of the 70 universities, only 23 now require English majors to take a course in Shakespeare. . . . The remaining 47 schools allow students to graduate with a BA in English without studying the language's greatest writer in any kind of depth. Among the Ivy League schools studied, only Harvard requires a course in Shakespeare."

Into this disciplinary vacuum, with a great whoosh, rushes . . . "cultural studies." The Forum notes some of these studies: AIDS activism, alehouses, atomic age, attitudes to marriage, big business, best-sellers, capture of the state, carnivals, CD-ROMs, cheap ballads, computer games, consumers—to regurgitate only the first three letters in the Forum's listing.

Well? Are we shocked out of our minds? Haven't we been headed this direction at least since the 1960s (longer ago than that in the view of cultivated experts like Jacques Barzun)?

What we've got, here at the end of the 1990s, is educational democracy—a phenomenon on which the ebonicists feast. It didn't have to come to this, but you can see how it did. Political democracy—the equality of all votes, however rational or perverse—suggested over time the need for equality in other departments of life, education among them. If all votes are equal, how about all outcomes in life? The educational revelers have kept their eyes studiously on just this goal: the denigration of talent, the watering down of the academically strenuous, the quest for the timely (hence the generally accessible).

Shakespeare and AIDS studies, Milton and film noir—yawn, what's the difference? No difference at all, depending on what your educational objective is: training minds to razor-sharpness or certifying twenty-two-year-olds for the job market.

The quest to lower educational standards is essentially a tearful protest against the nature of things. Even in the twentieth century, not all people have the same brains. Horrors! Can't have total democracy that way!

We can do something about it, though. We can teach in a way that downplays or blurs all those differences in mental capacity and aptitude, not to mention circumstances (e.g., background) that don't necessarily reflect aptitude. Can't speak good English? Throw over the English requirement. Don't care about dead white guys? Rather watch MTV? Out with Shakespeare (despite all the new movies based on him)—and, in time, all other writers and works that have shaped the way we think. Boy, do we get equal then—equal in our gapemouthed incomprehension.

Cheer up, though. It won't last forever. Water doesn't flow uphill, and two plus two doesn't equal five. The natural always reasserts itself. Standards will return when those capable of grasping their importance understand how the educational system has been cheating and lying to them. The problem, meanwhile, is the millions now being lied to—the pitiable victims coming slowly to fancy that between Shakespeare and John Grisham there isn't a dime's worth of difference.

December 30, 1996

The Used-Car Lots of Academe

Universities were founded originally for the purpose of studying and communicating truth. Well, guess what: That was then, this is now. The modern university is an academic used-car lot: Good or bad, beat-up or shiny, you can buy it.

Including condoms.

The university I have immediately in mind is the University of Texas, whose campus legislature, known as the University Council, is whooping it up for on-campus condom sales.

A couple of weeks ago, these successors of Socrates and Bacon called for marketing prophylactics as an AIDS-fighting device. Vending machines for said purpose are to be set up in such locations as the student union, the libraries, and, yes, the dean's office. They are in men's dorms already, and, when last I heard, were destined for the women's residence halls. Why not the football stadium next? You never know where students will find inspiration.

A coalition of faculty members protested that condom promotion "sends the wrong message to our students, promotes sexual practices which could lead to serious infection or death and misrepresents the values of our educational community to outsiders."

An Austin doctor objected that "Condoms are the poorest form of contraception. Study after study has shown that condoms have a failure rate in excess of 20 percent per year when a couple is trying to prevent pregnancy."

Supporters countered: Get real, you don't think kids are going to deny themselves a fundamental American right like premarital sex? Since they're going to Do It anyway, they should Do It safely.

We all know this argument. It is the argument of the shrug, of palms spread wide in futility; of what-do-you-expect-us-to-do-since-that's-how-things-are.

You hear the argument made elsewhere, of course, besides the University of Texas. Around the country, white flags flutter from the educational and moral ramparts. New York City and Los Angeles public schools distribute condoms to students. Recently the school board in upper-middle-class Plano, Texas, required that AIDS awareness teachers demonstrate the use of condoms.

In this climate of moral Vichyism, the University of Texas hardly stands out. And then, again, it does. Because a university, when it capitulates, creates more dust and din. Universities once were among society's formative institutions. Truth was their aim—the uncovering and the propagation thereof. To go with the flow was to betray the university's very mission, to undermine its authority.

What is the flow today? The flow is acquiescence, acceptance in the moral, if you call it that, spirit of the times. The University of Texas believes in consumer sovereignty. If consumers—students—want or need condoms, far be it from the university to tell them what they ought to want, such as the civilized gift of continence.

Today's university sees its mission not as the cultivation of virtue but as the tame, lame acceptance of the fact that, gee, not everybody wants to be virtuous. This must be especially true at UT, which has one of the highest HIV positive rates of any campus in the country.

The presence of condom machines on campus shows the customers how resigned the authorities are to being ignored. Abstinence, as the best means of AIDS prevention, gets lip service. The condom machines whisper of the lip-servants' despair that anyone is going to listen. Rather than witness, the authorities accommodate. Far from testifying, they make their peace with the spirit of the age.

It would be unfair to say they don't teach. What they teach is the relativity of the standards for which modern society supposedly thirsts. A campus condom machine is a whole seminar in cravenness and supine acquiesence to what is, instead of what should be.

Well, at Texas, thirty-one faculty members stood up against surrender: a remnant of sorts, a light in the moral darkness. If Austin is Vichy France, a resistance movement is afoot. How soon the Normandy landing?

July 22, 1992

X

Matters of Life and Death

ULTIMATELY, THE DIVINE ORDER guides and enfolds us—or there is no order, including that variety the politicians would impose by fiat. Matters of life and death are the province of God, in my own, admittedly unfashionable, understanding.

Smoke and Mirrors

The anti-smoking crusade is becoming . . . I grope for a word . . . silly. A second word comes simultaneously to mind: counterproductive. I speak, by the way, as a lifelong nonsmoker. I would as soon chew on a used wash rag as light the finest Cuban see-gar.

And yet the crusading aspects of the whole enterprise start to suggest cheap show biz. All we need at this point is horses, armor, and Cecil B. DeMille.

The Food and Drug Administration presses for the right to regulate tobacco as a drug. FDA investigators, according to the *Wall Street Journal*, have conducted "an intensive two-year search for testimony from tobacco insiders," concerning the industry's imputed desire to hook teenagers on cigarettes. The testimony of several ex-industry officials—untested in court—is retailed by the crusaders as Gospel Truth.

Six attorneys general have begun filing amply publicized lawsuits against the companies. The states—Texas joined the parade last week—demand mega-billions for the cost of treating tobacco addiction under Medicaid.

It's all very odd, this matter of social priorities. The deadly effects of tobacco are much remarked. However, the deadly effects of abortion are more pronounced by far: approximately 1.5 million victims a year. The illegitimacy rate in the United States is 30 percent, compared with 5 percent in 1960. Divorce—a paramount social evil—is more than twice as high as in 1960. Much of popular culture degrades the whole of society. Pornography flourishes.

We're at war with *tobacco*? Give me a break. True, the hard-shell Baptists who seemed so risible to H. L. Mencken and his contemporaries never approved of tobacco. Or dancing or card-playing.

Our modern crusaders brush aside this species of objection, based as it is on religious understanding ("What? Know ye not that your body is the temple of the Holy Ghost . . .?"—1 Corinthians 6:19). Physical fitness, though, as opposed to spiritual well-being: That's something modern crusaders understand in their bones.

The anti-smoking crusade is determinedly secular. The sort of people who wear earth shoes and sport double surnames figure prominently in the war against tobacco. This reminds us why few if any anti-tobacco crusaders have joined the battles against abortion and illegitimacy. In both battles you commonly—though certainly not always—find yourself grounding your analysis in religious truth.

Well, crusading spirit must be served, even in what today's Supreme Court clearly regards as a non-religious nation. We need to march, we need to exult. Tobacco! Why not the makers and purveyors of tobacco as our late twentieth-century infidels?

It works for the crusaders, though not without causing complications for others. For instance, there's the perception that if we just stubbed out every cigarette butt in America, we'd have it under control—when the sparing of 1.5 million unborn lives would serve us better.

Then there's the sheer weight and mass of the crusade. A former investigator for the FDA, Jim Phillips, complains that under Commissioner David Kessler, anti-tobacco crusading is draining the agency's resources.

According to Pennsylvania Congressman James Greenwood, who is trying to overhaul the FDA, it is deadly slow in approving new drugs and treatments. "From the moment a new drug is developed in an American laboratory," Greenwood says, "it takes 12 years and costs $350 million before it can be prescribed to the first American patient who needs it. For the past five years, two-thirds of the new drugs approved by the FDA were first approved in another country."

A California cardiologist meanwhile denounces the anti-tobacco movement for focusing so narrowly on teenagers as to let the country's 40 million adult smokers off the hook.

As the crusaders flail about with their lawsuits and press releases, questions arise. Is this the highest we can stoke our moral indignation? The thing that most agitates the crusaders is ... smoke? Gosh, the original crusades, eight hundred years ago, would have bored us to death, wouldn't they?

April 1, 1996

"Safe Sex" and Other Absurdities

Suppose, just to be supposing, that Magic Johnson had used a condom in that now-notorious encounter with—whomever. Would that have made everything all right?

From all the babble about Magic's infraction, one gathers, yes, a condom would have made everything fine, not to mention politically correct.

Magic would have been practicing "safe sex," a very 1990s thing to do.

"Safe sex"—what a clangorous misnomer! When was sex ever "safe"? The relationship between men and women—and all variations on that relationship — are as combustible as gunpowder. Magic has been blown sky high by an explosion he never anticipated, and so have millions of others, not all of them from contracting AIDS.

Look at Clarence Thomas and Anita Hill, whatever they did or didn't do. Their confrontation was electric with sexual tension. Look at the divorce statistics, the "date rape" controversy, the homosexual rights movement, the big-time press that "sexual harassment" is currently receiving.

My friends, this is heavy stuff. It goes far beyond condoms: synthetic items, procurable at the corner 7-Eleven. There is nothing synthetic about sex. It touches what is elemental in human nature— foremost, the reality that we are different, we men, we women; different and yet the same; apart but yearning for unity. How we get there is the stuff of a thousand million love songs, poems, sermons, letters, self-help books, and *Readers Digest* cover stories.

A great, unfathomable mystery is sex, involving not just flesh, which we can all see, but spirit and emotions, which we can't. This is why we have to tread carefully.

Fortunately, there are rules—the equivalent to "no cigarette lighters around the gunpowder." Maybe the word "rules" grates on the nerves of an increasingly undisciplined society. Fine; "signposts" will do as well. These have been carefully erected and creatively illuminated over the centuries. Experience has shown them to be grounded in the knowledge of what human beings actually are, instead of what they wish they were.

And what paths do the signposts point us down? Where is the sure ground, the firm footing? In marriage, for starters—this man, this woman pledging lifelong love and allegiance to each other "for better for worse, for richer for poorer, in sickness and in health . . . "

Of course, the partners must mean what they say. Today's divorce rate attests to the inability of many to take seriously even the most solemn pledges.

At that, cohabitation—today's trendy substitute for marriage— is no substitute whatever. There is no long-term commitment in it. Short-term, tentative commitment, alas, doesn't work. Even worse is the one-night stand, which is wholly empty of commitment.

Sex, which involves at its deepest level the partners' sense of individual and mutual identity, is too serious a matter to fit into a your-place-or-mine context. In sex, we are all of us deeply at risk. We cannot offer all that can be offered without some guarantees for the long-term continuance of the relationship. The signposts tell us so.

They tell us even more: such as that promiscuity, which begins in openness, is the deadest of dead-end streets. To switch metaphors, it sprinkles ashes on the gunpowder kegs. Nor, as Magic Johnson reminds us, are its consequences solely emotional. Promiscuity—heterosexual or homosexual—kills.

The lesson of Magic Johnson, with due respect to an otherwise wonderful human being, is not to practice safe sex, there being no such commodity. No, the lesson is to rejoice in the insecurity, the instability of sex, which impels us toward a security and stability no package of cheap, disposable, man-made goods could ever provide.

The great sexual standard of the human race, now, as two thousand years ago, is lifetime heterosexual monogamy, undertaken for mutual fulfillment and the procreation of children. It works and always has worked; the other alternatives don't and never will, barring a radical, and altogether improbable, transformation of human nature. The matter is as simple, as joyous—and as dangerous—as that.

November 12, 1991

Condomism and Confusion

Cute little condoms scamper into bed with people, and passion is thwarted when one prospective partner—isn't that the phrase?—tells the other prospective partner, no way unless you come up with Protection. All this, courtesy of the federal government. On television, no less.

The government, to widespread delight, is touting condom use through TV commercials. The government wouldn't do this under Ronald Reagan and George Bush; but as everyone knows, the decade of greed and insensitivity is over, so here comes our cute little condom.

As it happens, the new ads aren't perfectly in sync with the wishes of the coalition that tossed out Bush and gave us Clinton. Some homosexual activists lament the pitch to heterosexuals, relatively few of whom ever will contract AIDS (although heteros are the only ones who ever seem to get pregnant).

Moral traditionalists naturally have expressed outrage, but in Washington today, no one listens to their like. All that yammering about sexual abstinence! The condom campaigners start with the assumption that preaching about something no one's going to do anyway isn't very profitable. First, you figure out what people are willing to do, or at least to consider. Then, you urge them to do it. Bold, wouldn't you say? No doubt that's how the Renaissance and the Reformation started.

But you have to see the thing in context. Why do people who wouldn't sit still—supposedly—for a discussion of abstinence listen to pitches for condoms? Because if you're pitching condoms you're not questioning or, worse, denying modern people's right to self-expression come what may, and no telling what will. You're suggesting merely that the folks in question modulate the exercise of that right through prudence and caution. Who could object to caution? It's not as though you were telling people that wedded sex is wiser, better, *righter* than anything else! That would be preaching—a pastime we twentieth-century folk reject absolutely.

So abstinence, in the sexuality debate, takes a back seat. But from where it sits, we can see better what's wrong with the modern world. What's wrong is the notion, generally believed or else just randomly assailed, that one human choice is about like another human choice. The choosing, it seems, is the main thing. Different strokes for different folks. That one choice might be good and another bad—that sounds like something one's parents would have said, back when it was assumed there was a moral order.

Abstinence good? How could a form of denial ever be good? Well, because, on the medical level—at which the government's ads address us—abstinence prevents 1) unwanted pregnancies and 2) AIDS (unless contracted through a dirty needle or some such). Isn't this the point? Are not these the results the government wants?

Take it further, though. Abstinence—as understood by our culture until recently, and by the religions, Judaism and Christianity, that formed our cultural consciousness—shores up marriage and the family. As a pre-marital principle, abstinence reinforces the teaching that marital fidelity is of the utmost urgency. Do I hear someone say it's not? Maybe he'd tell me, then, why half of all modern marriages end. If there's not a fidelity deficit, what's the explanation? Physical infidelity, emotional infidelity—it's pretty much the same.

With the ripping apart of the family come heartache, a soaring crime rate, poverty for most single mothers, and devastation for the child-victims. Lately, the sociologist Charles Murray has been warning that what happened to black families, once illegitimacy became rampant, may soon happen to white families, in which illegitimacy is burgeoning. (Twenty-two percent of white births in 1991 were illegitimate.)

Give me a break: Does one single sociologist anywhere see Condomism as the launching pad for family renewal? I'll buy him a beer if so. Or is Condomism just the safe, oh-so-politically correct way of addressing a problem that politically correct folk won't face up to, thanks to intestinal fortitude deficiency? I say the latter. And I'll buy another beer for the reader who can show me why I'm wrong.

January 10, 1994

What We Need Is Some Stigma

Illegitimate births are up 54 percent since 1980, according to a government report. The reason, according to the report's author, is "a tremendous decline in the stigma" that was formerly attached to illegitimacy. In other words, modern society greets occurrences of bastardy with a great big yawn. Who cares anymore? And how's the O.J. trial going?

If anything, a sort of stigma attaches to the use of the word "bastardy," which has become, well, impolite. We don't want to tar people in that condition, *do we?*

Of course we don't. What we want, I would hope, is to prevent the spread of that condition. The routine acceptance of illegitimacy, as if it were a hair style or musical trend, is a social menace of the first magnitude. We need that stigma back. We need to start saying once more that illegitimacy is wrong.

We certainly used to. Remember "shotgun weddings"? They were the informal answer to situations wherein ardor had outrun morality, not to mention common sense. "Doing the right thing" by the girl one had impregnated didn't mean paying for her abortion or registering her for welfare benefits. It meant marrying her so that the offspring of the union, however prematurely conceived, might have a legal name and the prospects of a normal upbringing in a household with two parents.

A different moral understanding governed that society. The understanding was that single parenthood, as we have come to euphemize it, is inferior to traditional family life, with mother and father legally pledged to each other. A couple careless enough to conceive a child "out of wedlock" is apt to be careless in other respects—if indeed the two endure as a couple. Where's the incentive nowadays to regularize a relationship they probably never assumed would last more than a few months anyway?

If Mom doesn't object, and Aunt Flo couldn't care less, and the minister doesn't make a big deal out of it, and newspaper feature stories and TV talk shows encourage the view that illegitimacy is no more than a "lifestyle" choice—hey! Illegitimacy, more and more of it, is what you will have. According to the National Center for Health Statistics, a third of all U.S. births are illegitimate, with blacks and Hispanics leading the way but white women rapidly closing the gap.

These aren't Murphy Browns for the most part; they are women with less income and education than other mothers. Their children accordingly have a rougher go than the children of traditional two-parent households. With only one adult under the roof to provide counsel, direction, and discipline, the children are likelier to raise themselves—and likewise to get into trouble with the law. The number of criminals from single-parent homes is disproportionately large.

The illegitimacy rate, once very low, has been skyrocketing since the mid-1960s, thanks to the boost it got from the liberalization of welfare and the suffocatingly permissive moral climate. It is time to restore the stigma—even if that means pointing fingers and hurting feelings. The unkindest cut of all is assenting to habits and viewpoints, sometimes called "lifestyles," that degrade and undermine.

Vice President Dan Quayle felt the scorn of the fashionably permissive when, in his famous "Murphy Brown" speech, he chided those who would destigmatize illegitimacy. A few months later, *Atlantic Monthly* ran a devastatingly detailed report on single-motherhood. The headline: "Dan Quayle Was Right."

Illegitimacy isn't a morally or ethically neutral phenomenon. It's wrong, it's harmful, it's destructive. The trick is getting society to say so. The social liberals who dominate the entertainment and communications industries, and therefore the culture, don't believe in stigmatizing anything—save maybe "racist" jokes and school prayers. "Be yourself, live it up," they say to the young and restless. Who've been listening all too well, it would seem.

June 8, 1995

Yes, It Was a Baby

While Republican political candidates weather the pro-choice lobby's choicest wrath, a jury in Corpus Christi, Texas, complicates the lives of all who regard "pro" and "choice" as ends in themselves.

Last week, the jury convicted Frank Flores Cuellar of intoxication manslaughter. Whom had he slaughtered? A baby. Or was it? It hadn't been a baby in the instant his vehicle collided with a car driven by Jeannie Coronado, who was seven-and-a-half months pregnant. But, on the other hand, if it was a fetus and not a baby, why the strenuous attempts to save its life and why the manslaughter charges when those attempts proved futile?

Cuellar's lawyer, Anne Marshall, objected vigorously to the charges. How can you kill a person who, under state law, isn't a person at all—"person" meaning one "who has been born and is alive"?

Other definitions asserted themselves in the course of the trial. Born—delivered from the mother's womb. Alive—breathing air, exercising human functions. Dying—giving up life, a thing difficult to do without first having experienced life.

The jury took an hour to find that Cuellar had killed the baby and six hours to agree he should serve sixteen years in prison.

"Pro-choice." There is an appealing simplicity to the slogan: which is why it became a slogan. Ann Richards wields it with the bland sincerity of a washing-machine salesman. "Clinton," writes the former governor of Cuellar's (and a few million other people's) state in an op-ed piece, "believes the decision to bear a child must be left to women—not legislators, bureaucrats or judges." (Or juries?) Our Leader, Richards reports, "has consistently supported a woman's right to choose."

Well, I mean, if it's all that simple—and it could hardly get simpler—what's the problem? One problem might be Frank Flores Cuellar and the violence he and his kind do to ideas hardly less than to individuals.

The specific idea he steps all over is that there are different kinds of life—one growing visibly, another growing invisibly—and that the two exist on different planes, and that the rules for dealing with them are different. Frank Flores Cuellar, against his will, makes us grapple with a real-life understanding—that life is life is life, that politically or judicially contrived distinctions between born life and unborn life don't hold water. Or amniotic fluid.

President Clinton's veto of the partial-birth abortion bill was an attempt to quiet reality with a rhetorical massage. If I don't want to believe a partial-birth abortion extinguishes real life, I don't have to, Our Leader said, in effect.

Reality didn't count because Clinton's self-assigned task was to placate the pro-choice lobby he used to irritate as a moderately pro-life governor of Arkansas. He wanted not only the lobby's votes—he wanted its unremitting hostility to the Republican authors of the bill. Well, no problem there. More than a few pro-choice Republicans, if media accounts are reliable, have announced their intention of voting pro-choice Democratic. Hard-core GOP loyalists might be moved to exclaim: What a bunch of phonies! But all these impending defections really prove is that willful blindness is no partisan affliction. Republicans and Democrats alike can catch it.

The blindness immediately in question has to do with the indivisibility of life—old life, young life, impaired life, healthy life, born life, unborn life, all such lives enjoying the common denominators of breath and potential.

The pro-choice lobby, in both political parties, shuts its eyes tightly to reality. Sometimes, however, tight isn't tight enough: as when a drunken Frank Flores Cuellar barrels into a pregnant Jeannie Coronado and disturbing evidence of a third, emerging life draws public notice. Jeannie Coronado's baby wasn't a real, sure-enough, genuine, flesh-and-blood baby girl? Tell it to the jury.

On second thought, don't bother. The jury has heard, considered, pronounced. It *was* a baby.

October 21, 1996

Fetal Attraction

So just what do we do here? As doctors read the medical evidence, an unidentified pregnant woman in Chicago needs a Caesarean section. Failing that drastic intervention, her baby is likely to be born dead or brain-damaged. Her religious principles forbid such a step. She counts on God for a miracle.

Enter at this point Cook County's public guardian—a Big-Brotherly job title if ever I saw one. He has hailed the lady into court, demanding that the Caesarean be performed and the fetus, if possible, saved. Lower courts have disagreed, but the public guardian is appealing to the state Supreme Court. He calls himself "lawyer for the fetus."

It is one of the most arresting situations on view in an arresting time. All kinds of contradictions struggle for supremacy.

Under the U.S. Constitution, as presently interpreted, our unnamed mother has the right to—well, let's be sanitary about it—"terminate" her pregnancy. Sovereign of the womb is she: mistress of all she feels kicking within her. The U.S. Supreme Court says so. What is the public guardian's problem here? That the fetus, in legal-clinical terminology, is in for a bad time? On what basis may such a claim be lodged?

Yes, the baby is full term, but *Roe v. Wade* accords full-term babies no constitutional rights larger or higher than the rights of six-month-old fetuses, month-old fetuses, fetuses as big as a minute, as Southern ladies of the previous generation used to say. States are permitted, under *Roe*, to ban abortion during the third trimester of pregnancy, but that's local option; either way you do it is cool with the high court.

Notice: The public guardian doesn't call the fetus a baby, which would be politically incorrect. Feminist orthodoxy posits the otherness—the sub-humanity, one could say—of The Thing In The

Womb. But this being so, what right has an official to speak up in behalf of The Thing? Surely it's OK for the mother to do as she likes with her unborn. Such is the plain meaning of *Roe v. Wade*: choice, autonomy.

The public guardian's plaint disappears, or will in due course, like a drop of cream in Lake Michigan. Legally, he exceeds himself. The mother's sovereignty under *Roe* is well-nigh total. And yet . . . and yet . . . , he can't help wanting to interfere.

This cannot be wholly out of bureaucratic pride or malice. Confusion, perplexities, ambiguities abound in the realm of abortion law. Now and again a pregnant woman is shot or injured badly in an auto accident. News accounts note: "Doctors worked to *save* the unborn baby," or "The fetus was *killed* by the bullet." Save? Kill? How so? Isn't the Thing just a piece of protoplasm, no more? Why work to save it? Why care?

The pivotal issue, it seems, is whether The Thing is wanted. If so, let's save it; if not, let it go. The Chicago baby is wanted very much. This is why mother and public guardian dispute its route into the world.

Hold on, though: What makes wantedness the criterion for birth? A mental disposition determines who lives and who dies? Such is the law of the land: a harsh, cruel, and ultimately unworkable law. You could, with equal rationality, play spin-the-bottle to see who lives and who doesn't. Why not flip a coin? One arbitrary outcome is as defensible as another.

Roe v. Wade, the worst decision in American legal history, leaves us bereft of official guidance in matters, quite literally, of life and death. The tyranny of whim—that is what *Roe* reduces us to. The rule of law is over, where life is concerned. Dr. Kevorkian is the wave of the future: life and death as the merest options. Today, *for* us; tomorrow, maybe, *in behalf* of us.

December 16, 1993

Life, Death, and the Abortion Movement

Two wrongs don't make a right, our mothers used to inform us whenever, in childhood, our vindictive impulses threatened to get out of control. The solemn, civilized arithmetic holds up today. You don't shoot an abortionist in the back, as Michael Griffin, thirty-one, of Pensacola, Florida, allegedly did in a ghastly incident that will reverberate for a while in our national consciousness.

If Florida ultimately executes Griffin, blame should attach not to the Florida justice system but to the prisoner, and to him only. No provocation justifies the cold-blooded murder of a defenseless man.

Yet, when all's said and done, an urgent question will remain: What about all the lives that continue to be extinguished in clinics such as Dr. Gunn serviced in his ceaseless perambulations?

If the life of an abortionist matters—and it does, profoundly—what about the lives an abortionist extinguishes in the way of business?

The "pro-choice" movement will not, I think, admit the equivalence of these questions. An admission would not serve the movement's purposes. Once you start equating the life of a forty-seven-year-old doctor and the life of a forty-seven-day-old "fetus," you run into major difficulties in defending abortion.

The operative word is "life"—one life lived and lost outside the womb, the other inside it, by being constructed alike, sharing the same complex, mysterious origin. What about these lives? Is it so easy really to differentiate them—to say that, based on mere circumstance, one is valuable, the other beneath notice? And who decides? People with guns and surgical equipment? A fine argument, that, in a civilized society!—assuming that modern society still qualifies as civilized.

Those who, prior to his brutal murder, never heard of Dr. David

Gunn—this is 99.9999 percent of us—have no way of accurately appraising the value of his life. His dubious occupation aside, any abortion opponent has to concede Dr. Gunn the benefit of the doubt. He was human. He possessed an immortal soul. From the pro-life standpoint, it was conceivable that, with prayer and time, he might have experienced conversion. Such things have happened before. And, oh, what a mighty witness he might then have offered! Has the Pensacola vigilante never heard the name of that erstwhile persecutor of Christians, St. Paul?

By contrast, the subjects of Dr. Gunn's ministrations—the developing human beings he, shall we say, terminated—enjoyed no such presuppositions of worth. They were—well, what? Blobs? Even thumb-sucking, breathing, stimulus-responding blobs?

No adult figure in their brief lives seems to have asked or, anyway, to have asked with interest, what about this one and that one? Who might he or she turn out to be—poet, preacher, plumber? Or just worthy citizen? A mother? A father? Forbear of someone extraordinary and world-changing? You can't know. The presupposition of worth—that same presupposition to which abortionists are entitled—should benefit born and unborn alike. Not these days, though.

Abortion clinics are not in business to extend the benefit of the doubt; they are there to withhold it—in the same way the Pensacola vigilante withheld it.

Those who liken abortion clinics to the Nazi death camps are less extreme and impolite than the pro-choice movement would indignantly claim. The camps were places of anonymous, impersonal death: nothing against this Jew or that one, save membership in a class marked down for destruction. Are unborn babies the new Jewry—a victim class all the easier to impose upon because silent and unseen?

Modern life's rock-bottom cheapness is not the work of the abortion movement, which post-dates Auschwitz and Buchenwald by nearly three decades. The secularization of modern life and thought is the villain. Out of the secular ethic flows disregard for lives that, in the old religious dispensation, were deemed the gifts of God.

A gift of God had meaning, purpose, destiny; it was no accident of biology. Every day we see what happens in the new moral environment, where man, not God, is on top. What happens is, man plays God.

March 11, 1993

The Power to Make Life

Clearly life is no bowl of cherries. What it is, among other things, is a biological and spiritual wonder perpetually full of challenges— never more so than at present. Witness the furor over cloning and partial-birth abortion.

Dr. Ian Wilmut is untroubled by his discovery that, lo, he now knows how, through genetic manipulation, to replicate a given sheep: and if a sheep, why not also a human? As little disturbance as this new knowledge causes Wilmut when the lights go out, others bite their fingernails, pondering what it all means. Is this what we really want—power to make life itself? And make it the way we want it, as though following a Jeff Smith recipe?

That may be what many want. Power over life and death is the unspoken issue in the partial-birth controversy, which an abortion lobbyist, Ron Fitzsimmons, re-ignited the other day with his confession that he lied about these gruesome procedures. They aren't at all rare, Fitzsimmons said, contradicting the abortion industry's, and Bill Clinton's, rationale for defending the half-delivery of unborn children, capped by the suctioning out of their brains.

Congress will take another crack at banning the practice, which is presently legal only because Clinton last year vetoed a bill that would have ended it.

I would throw in some news on the euthanasia front, only, at just this moment, there isn't any. Dr. Kevorkian must have gone skiing.

Life being the rock-bottom, untranscendable human commodity, you might suppose recent events would catapult us into a prolonged discussion titled, roughly, "Who's in Charge Here?" Not quite. Such a discussion, if it ever got going, would confront the participants with unwelcome news: that in the matter of life—breathing, feeling, seeing, digesting, thinking life—having charge is no lark.

The power to create, the power to destroy: Here are the ultimate powers. Neither is unfamiliar. For a considerable period of time, humans have been having babies. Creation! For virtually as long, they have strained to define the conditions under which life may be taken away. Destruction!

Abortion is twentieth-century individualism raised to the Nth power. If you can work where you want to, and vote how you want to, and travel at will, and say almost anything to anybody—why can't you extend the permission a fraction farther? Why can't you decide whether to carry through a pregnancy or not? Aren't these privileges all of a piece?

The traditional answer is no, they aren't. Life—the underlying condition of existence—is qualitatively different from speech and travel and the franchise and such like. Different rules apply. Except that, by common consent, we rarely talk about these rules. To do so makes people uncomfortable; it hampers their freedom of choice. The horror of partial-birth abortion exists because of conversational squeamishness about the whole topic of who's-in-charge.

Now comes cloning, this time not as a comedian's throwaway line (as in the 1980s), but as a reality we must face. Who's in charge? Can humans create human life? Yes. Should they? Er, interesting question. However, it can't be ducked.

The real squeamishness in these matters has to do with *G-o-d* (a Being supposedly resident somewhere in outer space) and such conversation as a discussion of life's origins might generate. Who's really in charge here? Not Dr. Ian Wilmut, who resolutely sticks to his sheep. Not Ron Fitzsimmons, who by his own admission hasn't figured out whether brain-suctioning (as distinguished from lies about it) is a bad thing.

Are humans really in charge? What if the partial-birth furor and the cloning controversy and, yes, the "assisted suicide" mess (once Dr. Jack resumes his labors) lead us eventually to ask the fateful question: If humans *don't* make the rules of life and death, who does?

Only one answer is available. Secular minds won't like it. On the other hand, look where secularity got us: boxed in by perplexities we can't resolve without resort to—gosh, even today!—our knee-caps.

March 3, 1997

Gay Times?

What's this? Just *one* percent of American men are gay? One?

So says the Alan Guttmacher Institute—no religious-right think tank, to say the least—citing a survey it recently conducted. If true, this overthrows the figure of 10 percent, derived from Alfred Kinsey's famous study of 1948 and enshrined in gay rights rhetoric. ("Look around you—one of every 10 men you see is gay.")

Increasingly, it's clear that the Kinsey estimate—based on surveys of institutional inmates like students and prisoners—was wildly off base to begin with. We're a "straighter" society than we are led to imagine.

Guttmacher's study jibes with other recent head counts, domestic and foreign. The University of Chicago's National Opinion Research Center last year said 2.8 percent of American men were exclusively homosexual. Judith Reisman, in a 1990 book, came up with the same figure as the Guttmacher Institute—one percent. A French study initiated in 1991 says just 1.4 percent of respondents acknowledged homosexual relations in the previous four years.

Figures, figures! What do they mean, if anything? At a basic level, they mean something the homosexual rights movement finds embarrassing—that the movement constituency is far smaller than depicted. The TV networks confront a similar set of realities: The more viewers you deliver, the higher the rates you can charge advertisers. Politicians and merchants pay closer attention to 10 percent of the male population than to 1 percent.

Of course, from the gay movement's standpoint, there's another way to look at it. A smaller percentage means a smaller threat, as perceived by the straight community. If just one percent are gay, why not open the military to them? Who'd notice?

Actually neither viewpoint—the more the merrier or the fewer the feistier—touches the root issue, which is, can society afford to smile on the homosexual lifestyle?

I didn't say "tolerate," I said "smile on." Tolerance, defined as do-it-if-you-must-but-don't-flaunt-it, is the traditional American attitude. Gay rights activists insist endlessly they have never experienced tolerance; but, in fact, given the human species' historic abhorrence of same-sex intercourse, homosexuals have enjoyed surprising latitude. Not even the AIDS calamity persuades straights that the time has come to herd gays into prison camps.

The homosexual issue—which became an issue only when homosexuals made it one—can't be considered in a vacuum; the push to legitimize homosexuality is part and parcel of the wider culture's push for the loosening of all sexual standards whatever. If straights freely can divorce, cohabit, and bear illegitimate children, why can't gays equally do what turns them on?

Fair enough: Logical consistency *should* prevail, but in a different sense altogether. Logic can compel not just a lower standard for gays and straights alike but a much higher one. (it would be hard to get a lot lower than we are now!)

The permissive moral climate of the late twentieth century can't be shown to have made anyone happier—men, women, children, gays, straights, bisexuals. The rapid breakup of families has produced little but heartbreak and poverty; serial homosexuality has as its most visible consequence the poison of AIDS. Maybe we're more "honest" and "open" than our forbears. Are we happier and more satisfied?

What's wanted surely is a return to the historic norms that our society—especially its liberal intelligentsia—has so thoroughly trashed over the past twenty-five years or more. The norms, which include lifelong fidelity to spouses and procreation as a principal purpose of sex, are not far to seek. They're in heavy, black-covered books such as our forbears used to take down and read on Sundays, if not more often. They're in the great songs, stories, poems, and sermons of our tradition.

Figuring out what to do isn't the problem. Doing it in a social environment that still prizes self-indulgence over obligation, restraint, and responsibility—that's the real problem here at century's end.

April 15, 1993

"Gay Marriage" and Power Politics

President Bill Clinton would like to have his Big Mac and eat it, too. On the "gay marriage" question, it won't happen.

Yes, he still supports gay rights—the abolition of legal distinctions between homosexuals and heterosexuals. No, he wouldn't veto a bill should it come before him, letting states outlaw gay marriage. Homosexuals and lesbians, recognizing in the president's declaration a logical gap as wide as the Great Plains, are outraged. They'll probably still vote for him, but with noses held and eyes shut tight.

The president, a born pleaser, has displeased mightily by taking a moral stand: one he knows is agreeable to a larger number of voters than those to whom it's not agreeable.

How'd we get to this point, anyway, when the institutionalization of marriage between men and men, women and women, figures large in our political deliberations? There has never been a moment in human history quite like this one, and that covers some territory.

The proximate cause of the disturbance is the likelihood that Hawaii will legalize gay marriage, obliging the forty-nine other states, under the Constitution's "full faith and credit" clause, to recognize such unions when performed in Hawaii.

With respect to gay unions, congressional conservatives talk of a pre-emptive strike. They would declare that no state had to accept such unions. Clinton indicates he would sign such a declaration. Hence, the furor.

That all this rates as *political* furor shows what we've come to in the 1990s. *Everything*, or next to everything, is a political question. Not just taxes and trade and fleets and armies but also culture and morality. The politicians have undertaken to decide what the people may believe. The natural consequence is political warfare.

It is not supposed to be thus. The people are supposed to tell the politicians what to believe, assuming the politicians don't know instinctively. A country's moral and cultural assumptions are deemed—anyway, they used to be deemed—as beyond the reach of politicians. Those assumptions stem from tradition, formed chiefly, if not entirely, by religion.

The weakening of religious commitment in our time, the waning of belief in absolute standards informed by the Bible and Judeo-Christian witness, has opened a huge gap. Through this gap, the politicians pour. Suddenly, cultural and moral commitments become matter for political exhortation. The politicians will offer one group one thing—abortion on demand, easy divorce, government day care. Another group gets contrary offers—an end to abortion, a tightening of divorce laws, a larger scope for parents as against government supervisors.

The commitment that prevails is the one whose backers command the most votes. The rightness of a thing, or its wrongness, doesn't matter; its relative popularity is what matters. Popularity isn't supposed to be the "summum bonum"—the highest good—but democratic politics knows no other way of mediating disputes than the counting of noses.

Enter President Bill Clinton, perplexed. How to keep *everyone* happy in the gay-marriage debate? It can't be done. Gay marriage—opponents insist there is no such creature—is, at base, a moral question, concerning which politicians have nothing to offer.

The bill that Clinton thinks—for now, at least—he would sign is a proper response to a mess cooked up by politicians. If "gay marriage" is a concept alien to civilized society, should the United States appropriate it on the say-so of one state? Talk about a prescription for cultural disaster!

The no-gay-marriages bill is a signal to politicians to step back and let the religious and moral communities handle this one. Divided these communities may be, thanks to the international gay-rights clamor. One advantage they have over the politicians: They don't ask, on the front end, where they votes are. They ask: What is right? What is wrong?

May 27, 1996

Divorcing the Divorce Culture

Michigan, according to the *Wall Street Journal*, is considering divorcing itself from the divorce culture. The proper response, wherever one lives, is: Do it!

Do it! was the exuberant squeal that landed marriage and family life (like so much else) in trouble from the 1960s through the 1970s and even beyond. Bored with your family? Tell 'em goodbye and good luck. Try something, and somebody, new. Do it!

All fifty states have enacted no-fault divorce laws. California was predictably the first to do so; its law was signed by Governor Ronald Reagan, the divorced husband of Jane Wyman. Michigan passed its own law in 1972. Just three years later, all but five states had joined the parade, freeing restless spouses to leave a union for any reason or no reason.

A chicken-or-the-egg question asserts itself here. Did no-fault laws cause the divorce explosion, or did growing pressures for freedom in marriage result in passage of the no-fault laws?

The true explanation, no doubt, lies somewhere in between. No-fault divorce laws were passed because there was a growing demand for loosening the marital knot. Looser and looser the martial knot grew as the new laws gave voice to the conviction that, heck, marriage isn't such a big deal any more.

It must not be, what with a divorce rate of around 50 percent. People slip in and out of marriage as easily as if it were a suit of clothes. Any old cause for separation will do. *People* magazine, reviewing the big bust-ups of 1995, noted Richard Gere's egregious behavior toward his wife, the ultra-glamorous Cindy Crawford. "He's spiritual," said a pal. "Cindy gave it a try, but she's not into eating yak butter."

Elizabeth Taylor's eighth husband walked out after the Liz of *A Place in the Sun* and *Cat on a Hot Tin Roof* had hip surgery and ballooned to 160 pounds. Tommy Lee Jones, while filming on location, fell for a camera assistant. So it goes.

It was otherwise, once upon a time. Marriage was a solemn occasion—a theological occasion, if you please. The happy couple entered into it "reverently, discreetly, advisedly, soberly and in the fear of God." They made great promises: to love each other "for better for worse, for richer for poorer."

No ethic of self-sacrifice was likely to survive the self-indulgent 1960s. This one didn't. Divorce soared, the law winked, and misery spread: female poverty, children isolated or ignored, feelings of irresponsibility and unconcern let loose.

Divorce there always has been. Not every marriage is good; some marriages are insupportable. Even the prince and princess of Wales, for one absurd reason or another, can't get along. But divorce as an isolated act of renunciation is different from a whole culture of divorce, as the American society has inadvertently become.

Michigan Representative Jessie Dalman is the author of the bill that would start hedging marriage with some of the lost legal protections. There would, for example, be a requirement for counseling before marriage and likewise before divorce. Governor John Engler, who is himself divorced, says he would sign such a bill if it arrived on his desk.

How much would this help? In a practical sense, maybe not that much. The state can't legislate love, respect, and forgiveness. What it can do, perhaps, is point up their transcendent importance, the law being a tutor of sorts.

The most consequential tutor, of course, is religion. The decline of moral standards based on religion (as distinguished from yak-butter spirituality) is the factor most responsible for the divorce rate. Covenants with the living God contrast powerfully with crossed-fingered chirpings about the joys of life together.

The Michigan no-fault debate is the latest sign that the cultural disorders of the past thirty years are—well, not finished but under attack. We've tried license; we've tried self-indulgence. Backward we look in despair. Where's that pathway we used to be on? If we could just locate it again!

January 8, 1996

White Broncos and the Marriage Crisis

The latest phase in the O.J. Simpson saga is the men-are-brutes angle—a possibly understandable attempt to dignify our national immersion in a murder story.

Mariah Burton Nelson in the *New York Times* calls O.J. "a product of a culture that allows more than two million women each year to be beaten by husbands or boyfriends."

The *Wall Street Journal*'s Al Hunt, not to be outdone by a woman, calls domestic violence "an epidemic in America." He advances statistics twice as frightful as Nelson's.

But the matter may be worse than we suspect. Put aside the physical injuries and suffering, hard as that may be to do. A wife-beater—or husband-beater—drives a fist into the whole premise of their union. It swells up and turns purple. Repeated blows multiply the damage.

Marriage is accounted a sacrament of the church—a "holy estate." The purpose is fusing two lives into one. Everybody is familiar with the stately promises exacted of the couple by the Book of Common Prayer, including: "Wilt thou have this Woman to thy wedded wife. . . . Wilt thou love her, comfort her, honour, and keep her in sickness and in health; and, forsaking all others, keep thee only unto her, so long as ye both shall live?" To the woman go the same inquiries. The expected answer in both cases: "I will."

"Love," "honour," "comfort," "keep"—no suggestion in all this of a license to convert a mate into a punching bag. We have got here not *just* a violence problem; we have got a family problem. The violent spouse esteems neither his partner nor the marriage vows made by both.

The family, as we know, is clearly in a bad way. The divorce rate is 50 percent. Illegitimacy abounds. Growing numbers shun the institution entirely, preferring life together without commitment. Life *with* commitment is tenuous enough; without, it can turn savage. Violence against mates, married or unmarried, is one more symptom of the lowly estate into which the holy estate has entered.

But of course one knows the explanation. Marriage is un-modern. It imposes sacrifices of will and appetite for a supposed greater good. The culture glorifies self-fulfillment, not self-restraint. Those with claims on our time and resources—a husband, a wife, a child—become hindrances, objects of resentment. Some of the resentment is sure to slop over into violence.

Putting wife-beaters, however famous, behind bars is the surface answer. More fundamental is the task of engaging society in a wholesale rethinking of marriage—its purpose, its obligations, its sacredness. It will not be easy. Purpose? we reply. The purpose is sex or money. Obligations? No one talks anymore about obligations. Sacredness? Puh-leeze—the Supreme Court put a stop to all that, at least in publicly supported facilities.

A venture in political incorrectness is essential. In the name of Nicole Simpson and Ronald Goldman, it's less important to gas "the Juice" than to undertake, at the societal level, the restoration of marriage and family life.

The churches should lead. As columnist Michael J. McManus counsels in an exemplary book, *Marriage Savers*, churches should intensify theological and psychological preparation for marriage. "The church," McManus says, "which too often is only a wedding-blessing machine, can in fact be a real blessing to every person it marries." It can explain, as no other institution can explain, the divine purposes for which marriage was instituted. Do you hit or kill one you have vowed sincerely "to have and to hold from this day forward, for better for worse, for richer for poorer"? In a pig's eye!

Society at large can help to keep families from splintering. All no-fault divorce laws should be irrevocably repealed. Staying together, not breaking up, should be the norm.

Only marriage makes a family; only families make a society. To lose the family is to lose all—as many of the ninety-five million who watched the Flight of the White Bronco through Los Angeles must by now have come flickeringly to understand.

June 23, 1994

XI

The Fourth Estate

INTO JOURNALISM I wandered more than three decades ago. I love it to this day, much more than journalism's more thin-skinned defenders probably suppose. If from time to time I flay my beloved profession, it is for the purpose of recalling it to a higher vision of what it could be with a little effort and a lot more ideological detachment.

In Praise of the Eighties

It's perpetually fascinating to watch the liberal media at work—even in stories on wine.

Here's one I caught the other day, in an otherwise harmless family newspaper:

"PARIS—Beaujolais nouveau, that fruity, ambitious, overpriced wine, was the drink by which we toasted the Party '80s.

"As with many other things from that decade of excess—financier Michael Milkin, shoulder pads and defense spending—Judgment Day has arrived.

"It will find little mercy in the Vengeful '90s."

The idea is that beaujolais nouveau, which is confected from new French grapes, is falling in price as it sags in popular appeal.

To tell the story, we have to drag in the Party '80s, besmirched and grimy, slap them about 'til they look sufficiently shamefaced, then compare them primly to the new, morally superior '90s—a time for settling accounts and putting aside nonsense. A time, if you want to know the truth, for rebuking the evil Republicans (Reagan and Bush) and exalting the virtuous Democrats (Clinton and Gore).

My beloved profession, as I say, can't even let a wine story pass without adverse comment on the debauched decade that gave us the end of the Soviet empire and the highest economic growth since World War II. To admit successes of this sort would be to nod civilly toward supply side economics and the splendors of lower tax rates and enhanced economic incentives. It would be—still worse!—to affirm the handiwork of Ronald Reagan; to admit that this exceedingly popular president may have deserved his popularity, by achieving important things for his country and the world.

My guess is that implacable anti-Reaganism is at the bottom of the anti-'80s cult. It certainly is at the bottom of Democratic attempts during the late presidential campaign to portray the '80s as the worst economic period in our post-war history.

Worst, my hind foot! It was the best. Robert Bartley, editor of the *Wall Street Journal*, marshals the relevant statistics in his new book, "The Seven Fat Years and How to Do It Again." Fat years—in your face, Bill Clinton. Bartley shows that the 1980s were fat indeed and, what's more, good for us, the s&l disaster notwithstanding. (The disaster was needless, Bartley says; Congress insisted on protecting risky as well as sound institutions.)

Alarming, to some of us anyway, is the media's easy complicity in spreading the false legend of the 1980s. A wine story, for heaven's sake! We are to take it as gospel, on the authority of a wine writer, that the 1980s were excessive and horrible? This shows how far the debunking process has gone. It has become part of common knowledge: If you call the snide chatter of TV talk shows hosts knowledge. The politically correct response to the 1980s is a big raspberry. This our wine writer delivers as if hers were the only respectable view in the world.

Look at the careless links in her story—Michael Milkin, convicted swindler; shoulder pads; defense spending; wine prices. Everything overdone, everything reprehensible. What decade the wine writer prefers isn't clear—a bubbly, amusing little time like the 1960s, when Americans lined up against each other in the streets; the 1970s, gulch-dry, with a sour finish, when interest rates and inflation soared into the double digits and Soviet interests advanced across the planet?

We don't need to see the 1980s as vintage, because they weren't. Nor has any other decade in human history been vintage, including my beloved 1950s: tail fins, Ike, and five-cent Cokes; but also drought, polio, and communism. We fat-headed humans keep making the same mistakes, no matter what opportunities are handed us; but somehow in the 1980s we made fewer mistakes and did more things right, than in quite a long time. Including, yes, the higher defense spending that contributed to Soviet communism's collapse.

Ronald Reagan, a gifted speaker and performer, proved a gifted molder of minds and policies. His foes seek to pull him down from the lofty place he still occupies in ordinary people's hearts. I say fie. I say, as any decent wine critic would, sipping any spoilt and vinegary vintage: Burp.

November 19, 1992

The Media Strike Again

The Fourth Estate, as we used to call the press, supposedly got its name from Edmund Burke, who said its power exceeded that of the realm's traditional "estates"—church, lords, and commons. But Burke never met the massive media.

The media this week helped break up a royal marriage and covered the Marine landing in Somalia as if filming a mini-series. There's power for you: the power of the snoop, determined for commercial reasons—with maybe a soupçon of public spirit thrown in—to see all, tell all. Anything we don't see we can attribute, not to technological shortcomings, but rather to the media's lack of appreciation for the story. Pandering has been raised to an art form.

Mind: Pandering—i.e., giving people what they are believed to want, whatever it is—can be justified economically and politically. In public affairs, better too much light, the property of a democracy, than too much darkness, the property of an autocracy. But light—especially of the wattage necessary to make filming possible—can blind as well as illuminate. We sometimes see so much, we see hardly anything.

The media show what's there, but often what is there wouldn't be there except for the media. The royal breakup in England is a case in point. Bad marriages have afflicted the reigning classes in all countries, not least England, one of whose sovereigns famously took to himself six queens. There was of course no media scrutiny then. Is that an argument for encouraging it now? Before answering, try to imagine how much smoother in the present case the royal road to romance might have been if trodden far from the cameras, the outstretched mikes, the shrieking headlines.

The omnivorous British media would drive anyone nuts, including those whose job, like Charles's and Diana's, is mostly to endure the British media. This isn't to say a royal couple is without responsibility for its own happiness and health; rather, that the almost-complete loss of privacy takes its toll. The media have treated, and will probably go on treating, the Prince and Princess of Wales, not like future rulers but like chunks of red meat for hungry customers. One is all the more sympathetic with Bill Clinton's reported wish for a little privacy (though with Clinton, a born exhibitionist, you can't know if he means it).

And what about coverage of the Marine landing? No harm done perhaps, except to the dignity, if any, of the media, which needed only Cecil B. DeMille there, barking orders, establishing camera angles. An observer with a true sense of the occasion would have yelled "cut" once the beach was secured. Foreign policy was downgraded to show biz and probably will be again before the Somalian operation winds up.

True enough, the Pentagon had invited the media—obviously without anticipating how many would come and what they would do. There probably will be more restrictions in the future but not so many that the Pentagon, as during the Persian Gulf War, gets cross-wise with the media.

What do we do about any or all of this? Options in a democracy are few. We can't go around beheading cameramen and reporters or foreclosing their livelihood.

One thing we can do is to think seriously about such matters, beginning with a basic question: Why were reticence, dignity, and good taste more prevalent thirty or forty years ago than they are today? Was it for lack of the technology essential for sophisticated snooping? Or did there exist some widely held conviction that, although a free people need to know much, a sane people can't afford to know everything?

If the answer to the first question is yes, all is lost, because technology gets continuously better. However, a yes answer to the second strengthens the grounds for hope. We can look for means of restoring that lost, intensely civilized regard for reticence, dignity, and good taste. It won't be easy. One suspects that cold cash, the panderers' eternal reward, undermines privacy more thoroughly than cold technology. Where pandering pays, panderers multiply.

Pandering today pays plenty. Turn on The Box, sit back, and watch.

December 10, 1992

Madmen and Their Press Agents

One starts to wonder. Without the cameras, without the swarms of reporters and government agents, without the talk-show hosts weighing every nuance of David Koresh's ravings—without all this, would the Branch Davidian siege have turned into *Götterdämmerung*?

The chief characteristic of canny screwballs is exhibitionism. Hitler, that poised looney, had the movie cameras perpetually grinding, but he never enjoyed one advantage vouchsafed David Koresh:

instant access to the hearts and minds of the world. This, through the magic of media.

How David must have loved it—looking out the window of his jerry-built Valhalla; imagining the TV cameras; imagining his words and thoughts penetrating homes around the world. Here was power. Here was glory.

Oh, yes, he was crazy—like a fox. How many semi-educated country boys command audiences like his? Whatever he said, they wrote it down, studied and analyzed it, made it known to the world. Every detail of Koreshian theology came under scrutiny. What seminary professor has ever enjoyed such attention? What professor ever held the world hostage? Surely that's it. Day So-and-so: The World Held Hostage—by David Koresh, world-class manipulator.

The story, to be sure, was legitimate; you couldn't ignore it. The government blundered with its February foray that cost the lives of four agents. Unwittingly, the feds made David Koresh a media star and his followers a constellation. The exhibitionist had found his audience. Why, in fact, he will live on. At least two made-for-TV movies about the siege are planned; one began production some days ago in Oklahoma, the producers unsure how it would end but certain a financial bonanza awaited them.

Can it be said, then, in a metaphysical sense, that Ted Koppel and Dan Rather torched Koresh's Valhalla? Of course not; David and his poor, sad, doomed followers effected that awful result. Yet we can't ignore the baneful consequences of the new style of saturation coverage: exhausting, inexhaustible reports intended to Keep Us Informed. Lest some competing station do the honors.

All this wonderful, this historic, this transcendent capability for conveying knowledge—to the service of David Koresh it goes. But, then, we've been approaching this point for some time. The journey started in the 1960s with the student protest demonstrations. Mob leaders shrewdly realized the power that television coverage gave them, and sometimes held up the jeering and placard-waving, pending arrival of the camera crews.

Afterward, life became instant theater. Lights, camera, action! In Los Angeles a year ago, looters and murderers became stars of the extemporized television saga, "We're Mad as Hell." When the Marines landed in Somalia, the media were on the beach waiting.

News clearly must be covered. But covering it can mean playing into the hands of the exhibitionists: according them the serious attention so few really deserve. Failure to guard against this possibility distorts the viewers' understanding.

Is it that our world has gone mad, or is it that we simply think so, given the attention lavished nowadays on madmen? The normal, the reasonable, the honorable, the dignified—television has no interest in these attributes. It loves the Butta-whatever their names are, and Amy Fisher; it adores cheerleading moms who plot murder and transvestite accountants who jog with their sisters. Of course it loved, and still loves, David Koresh. David knew its love; rejoiced in it, sought to stoke it higher and higher so as to postpone the dreadful day when he, King David of the Airwaves, would be just another celebrity has-been.

What is the antidote for this our sickness? Certainly a huge dose of just those qualities television shuns: reason, dignity, love. But I have in mind also a passage from the book David Koresh made more famous than ever, the Revelation of St. John Divine, in which it is written, in the twenty-second chapter, "He which testifieth these things saith, 'Surely I come quickly.' Amen. Even so, come, Lord Jesus."

April 22, 1993

Another Newspaper Shuts Down

I had a job to come to this morning, and a place to write this, and I reflected: This was infinitely more than could be said for my brothers and sisters at the late *Dallas Times Herald*. The *Herald* expired Sunday of economic sclerosis. The funeral rites are free-form and ongoing. Indulge me while I rise from my seat with the family and claim the pulpit for a moment or two.

I sit in the family pew by virtue of long membership in the *Times Herald* alumni association. The *Herald* took me on twenty-five years ago—March 16, 1966. I stayed for seven and a half years, as, serially, oil editor/business writer, general assignments reporter, religion writer, statehouse correspondent, and editorial writer/columnist.

These were good times. The newspaper business was good, if underpaid at $135 a week. We loved what we were doing, and we loved—in that cynical, hard-boiled newspaper way of ours—each other. We were part of a great enterprise, that of telling readers what goes on, speaking secrets aloud, informing, illuminating, admonishing, castigating. I had trained in college to profess Southern history. The *Times Herald* newsroom wove its spell, and I never emerged from beneath it.

In due course, as happens with institutions, the *Herald* changed. Other doors opened. The *Dallas Morning News* graciously welcomed me into a new family, and here I have dwelt since. Yet the other day, I left my normal route in order to drive past, one more time—almost certainly the last time—the back door of the *Herald*, the door that I so often entered and exited, over so many years. I felt . . .

All right; enough snuffling. We are grown up around here. These things happen. The world goes on, and anyway I promised that my time in the pulpit would be brief. One thing more needs saying, nonetheless. It is that an unsettling trend is underway throughout society, and that this very trend contributed greatly to the *Herald*'s demise, and that the trend is increasing, not slackening, and we must do something.

People simply seem not to depend on newspapers in the degree they formerly did; indeed, they seem not to depend on the printed word—whether it is newspapers, books, or magazines—for information, edification, amusement. Or, if they do, it is for narrow purposes, as contrasted with the broad purposes served by the mass-circulation newspaper.

Circulation of printed journals rises in absolute numbers; as a proportion of total population, it declines. The printed word is—well, not dying exactly, but slipping from view. The *Times Herald* was a victim of the tendency to get one's news and views from the airwaves—or simply not to bother. We journalists are vendors of words, as St. Augustine put it; the market for our product, alas, is declining. Quickly—when was the last time you caught your teenager sprawled on his bed with a newspaper or, save the mark, a book; a book unassigned to him, a book chosen for its pleasure-giving capacities? You probably noted the occasion on the family calendar, so monumental it seemed.

Basic literacy in this, our nation, is on the wane. The problem is not the ability to read and write. The problem is the desire to do so, and the fault is—whose? Television's? The schools'? The home's? A little of each, probably. Television is everywhere, an ever-subtle temptation; the schools, in the 1960s, moved from reading and writing to experiential learning; parents probably don't adequately police the tube or enforce homework assignments. Maybe, for that matter, our product isn't all it ought to be. I don't know.

But I ask: What is more glorious than reading? Unless it is writing for reading? And what binds us more securely as a society than the printed word? The printed word is well-nigh imperishable; the spoken word is of the air itself; even taped, it loses accessibility. We have Homer's words, Virgil's words and Shakespeare's and Milton's and Mencken's and Reston's because they wrote them down, and others preserved them. Where will Ted Koppel's words end up?

Another newspaper gone and the world's supply of words correspondingly diminished. The pain is intense. We must do something. Yes, we must. But what?

December 9, 1991

Bomb the Journalism School!

The University of Michigan is dropping its masters program in journalism? The University of Washington is considering a similar move? And Ohio State? And the University of Tucson? As old Gabriel Heatter used to intone on nationwide radio, "Ah, there's good news tonight!"

The good news is that a much-needed redirection of American journalism training could be in the offing. Today's journalist, on whom the future of democracy depends, can turn a congressional debate into a pyramid-shaped story with a strong lead and snappy quotes. But has he any idea what the *Federalist Papers* contain or what caused the War Between the States? You sure can't take it for granted.

Concerning the inspiration to drop graduate journalism at Michigan U., the program director says, "It was an intellectual decision that the college should expose students to thought and not methodology." Brilliant! Why didn't someone think of this years ago? A program aimed at training journalists is about as socially useful as athlete's foot.

For a century, our academic institutions have been grinding out professional journalists, schooling them in reporting, ethics, headline writing, and a host of routine skills learnable on the job in, oh, two months. In return, we have the *National Enquirer*, *People* magazine, *Cosmopolitan*, *Soap Opera Digest* and *Geraldo*.

There's high-brow journalism, too: the *Wall Street Journal*, the *New York Times*, *National Review*, Jim Lehrer and Ted Koppel. But shallow and shoddy writing is much more the rule than the exception in modern journalism. And with journalism consisting more and more of chitchat, the tedium factor rises. We have people telling us the news who don't understand the news. They've mastered headline writing or speaking techniques when they should have been studying constitutional law or market theory.

Thus Charles A. Dana, whose *New York Sun* produced some of the nineteenth century's liveliest journalism, prescribed for his profession: "I had rather take a young fellow who knows the *Ajax* of Sophocles, and has read Tacitus, and can scan every ode of Horace— I would rather take him to report a prize-fight or a spelling match, for instance, than to take one who has never had those advantages." Why so? For the larger view, for the ability to make a prize fight or a spelling match fit its place and setting—and to recount it with clarity and economy.

However, there's a larger truth in all this. It is that would-be journalists are far from alone when it comes to snubbing liberal education. That's American higher education for you—the clipping and snipping of broad disciplines to specialty length, and the emphasis on careerism as opposed to knowledge.

Teachers learn to teach by taking education courses, prospective businessmen study finance, and future farmers and ranchers take "ag" courses.

It's the natural thing, you say. Well, sure. It's also sterile, time-wasting, and socially fragmenting. We've created a world of specialists: Everyone remains in his own niche, knowing hardly anything about anyone else's niche or about the sweep and the majesty of our culture.

What to do with journalism schools? Abolish them all. Pension off the faculties, and put would-be journalists to work studying history, literature, political philosophy, and economics. And the *Ajax* of Sophocles. Teach routine skills in summer on-the-job programs.

What to do with colleges of education? Fit them up with dynamite. Warn away innocent bystanders. Sow the sites with salt. Immerse prospective teachers in the subjects they intend to teach, not omitting history, literature, etc., etc. Inculcate in them love of the subjects—and a burning desire to communicate that love.

Schools of medicine? Wait. You can carry a good thing too far. A specialty dedicated to keeping us breathing requires specialized knowledge. But someone remind Doc occasionally to plug in a tape of the *Federalist Papers*—just in case Ira Magaziner gets another high government job.

October 30, 1995

Wanted: Blatant Censorship

An industry-initiated system for rating television? Never mind what the television industry announced the other day at a White House meeting. That's not how TV programs deserve to be rated.

Here's how TV programs deserve to be rated:

"Mom, I'm going to the den to watch *Let It All Hang Out.*"

"You're going to watch *what?*"

"*Let It All Hang Out.* It's cool. All my friends watch it."

"Your friends aren't members of this family. I don't care for that kind of program. My goodness, if you're going to waste your time watching television, let's watch something fit to be watched."

"But Mom . . ."

"But nothing!"

Blatant censorship—that's what we need. By parents.

Yes, I know. All together now: "This Isn't the 1950s Any More!"

There are no mothers wearing pearls and high heels as they sweep the floor. Robert Young and Jane Wyatt are dethroned as our parental role models.

This is in part a function of divorce and family breakup. It is in still larger measure a function of the broad decline of standards throughout the whole of society. The old no-nos, the traditional concepts of right and wrong no longer win the unreserved admiration of our authority figures—such as they are. Network presidents, in the old days, would have been lynched for some of the fare that today raises scarcely an eyebrow. No, this isn't the 1950s anymore.

But one thing is the same: Parents still are parents—givers of life, nurturers of norms. The fact that a parent doesn't want such a job is no reason to excuse him from it. That's what parents do—teach standards, *their* standards.

They teach what *this* family—not Joe's or Susie's family, but this one—does.

Of the TV industry figures who pledged at the White House to develop a voluntary ratings system, President Bill Clinton said: "They're handing the TV remote control back to America's parents."

Horse feathers! America's parents hold the remote control already. They just don't always choose to use it with vigor and authority.

That's a sympathetic statement, by the way. These are tough times for parents as I should know, being the father of two high school students. The parental voice, in these fallen times, no longer rings through the house with magisterial authority. When it tries to, back comes the righteous rejoinder: "Oh, come on, Dad, get real." Which is just for starters.

On television-watching, there have been pallid compromises at the Murchison household—some giving here, some giving there—in the interest of arrangements that work more or less to the benefit of all. The children watch the sometimes subversive but always clever program *The Simpsons*, and on other occasions, the set goes off when language or situations become too graphic.

It's not the bald, unapologetic censorship our own parents would have exercised in the 1950s, but, then, need I say it again, this isn't the 1950s. You do what you can and hope for the best.

The point is that there are no adequate substitutes for families, working together in love and mutual concern. Not the benevolent world of commercial television. Not even the White House.

How do we really, truly, convincingly reform television? The means are at hand. I am not talking about the power button on the remote control. The minute—the split second—the families of America decide that we deserve the guidance and scrutiny of abiding moral norms, the TV problem will take care of itself.

Why does television push the envelope? Because a society receptive to illegitimacy, abortion-on-demand, drug-taking, and moral laziness of every description has been pushing the envelope. Popular entertainment doesn't exist in a vacuum: It reflects as well as creates. What it reflects isn't very edifying, but whose fault is that if not our own? When we're ready for something radically different, you can go to the bank on our getting it.

March 4, 1996

From Bach to Bochco

Inevitably, the *NYPD Blue* fracas turned up on Phil Donahue the other day. In fact the cast turned up en masse in order to tell the world what a superb contribution to television drama is this new frank, candid, a-bit-of-nudity-here, a-lot-of-obscenity-there effort from Steve Bochco of *L.A. Law* fame.

"It's an intelligent and adult drama we feel proud of," said the cast member with the bald head and mustache. Minutes earlier, in a sequence from the program, he had been depicted grabbing the, ah, area between his legs and uttering a phrase that the prudish producers of the Donahue show saw fit to bleep out.

"It's realistic, is the point," said Phil, as if that explained everything.

Another cast member—this one a woman—chimed in: "It's real, it's happening."

Oh, it's happening all right. We get more "adult" every year. Why, we're growing up so fast, becoming so big and mature, we'll be ready in a few years for the cultural twilight home.

From the hot letters concerning censors and blue-nosed Puritans and all the other phonies Phil despises, I gather much of America is ready for *NYPD Blue* and its vaunted "realism."

We're frank, we're bold, we're free, and television delights in showing us so. There's just one question, says the pundit in the derby hat and celluloid collar: Should we be proud of it? We're to pin a medal on Brother Bochco for showing us that life is grimy? Certainly it's grimy. Do we like it that way? Shall we let it get grimier and grimier until, beneath all the filth, no one can recognize any longer the race (viz., human) that produced Michelangelo and Mozart and Augustine and Dante?

From Bach to Bochco—what a civilizational journey. It makes you want to peel a banana and scratch. Maybe swing by your tail from a tree.

It's real, it's happening, and so is our cultural descent, step by relentless step. We've gone in thirty years from actors who acted like people to actors who, considering what they do on-screen, would seem more at home in a nice zoological garden. Movies began their own descent, circa 1968. Television, a primmer medium, joined in more recently, with sitcoms heavy on sexual innuendo. Now, with *NYPD Blue,* the mask of innuendo falls! Reality shines forth! Oooooooooh, baby!

A woman in Donahue's audience voiced in a hopeful way the view that characters on television should serve as role models for our children. A cast member replied, no, that's not what we're up there for, and the celluloid pundit replies: Right. Up to a point.

Literature and drama *do* exemplify life. There are two ways of doing so. One is holding up the good (virtue, justice, courage, etc.) for admiration and imitation. The second is holding up the crude and raunchy and questionable—a canvas of scrawls and dark colors—refusing proudly to contrast it *unfavorably* with the good.

The problem with *NYPD Blue* is a civilizational problem—a regnant cynicism about good and bad, beauty and ugliness, truth and falsehood; an inability not just to distinguish between such opposites but even to admit the possibility of a distinction. Call a bad thing bad? Not in this fine, egalitarian age where we are ever voting our preferences, with ballots or TV knobs, and what counts isn't the outcome, merely the voting. On this squishy, squashy ground, Brothers Bocho and Donahue stand tall, for the moment.

What makes the "NYPD" debate so odd a thing is the background: the shrieks of murder victims and sobs of pregnant teenagers; guns on school campuses; child abuse; abortion for any reason or no reason; Dr. Kevorkian. Reality? Here it is. You'd think at this time of crisis our artists would like to show us the alternatives—good people doing good things, as living commentary on the bad. Nope, the artists, the TV-talk show hosts, wallow happily in the mud, oinking at those who dare suggest man has a higher destiny than grabbing himself below the belt, blurting out a word too strong—at the moment—for Phil Donahue's show.

October 11, 1993

Real Elitists

Former Education Secretary William Bennett's frontal assault on trash-talk television ticked off—surprise—the trash-talk hosts. These see themselves as prospective victims of a Puritan backlash.

Sally Jessy Raphael was particularly exasperated. "It's a real elitist view," she said, "for a guy like this to stand up and say, 'I don't think 4.5 million people should watch this.'" Geraldo Rivera, unwilling to tout his endeavor as *Masterpiece Theater* for the blue collars, nevertheless allowed he didn't need the help or advice of outsiders like Bennett and the two co-leaders of his highly publicized endeavor, Connecticut Senator Joe Lieberman and civil-rights activist C. Delores Tucker.

The purpose of the endeavor: cleaning up daytime TV through pressure on networks and sponsors. If enough viewers complain—so Bennett & Co. reason—sponsors may withdraw their support or the network, to head off such a prospect, will decree kinder, cleaner programming. No more "Women Who Use Men for Sex," "Woman's

Fiance Lives a Secret Life," or "Love Triangles" (a selection from the November 2 line-up).

The same clean-up crew worked with impressive effect to chasten gargantuan Time Warner, one of whose subsidiaries distributed "gangsta rap" videos and CDs that were filthy-mouthed, raging with malice toward policemen and contempt for women. Time Warner, rather than stick up for debasement, sold its stake in the label.

What have a best-selling author, a politician, and a battler for civil rights got against the television networks' right to sell lust and degradation—and against our freedom to choose such commodities?

Let's put the question another way. What are the consequences of television's pandering to the baser human instincts? They can't be nice consequences. One I can think of is the implantation of a thought: Hey! There's a lot of fun stuff going on out there, and I'm missing out. As the "fun" stuff consists of adultery, illegitimacy, incest, and the like, the last thing we need is more dabblers. There are enough expert practitioners as it is.

Moreover, if we are what we eat, so we also are what we enjoy. Squalor can make us squalid. It's like living at the base of a trash heap. After a while, you think that's how the world is.

The argument against that proposition comes from those who insist that in life, everything is just about equal. One man's squalor is another one's turn-on. Which may be true, but it doesn't render squalor and degradation the moral equivalents of love and honor and beauty. One problem here is that modern society is afraid to make such a bald declaration. Say that one thing—particularly one "lifestyle"—is better, righter, or truer than another, and you get in trouble fast. You are backward. You are repressive. You probably want to support Bennett and Lieberman and Tucker.

As a matter of fact, I do, and we all should. Not with the expectation that their battle against one spectrum of programming in one (albeit highly influential) medium is going to prove pivotal in the culture wars. But you have to start somewhere. Bless their hearts, Bennett, Lieberman, and Tucker are starting on high ground.

Are they also engaging in that most un-twentieth-century pastime, censorship? Censorship is what governments practice. Official suppression of free speech—if you call "Love Triangles" speech—isn't the issue here. Marketplace action is: Pick up the phone, write a letter, complain, urge, picket, boycott. No one in his right mind could gainsay that this, too, is free speech—in at least as exalted a form as that practiced by Sally Jessy Raphael.

Yes, certainly, the Bennett-Lieberman-Tucker objective is to inhibit what might be called viewing choice. Fine—provided the choice in question degrades, debases, incites. Maybe Sally Jessy can show us why "Transvestites Who Marry Their First Cousins" is essential entertainment. It's her American right to do so. And wouldn't it be fun watching her try?

November 2, 1995

XII

Freaks of Culture

WE ARE ALL NUTTY to one degree or another, I have concluded after a few decades of intensive observation. What else should we expect if the scriptural account of original sin is accurate—as I believe it to be? If I point out others' problems, I hope I do not imply that "others" are the only ones with problems!

The Great American Meatout

This is for the perpetrators of the Great American Meatout. Generaled by Doris Day and Caesar Chavez, these advanced social thinkers request abstention from beef today, in favor of "a less violent, more wholesome diet": bean curd, I suppose, topped off with alfalfa sprouts.

What a good day, it strikes me, for a juicy hamburger with onions!

For supper, I may follow up with a rib-eye steak and a baked potato.

If I smoked—which I never have and never will—I would top off the experience by inhaling two or three of the most odoriferous cigars procurable on the open market. If I owned an Uzi sub-machine gun—which, again, I never have and never will—I would prop it by my plate, maybe taking the opportunity to perforate the walls, Sherlock Holmes-like, with patriotic motifs.

Anything to aggravate the new Puritans, I always say.

Politics, which formerly was confined to matters governmental, is creeping incrementally into the shrinking sphere of private life

and action. People are trying to change those who, in their own refined view, need changing.

The new Puritanism—anti-meat, anti-fur, anti-tobacco, anti-gun,
and all the rest—marches in the same joyless parade as the Political
Correctness movement on college campuses (anti-racism, anti-sex-
ism, anti-lookism, anti-ableism). We, the unenlightened, are invited
to salute as their fashionable concerns pass in review.

Granted, it is common sense that certain things visibly hurt us
and should therefore by shunned. Drugs kill. Child pornography
degrades subject and viewer alike. But a Big Mac, for the love of
Allah! A Whopper-cut-the-onions-heavy-on-the-mayo!

Homer, Dante, Bach, Babe Ruth, and John Wayne ate meat. Who
are the Meatout people, in the face of this definitive experience, to
interpose their peculiar insights? (Sample: "The holocaust of animal
agriculture goes on every minute of every day of every year. The
four 'horsemen' of this latter-day apocalypse are: animal suffering,
diet-induced chronic disease, world hunger and devastation of natural resources.")

The new Puritanism is pushy and bumptious. We are going to
reform smokers and gun owners by legislation, fur-coat wearers by
ridicule, beer drinkers by "sin taxes," drivers of large automobiles by
increased levies on gasoline. We are going to make them pure and
righteous. In other words, we are going to make them like *us*.

Who thinks these things up? The upper middle classes prima-
rily: the people with college-derived verbal skills and fax machines.
Many of them work in my own profession, the mass media. They
may not understand real life, but they sure know PR.

The new Puritanism amounts to class warfare levied against the
uncultivated, the insensitive, the boorish—people who look like Rush
Limbaugh and think like Jesse Helms.

Our perfervid class warriors don't have much good to say about
free-market processes. Which isn't too surprising. The free market
lets people choose freely—to gobble a hamburger, say, in preference

to a raw carrot; to shoot birds rather than watch them. Obviously, we must shame and hector these people into doing the right thing. That is what events like the Meatout are designed to accomplish.

The most fascinating datum about the new Puritanism is its secularity. It concerns itself, not with souls—that was the old Puritan's obsession—but with bodies. The only sins today are sins against the body.

Don't talk about damnation and redemption—which fashionable people don't believe in anyway; talk instead about cruelty to rattlesnakes. What use harps and golden streets, when the wetlands are perishing?

The timing of Miss Day's Meatout—the fifth week of Lent—is particularly poignant. In Christian tradition, Lent, the period of preparation for Easter, is adorned by acts of voluntary self-denial; acts that may include abstention from meat. However, this is for purely spiritual reasons. What's the life of the spirit got to do with sticking it to the cattle raisers, the sheepherders and the Golden Arches crowd?

Not much, to tell you the truth—which is one of the nicer things we may have heard lately about the life of the spirit.

March 20, 1991

Morally Concerned Artists

Get out the handkerchiefs and smelling salts for the doleful tale of Karen Finley, "morally concerned artist," to borrow her self-description.

A federal grant to Miss Finley had been approved by a peer panel of the National Endowment for the Arts, but higher authorities within NEA vetoed the grant. "I am suffering," Miss Finley told a New York audience of public and cultural figures. "A year ago I was in a country of freedom and expression; now I am not." She dissolved into tears. Then the audience began to cheer her sallies against censorship. In short order, reports the *New York Times*, Miss Finley was "laughing boisterously and shouting at the top of her lungs."

Would you like a single argument for abolition of the National Endowment for the Arts? There it is. The cultural establishment can't be trusted to know arts from warts.

The "Art" of Karen Finley consists of appearing on stage in her birthday suit, over which she smears chocolate and bean sprouts; there's also some business with vegetables, "which Miss Finley inserts into her body," as the *Wall Street Journal* delicately phrases it.

This is "Art"? This is what the cultural community thinks American taxpayers should pay for? If Miss Finley is an artist, then I am a Wagnerian *heldentenor*, and would the taxpayers please indulge my desire to sing *Siegfried* at the Met?

Congress next week takes up the much-vexed question of what to do about the National Endowment for the Arts—extend it without changes, restrict its ability to make controversial grants, or abolish it outright. A heated debate is assured during the sultry weeks ahead. We will be reading again and again about "morally concerned" artists like Karen Finley.

On the one hand, it will be said, see, we can trust the NEA to defend the public interest in moral art. Did not the NEA thrust Miss Finley and three other underground artists away from the public feeding trough?

On the other hand, it can be said, look, Miss Finley's peers seem generally agreed that her act is swell, and that the taxpayers should finance it. "This is a battle for the soul of America," says New York City's cultural affairs commissioner. "We need the peripheries of art," declares Joseph Papp of the New York Shakespeare Festival. "It's like the shoreline of this country. We need this!"

Oh? Just why do we need Miss Finley and her bean sprouts? And, equally to the point, what's this "we" business? Who presumes to address so authoritatively the American people's cultural needs?

Why, the cultural establishment does. For the benefit of the great unwashed—you and me—the Truly Cultured will spaciously define "culture," disclosing to us which activities should be financed by government, and which should not be.

I have a better idea. Let the unwashed—a.k.a. the everyday taxpaying citizens—decide for themselves what cultural events are truly worthwhile. Let them decide by buying tickets to this or that event, or donating money to this or that institution. Joe Doaks doesn't toil at the feed store or the backhoe so that curvaceous (let us hope) Miss Karen Finley may demonstrate the artistic possibilities inherent in bean sprouts and vegetables.

A cultural establishment unable to see the difference between Miss Finley's right to dance and the taxpayer's right not to subsidize her is an establishment sorely confused, seriously adrift from traditional moorings. Why take any more chances with these people, who have so many arresting ways of spending our money?

Defenders of "culture" sometimes respond that *they* don't like supporting the Pentagon, but just as the government makes them support it, so the rest of us should be made to support their interests.

That ole dog won't hunt, as we cultured Central Texans say. Defense is the basic responsibility of any government, and is constitutionally mandated; support of the arts is, at best, a tangential function.

Representative Dana Rohrabacher of California has a bill to abolish the NEA outright. Congress probably lacks courage to do anything so sensible, but certain aesthetic possibilities suggest themselves.

As twilight fell upon the National Endowment for the Arts, Karen Finley, with chocolate, bean sprouts, and vegetables, could ceremonially dance farewell to the cultural free lunch.

That, I might subsidize myself.

July 14, 1990

The Man Who Never Heard of Longfellow

One hears about student test scores starting to rise from the basement floor. But one hears meanwhile about Mark Holmes's noticing the signature "H.W. Longfellow" on a manuscript inside a frame bought at a Houston garage sale—noticing it, then saying blankly to himself something on the order of, "Who's this Longfellow?"

"I wasn't familiar with him," Holmes told a wire-service reporter. He called a library. Any books on a dude named Longfellow? He called a University of Houston English professor. "Have you ever heard of Longfellow?" the professor recalls Holmes asking her. Would you believe it? She had. The manuscript is a working copy of "The Village Blacksmith"—probably the copy submitted to the magazine that published it in 1840. Holmes plans to auction it off. He has been encouraged to believe Ol' What's His Name might have enough residual fame to command seven thousand dollars.

The story relating Holmes's serendipitous find doesn't mention where he went to high school. No matter. You can probably go to most American high schools these days and escape serious acquaintance with Henry Wadsworth Longfellow, among numerous other ex-greats.

A hidebound, hard-bitten old pundit recollects from his own school days, back in the fifteenth century, that Longfellow was an inescapable deity. In Corsicana Junior High School, under the tutelage of Mrs. Geraldine Johnston, we not only studied "Evangeline," we cut up the *Saturday Evening Post* in order to illustrate notable passages therefrom. Passages like: "This is the forest primeval/The murmuring pines and the hemlocks."

Ol' What's His Name was deemed a rich source for student memorization — not least because he was something of an exhorter, always telling the reader to get up, get going, work hard, keep his nose clean. In "A Psalm of Life" he enjoined:

> *Let us then be up and doing*
> *With a heart for any fate;*
> *Still achieving, still pursuing,*
> *Learn to labor and to wait.*

"The Rainy Day" instructed:

> *Be still sad heart and cease repining*
> *Behind the clouds is the sun still shining*
> *Thy fate is the common fate of all*
> *Into each life some rain must fall*
> *Some days must be dark and dreary.*

"The Village Blacksmith," so unfamiliar to Master Mark Holmes, told the tale of a man who would have eaten red-hot coals as soon as a government-subsidized meal:

> *His brow is wet with honest sweat*
> *He earns whate'er he can,*
> *And looks the whole world in the face,*
> *For he owes not any man.*

Imagine moral earnestness of this caliber firing up the modern educational establishment, whose affection for dead white males like Longfellow isn't strong to begin with!

In the olden days, such considerations hadn't arisen. The poetry of Longfellow was a vital organ in the corpus of American literature. The schools would no more have let us escape knowing him, if only in bits and pieces, than they would have spared us the multiplication tables and the Declaration of Independence. Certain things you had to know because you had to. Such as:

> *Listen, my children, and you shall hear*
> *Of the midnight ride of Paul Revere*
> *On the eighteenth of April in Seventy-Five;*
> *Hardly a man is now alive*
> *Who remembers that famous day and year.*

In twenty or thirty years, if the educational system doesn't get a grip on itself, hardly a man will be alive who remembers those pulsating lines, far less their author, Ol' What's His Name.

Not that poetry, as Senator Bob Dole reminded us in his recent front-page jab at Hollywood, is dying out. There's always the rapper Tupac Shakur, in "Strugglin'": "I'd rather use my gun 'cause I get the money quicker . . . got them in the frame—Bang! Bang! Blowing (expletive) to the moon."

Oh, Tupac, what lyricism, what expression! There must be academics around who are ready to embed such luminous lines in the curriculum. Quite a job their type has done already in embalming writers who wrote with a vividness and inspiration we once supposed would live forever. Ol' What's His Name has, if nothing else, plenty of distinguished company in academic limbo.

June 5, 1995

Of Tortillas and Experts

The assorted snobs, busybodies, and killjoys who make careers out of running other people's lives have struck again. The target this time is Mexican food, which, according to the Center for Science in the Public Interest, is a mass of fat and sodium waiting to rise up and slay us all.

The center, a Washington, D.C., outfit, is best known for its recent assault on Killer Popcorn, which, in movie theater versions, was deemed unacceptably high in fat. Chinese and Italian restaurants have also tasted the center's wrath.

Among the Mexican food findings:

1. An order of chile rellenos gives the diner a day and a half's worth of fat.

2. Cheese quesadillas with sour cream, pico de gallo, and guacamole are laden with nine hundred calories, fifty-nine grams of fat, and 1,628 milligrams of sodium.

3. A half day's worth of salt comes with every savory basket of hot tortilla chips—not counting the sauce.

The center's researchers waggle their fingers like Puritans in the pulpit. Sinners, repent! Leave off from fat! Henceforth eat low-salt, low-fat, low-calorie enchiladas!

Is the center's fat-sodium analysis wrong? Probably not. A scientist presumably can count calories. What rankles is when the scientist puts down his test tube and starts telling the rest of us what to do with our lives. Modern Americans rarely permit clergymen to do any such thing. Why do they take it from scientists?

It isn't enough for the killjoys to publish their findings and invite professional agreement. They have to hold preachy press conferences, instructing us with white-coated solemnity that the things we like, we really shouldn't like. They appear to enjoy scaring the bejabbers out of us, these Lugosis of the lab.

If they were right, that might be one thing; but hardly do they form a consensus before it shifts and buckles. Thus eggs, a few years back, were said to be our ruination; millions quit, or cut back, on eating them. This was until Further Research revealed that eggs are in various ways good for us. The same with whole milk, a onetime menace now enjoying restoration to favor. Butter, for all the bad PR it has received, now is seen as more useful in some ways than that awful stuff, margarine.

Not the least problem here is taste. Fat makes things taste good. The experts don't worry about sensuous enjoyment. They'd rather we wrinkled our noses at the table than smiled with delight over a buttered baked potato.

The killjoys seem to believe in a single rule for everybody: this dish good, that one bad in all circumstances, for all people. Yet even in the scientific community there is not just one school of thought on food. For instance, can you salutarily knock off a couple of glasses of wine with dinner? Some scientists say, yes, please do; others say, no, certainly not. Moreover, (fortunately!) we're not all made the same internally. What one diner can't accommodate, another tucks into rapaciously. Every consumer of food is entitled to judge his own needs, heedless of persnickety experts.

You can of course thumb your nose—and fork—at the experts, but thereupon they encourage you to feel guilty. They would have you know that, when you insist on the immemorial culinary preferences of your ancestors, such as butter, whole milk, salted popcorn, enchiladas, you're digging your grave. Well, think of it—aren't your ancestors dead?

We're an odd people in some ways, we Americans. Liberty we profess to prize; but then we cede large portions of that very freedom to experts who lecture and browbeat us. An expert who tells us fire burns, water drowns, knives cut—fine. But experts who take cocksure stands on what's good for us are as useful as beer mugs in a Baptist pantry. Pass the tortilla chips, please.

July 28, 1994

Woodstock Revisited

Are all us old coots who vividly remember the Woodstock Music Festival turned on about its twenty-fifth anniversary? Why, sonny, we're so turned on—a few of us at least—we'd just as soon lie down 'til it all goes away.

Among this summer's quarter-century observances, including the moon landing and Ted Kennedy's nocturnal dip at Dyke Bridge, Woodstock deserves status as the ultimate bad trip. Not so much, perhaps, for what it was as for what its propagandists made it seem.

If, as at Woodstock, four hundred thousand young Americans want to wallow in the mud, smoke pot, listen to rock music, and unreservedly express their sexual yearnings, why, Western civilization can survive. Provided we don't, as with Woodstock, credulously receive the event itself as the replacement model for Western civilization.

The legend of Woodstock, much more than the reality, damaged us all, and our society. The legend was of liberation and its manifold possibilities. "Overcoming conditions that could conventionally be described only as disastrous," writes Allen J. Matusow, "the crowd (at Woodstock) created a loving community based on drugs, sex, and rock music."

Observe the oddness of this juxtaposition. A community. Based on drugs. Based on sex. Based on rock music. Where is the community? The purpose of drug use is release from communitarian restraint. The sex of Woodstock was, of course, the "free" sex so highly touted in the 1960s—free of commitment, indiscriminate in expression. Where is the community here? "Rock and roll," Matusow writes, in *The Unraveling of America*, "was the principal art of the counterculture because of its demonstrable power to liberate the instincts." Liberation again. Where is the community?

The Woodstock "community" of legend fell apart when the rain-soaked fields dried out. The civilized community the counterculture despised so intensely received near-mortal wounds from the frenzy that was the late 1960s.

Did this make Woodstock the central event of the 1960s? By no means. The old social order of Casey Stengel, Norman Vincent Peale, and *I Love Lucy* was weakening anyway: the call to community growing feebler, the summons to individual expression (à la Jack Kerouac, Elvis Presley, Andy Warhol, and James Dean) growing more powerful all the time. The legend of Woodstock no more than hastened the crash of the old order.

Today's maladies and pathologies followed in sequence. No more rules anymore? No divine presence enjoining on humanity the behavior consistent with their humanness? Wheeeeee! And a long slide it's been, to the disordered jumble we call modern life, where we answer every day, it seems, the jangling call to self-expression, self-exaltation.

The Woodstockians—or anyway their self-anointed spokesmen—preached a creed for which flesh-and-blood humans have proved remarkably unsuited. The one rule the rule-breakers can't repeal is that actions have consequences. The exaltation of drugs created a culture of drug dependency; sad victims of the 1960s, or the culture the 1960s engendered, stand on street corners with hand-lettered signs advertising not their freedom but their dependency.

The cost of "free" sex has not been fully tallied. The surge in illegitimacy is part of it; the surge of divorce; the scourge of AIDS; the breakdown in trust between men and women.

The explosion of crime is part of it. What you feel like doing, you do—right? If not, why not, when the rule is, no rules.

It all could be foreseen at the time. It *was* foreseen. Voices were raised in protest. The wind carted them away and scattered them. A new age was aborning at Woodstock, we heard: the Age of Aquarius. It was not the first instance of premeditated hype and cultural salesmanship, nor the last. And it goes on, this oversell of a garish event hardly anyone today would remember but for the oversell of twenty-five years ago. The event *is* worth remembering, profoundly so—but not for what we're likely to hear as the hype merchants coax from the nostalgia machine the comforting sounds they desire.

August 4, 1994

Christians and Pagans

As the second millennium of the Christian era winds down, paganism reanimates itself, rises, stretches, takes a few wobbly but thoroughly unapologetic steps. The pagans don't call themselves pagans. But that's what they are.

Take the recent account of a large conference in Minneapolis titled "RE-imagining." What is being "re-imagined"? Why, nothing much—just Christian belief. According to the account, "Participants called on ancient religious customs outside the Christian tradition, broke into a spontaneous celebration of lesbians and cheered the unilateral (if unofficial) renaming of a mainline denomination."

The denomination is the Church of the Brethren, and if you don't appreciate the scandal such a name causes, well, brother, you've been asleep for about two decades. Offended by the blatant sexism of "Brethren," the sistren came up with a substitute name—Church of Reconciliation.

In the same spacious spirit, the conferees decided to junk the Trinitarian formula of Father, Son, and Holy Ghost. "Bless Sophia/ Dream the vision/Share the wisdom/Dwelling deep within," they chanted. Sophia means divine wisdom, which is fine; Constanti-nople's great Christian church was Saint Sophia. One would like to know, even so, how the Doctrine of the Trinity became an irrel-evancy. The male thing, right?—Father and Son. Apparently we can't have that any more than we can have traditional Christian moral belief, where such belief impinges on, ah, self-expression. If Chris-tian morality puts down noncelibate lesbianism, we'll simply "cel-ebrate the mystery of being lesbian, Christian and out together."

An aberration of the Frozen North, these Minnesota goings-on? By no means. The attentive reader of religious news finds this sort of thing happening everywhere. In good old conservative Dal-las, just a few months back, there was another such conference. Among the propositions voiced: "There is really no sin. . . . We can never know God. . . . It is blasphemy to call God 'He'. . . . Women have trouble with the Trinity. We need to soften the edges of the triangle to make a circle." Symbols of Hinduism and witchcraft adorned this supposedly Christian affair.

The force behind the new paganism is feminism, which so far lacks the courage to admit what is afoot—not the opening up of Christianity but its shutting down in behalf of subjective, feel-good theology. The old Christianity emphasized repentance and confes-sion of sin, followed by forgiveness and reconciliation; it downplayed the self, that dirty little noun employed as a prefix in so many disagreeable contexts: self-worship, self-aggrandizement, self-deceit, self-betrayal. The new paganism, by contrast, adores the self—and the selfish. As between me and thee, Mac, are you trying to tell me there's a choice!

It comes at an odd time, this pagan resurgence, and maybe not so odd at that. Odd, because a burned-out, run-down secular society, one that views sex as something you do with condoms and crime as the outcome of social frustration—this society can't handle its own problems. The time for a little pre-pagan repentance might seem to be at hand. Yet isn't the spirit of the new paganism—the spirit of self-worship—the very hallmark of this age?

Who's surprised really to see perpetrated in religious circles the same dreary self-delusions that drag down the secular society? Such as the delusion that religion itself is exclusively a personal thing, the creation of individuals, no authenticity of its own, nothing to do with civil society, and—wait! That man over there! What's he doing? *Ohmigod*, he's praying on public property! Quick, call the cops! Alert the ACLU!

So it goes in the pagan era, as we may come to denominate the 1990s and who-knows-what beyond that? You have to say one thing for the new paganism: It's cheap. No bejeweled idols to go visit on stated occasions, no costly incense to hurl into the fire. All the new paganism demands is a mirror; and, of course, a good overhead light helps, too.

November 17, 1993

Cool, Hip Virgins

At a football stadium in Denton, Texas, thirty-five thousand young men brave a fierce thunderstorm as they affirm their commitment to postponing sex until marriage. And a week or so later comes a *New York Times* story noting that—wait, sit down, it is possible you are not ready for this—virginity is "cool."

Cool here and there, anyway. Often enough, and in a sufficiently large number of venues, to attract the notice of the media.

Says the *Times* story: "The *idea* that virginity is in some sense hip is spreading through popular culture." A producer for the *Geraldo* show says: "Virginity has become the new sexuality." Television shows feature virginal characters, including Donna Martin on the ultra-cool *Beverly Hills 90210*. The author of a new book on love, Diane Ackerman, acknowledges that "it's definitely hip to be 'safe' and healthy."

There are even "reborn virgins." These are people who didn't actually wait but now wish they had, and so have recommitted themselves to the principle.

What goes on, a religious revival? Not entirely. No single motive can ever be ascribed to thousands and thousands of humans, functioning for the most part independently of each other. A variety of compulsions seems at work. The sexual revolution, having leveled every conceivable barrier to "fulfillment," would seem nearly to have run its course. Its debris—especially AIDS and teenage pregnancies—is calamitous. The point no sexual revolutionary can evade is that prior to the revolution, no one had heard of AIDS; as for the teenage pregnancy rate (according to William J. Bennett's indispensable *Index of Leading Cultural Indicators*, it was only 5.3 percent in 1960, vs. 29.5 percent, and rising, in 1991. A generation that has trouble with the dates of World War II may have discovered that, without sex, you don't get pregnant unless you're the Virgin Mary—an unlikely eventuality.

Practical arguments for abstinence, such as the above, are seen as non-religious in nature. But this, so to speak, is to misconceive. The religious commandment of chastity is not an abstraction—some airy-fairy declaration dropped from the clouds in order to make life closer and tighter. The commandment speaks, rather, to the human condition. It says, this is who you are (i.e., children of God); this is what you therefore have to do (i.e., keep the gift, for its own sake, whole and unsullied).

The perception that abuse of the body hurts the body (and often enough the spirit) isn't theology proper; what it is, is the intimation of a destiny transcending the hasty satisfaction of momentary urges and appetites. By such avenues the traveler passes—if he is of such a mind—to theology and the churches and the sacraments.

Or, again, perhaps not. The "coolness" of virginity is an ancient insight (as is the perennial temptation of lust). In all cultures, Christian or pagan, indiscriminate sex—sex whenever, wherever, with whoever—weakens and compromises such relationships as it doesn't sabotage outright.

The relationship between man and woman—the most delicate thing there is, based more than anything else on trust and sacrifice—presupposes commitment. This is what marriage is about—commitment; the fine, intricate web of promises and undertakings; "for better for worse, for richer for poorer." "Sexual freedom"—which proves in practice more to resemble slavery than freedom—undermines prospects for commitment. It puts the glint in the roving eye, elevates internal satisfaction over external responsibility. Mick Jagger can't get "no satisfaction"? Good. The big baboon is looking in all the wrong places.

Naturally, it could be just the latest fad, this virgin business: today's Transactional Analysis. But somehow one doubts that. It looks—thirty-five thousand people in the rain at the Promise Keepers rally!—to be the leading edge of the counterrevolution. The 1960s, and their sordid handiwork, are at grave risk. And isn't it a lovely, lovely thought!

June 20, 1994

Collective Necrophilia

So it's thirty years since The Assassination. Goody. And in 2003, it'll be forty years. And in 2013, we mark the golden anniversary.

Those of us with personal memories of the occasion can hobble in our walkers down to the Grassy Knoll and recount the shock, the horror of November 22, 1963.

And will we be better off for this, our extended memory wallow—a wiser people, more content, more at peace? Not with our gray cells in chronological gridlock.

Scarcely the least or slightest evidence of late twentieth-century America's cultural decline is its infantile obsession with the last half-century of its past: above all, with the Kennedy assassination, which we see somehow as the defining event of our times.

Our obsession is morbid—necrophilic, almost. Just what is it about this need to review and assess, over and over and over again, our relationship with a dead president, our feelings about him, The Difference he made to us, or didn't make? What's it all got to do with the price of eggs? Our living nation, rather than haunt the cemetery every November 22, in a sort of post-Halloween orgy, needs to bury the past and move forward. John Fitzgerald Kennedy's dreams and schemes are of infinitely less consequence to us than is the socialized medicine plan touted by the incumbent president who attributes to JFK's example his own fascination with electoral politics.

And yet how typical, this lugubriousness—typical, I mean, of our present culture, which seems bent on reliving the good old days rather than doing anything concrete about the bad new ones.

I've never heard of a society as obsessed with the recent past as is this one. Reverence for one's forbears, and especially their principles of thought and action, is meet right and our bounden duty. "They will not look forward to their posterity," Edmund Burke instructs us, "who will not look backward to the ancestors."

Very well. Reverence, all the same, doesn't mean suspension of creative faculties. The continuity between the 1960s and the 1990s, culturally speaking, is extraordinary. Ancient—meaning they are my own age—rock stars still bestride the stage. Hollywood revives antediluvian TV series like *The Fugitive* and *The Beverly Hillbillies* as movies, on the assumption that's what we want to see. Television itself stages reunions of characters from long-dead series—one more chance to replay the jokes we used to laugh at, the situations that caused us to produce Kleenex and dab at our eyes. Radio stations blare the Golden Oldies. Whop-bop-a-lu-bop.

Meanwhile, no literature of any significance gets written. *The Bridges of Madison County*, for Hemingway's sake! This is what turns us on? Quick, name a modern poet. A composer, then. A sculptor? Any visionary will do in these culturally straitened circumstances.

Fresh out of ideas, we live by the only ideas we know of in this post-literate age—those we remember at firsthand. Kennedy. Camelot. The counterculture. Elvis. The Beatles. Billy Graham, age seventy-five this month, marches on, no successor in sight.

Even our political heroes have a musty fragrance. Clinton apes Kennedy. No black leader of Martin Luther King's stature has emerged since King's murder. Margaret Thatcher, plugging her political memoirs, excites admiration partly because of her moral resemblance to Winston Churchill.

We're due—overdue—a cultural renaissance. It's coming, though no one knows when or can predict its dimensions and character.

Crank up the Camelot Machine, meanwhile. So the record is wobbly, the needle scratchy, the sound flat and unengaging. Hey, it plays! And we 1960s survivors swing into action: left, right, left right; whop-bop-a-lu-bop. Or whatever.

November 22, 1993

The Meaning of It All

You acquire after two or three years in this business a deep suspicion of anything identified twice in print, or once on *Entertainment Tonight*, as a Hot New Trend.

The reason is that, as you ponder said trend, you seem to recall having seen it before. You note with arched eyebrows that we'll see it all again twenty years from now. If of an intellectual turn, you may comment drily, *Plus ça change, plus c'est la meme chose*—French for "yawn."

So here's all this current publicity on country music—on the record buyers' exalting Garth Brooks to the top of the album charts, the first time ever for anybody in a cowboy hat; on the start of a new televised country music variety show; on the country music stations knocking Top 40 out of third place; on the relative youth of an audience you might expect to see lined up for Guns 'n' Roses. Ph.D.s in sociology or American Studies take calls from journalists seeking to learn, so as to report, The Meaning of It All.

Ah, yes. The Meaning. The *New York Times* characterizes country songs as "lyric-oriented narratives that speak plainly about love, work and home." Does this mean the United States is turning back to love, work, and home?

It couldn't possibly be that simple. Nothing is that simple. But it is also true that music reflects the values of artists and listeners alike. Are we not a consumer society? We buy what we want. We get what we demand.

What's interesting is watching us demand with our dollars the celebration of particular values—love (as aforesaid), loneliness, heartbreak, jealousy. The human values, if you will, as old as Homer. The Greek poet, I mean; not the Homer who plunked along with Jethro.

Country music is crafty in sticking to the essentials, the unchangings, the everlastings. We know that so-called popular music changes. We have gone, in my middling lifetime, all the way from, "See the pyramids along the Nile, watch the sunrise on a tropic isle, just remember, darling, all the while, you belong to me"—all the way from this to "Rowwwwwwr, yehhhhhhhh, gilugg, gurgle," if I rightly translate the lyrics of Guns 'n' Roses.

The fundamentals of country, like the law of the Medes and the

Persians, altereth not. Hank Williams Sr., way back when, was advising us how your cheatin' heart would make you weep, you'd cry and cry and try to sleep. Moreover, he made clear, your cheatin' heart would tell on you. No theologian—at least no 1990s theologian—could put it more compellingly.

Not that country music exists in some twangy time warp. I recall a tender ballad of forty-odd years ago entitled, "Slap Her Down Again, Pa (Make Her Tell Us More, Pa, Tell Us Where She's Been)." I have the flicker of a suspicion that "Slap Her Down Again, Pa" would not go over big in the music marketplace of the 1990s.

That aside, love goes over big, and with it the emotions that move in love's turbulent wake. I'm not saying anything new here. Did my old friend Hank Williams speak more poignantly than the anonymous swain in "Greensleeves": "Alas, my love, for you do me wrong, to cast me off discourteously"? What about Sweet William, who turned his face to the wall and died "for love of Barbara Allen"?

Folks, you see, got the blues even before AIDS, date rape, sexual harassment, and the biological clock. When it happened, many wanted a strong belt of something stimulating. Many had "friends in low places" with whom they could consort. No, whatever happens to political systems and economies, the things that matter most to people don't change.

As country singers unearth and declaim on these things, we gather round, patting our feet, nodding our heads. We can't help it. We are constituted, God bless us, to remember and care about fundamentals.

Country music goes to town because it remembers who people are and what makes them tick. Them old boys and gals with the gittars, they didn't come to town on no load of hay. The financial hay they're reaping is theirs by right of conquest and good old American smarts.

January 6, 1992

A Unisex Military

You ask the purpose of the armed forces. Well, it's, it's . . .

I got it . . . The purpose of the U.S. armed forces isn't macho stuff like preserving national liberties through the intimidation or defeat of national enemies.

No, the purpose is providing career advancement and cultural therapy. Were it otherwise, we wouldn't have all these sex scandals—Tailgate, Aberdeen Proving Ground, and the like. We wouldn't have all these sex scandals because, as in days of yore, the armed forces would be populated wholly with folk of the male persuasion.

No female soldiers, sailors, and airpersons, no sex scandals. Not on base or on board, at least.

What follows, gentle reader, is political incorrectness of the first magnitude. Women and men belong in distinct military units, doing distinct but complementary things. The unisex military is a hoax and a danger.

The WACS, fine; the WAVES, fine; and so forth. Men and women integrated in the same unit—only modern Americans, scared of the social egalitarians who control public discourse, could tolerate this dismal state of affairs.

Gentle reader, this is the truth, and you know it. Water is wet, the sky is blue, men fight wars, women don't—here are basic truths about the natural order. Sexual politics can't alter or amend such truths, however vigorously the sexual politicians (Pat Schroeder comes to mind) chew the scenery.

None of this is to depreciate the valor and hardihood of women: traits demonstrated so many times as to require no proof. It is to say the United States needs to abolish the unisex military before our country really gets in trouble.

The unisex military is just so quintessentially post-Vietnam. In post-Vietnam America, evvvv-erybody, for public purposes, is an interchangeable unit. What this means, in military terms, is that if men can be soldiers, so can women. We must affirm them and their pursuit of Opportunity and Career and Satisfaction.

Well, why not, supposing the military to be just another career path, like law or oral hygiene? When sexual harassment (Tailgate) or rape and sodomy (Aberdeen) debase the workplace and the workers, you deal with it as the civilians do—as indeed, the military is dealing with it now; with reprimands, investigations and censorious newspaper editorials.

There is one problem here: The military is more than just a workplace. Its job is preparing for, fighting and winning wars. Whatever retards or undermines that job, such as on-the-job social ruction, is by definition prejudicial to the country's security.

Military unisex, as we see, weakens discipline, hence performance, hence prospects for victory. In the post-Vietnam military, where the worst threat comes from irate Bosnians thousands of miles away, Schroederian liberals forget all this.

True, earnest efforts can be made to scrub the military clean and pure of, ah, sexism. On the other hand, such efforts are expensive, time-consuming, and divisive. It will be recalled that no such efforts had to be expended back when the military was all-male.

Nor—an equally fundamental point—have Americans in these times of peace faced the matter of women in combat. Have the Schroederians ever read the *Iliad* or any intelligent account of Gettysburg or the Somme or the Marne or Ke Sanh? Do they know, for instance, that soldiers don't just topple over, they disintegrate when hit directly by shells? If the Schroederians want that dubious privilege extended to American women, they should come clean about it instead of pretending the whole unisex military thing is about Job Opportunity.

Job? Vocation? Career? Yes, offering to let an enemy blow your head off is a job; more than that, it's a public service requiring maximum efficiency and minimal distractions. The efficiency of the U.S.

military isn't noticeably high on the Schroederian Hit Parade. Sociology, consciousness raising, cultural metamorphosis—that's what the Schroederians value.

Patton, thou shouldst be living at this hour!

November 18, 1996

A Note on the Author

William Murchison, whose columns are nationally syndicated by Creators Syndicate, holds degrees from the University of Texas and Stanford University. He is a senior columnist at the *Dallas Morning News* and a contributing editor of *Human Life Review*. A frequent contributor to *National Review*, he has also written for the *Wall Street Journal*, the *American Spectator*, *Policy Review*, and *Human Events*. His previous book, *Reclaiming Morality in America*, was published in 1994, and he is currently at work on a book about the Episcopal Church. He lives in Dallas with his wife and two sons.

This book was designed and set into type
by Mitchell S. Muncy,
and printed and bound
by Thomson-Shore, Inc.
Dexter, Michigan.

❦

The cover was designed by Stephen J. Ott,
with a photograph by Edward R. Holmberg.

❦

The text face is Adobe Caslon,
designed by Carol Twombly,
based on faces cut by William Caslon, London, in the 1730s,
and issued in digital form by Adobe Systems,
Mountain View, California, in 1989.

❦

The paper is acid-free and is of archival quality.

10